AF292025

# LUCAS CRANACH

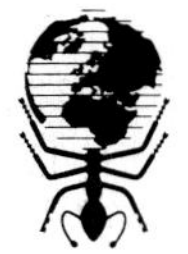

Books in the RENAISSANCE LIVES series explore and illustrate the life histories and achievements of significant artists, rulers, intellectuals and scientists in the early modern world. They delve into literature, philosophy, the history of art, science and natural history and cover narratives of exploration, statecraft and technology.

Series Editor: François Quiviger

Already published

# LUCAS CRANACH

## From German Myth to Reformation

### JENNIFER NELSON

REAKTION BOOKS

Published by Reaktion Books Ltd
Unit 32, Waterside
44–48 Wharf Road
London N1 7UX, UK
www.reaktionbooks.co.uk

First published 2024



Printed and bound in India by Replika Press Pvt. Ltd

A catalogue record for this book is available from the British Library

ISBN 978 1 78914 848 0

# CONTENTS

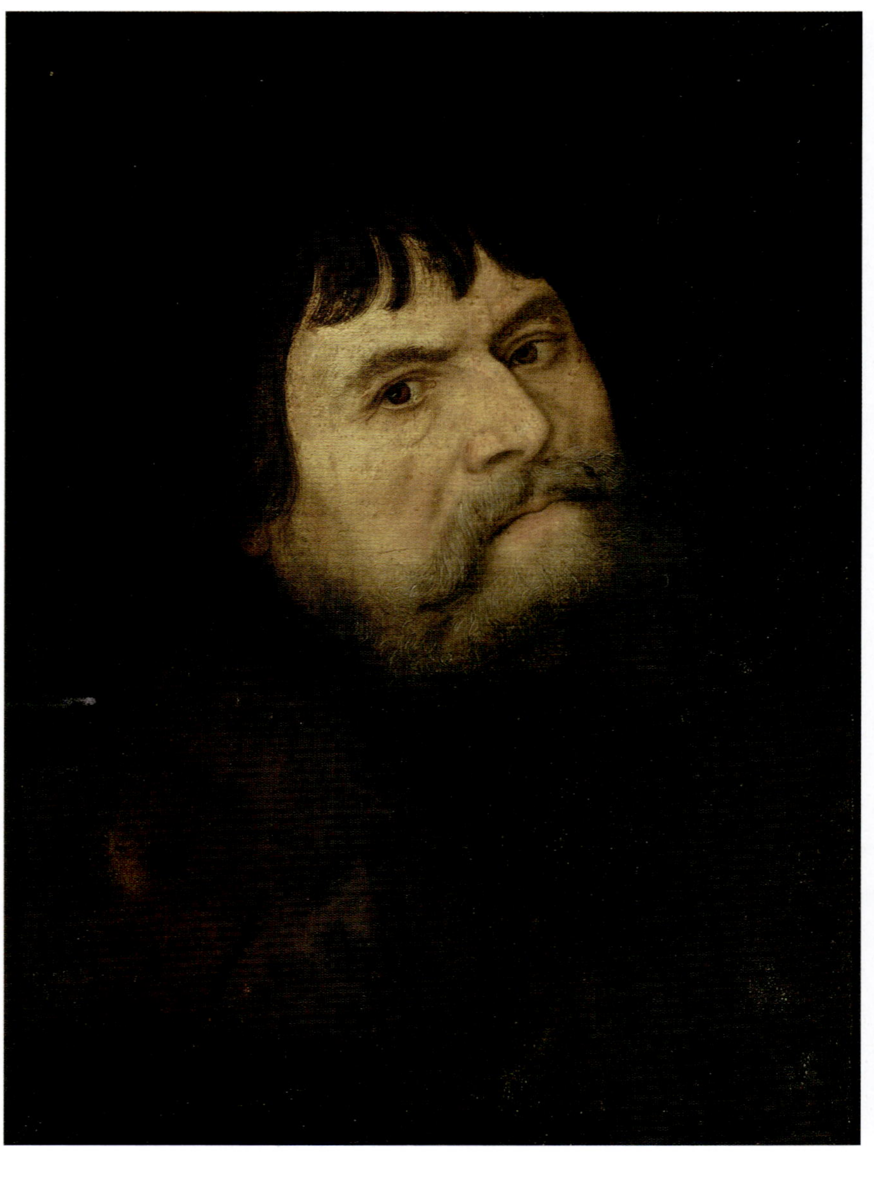

# Introduction:
# The Godfather
# of the Reformation

On the afternoon of 7 June 1526, Lucas Cranach the Elder was with one of his closest friends, the reformer Martin Luther. They were standing together in the Wittenberg City Church, also called the Church of St Mary. The occasion was the baptism of Luther's first son, Johann, or, as Luther called him, 'Little Hans'. With two sons of his own already, Cranach was about 54 years old, 10 years older than his friend. Little Hans had been born just that morning.

This day solidified a project of many years: it marked hope for the stability and future of the massive cultural shift in the history of Europe and the history of Christianity now known as the Reformation. Broadly speaking, the Reformation was a movement that claimed to adhere to the earliest texts of Christianity – in particular, the Gospels – and thus disputed the Roman Church's authority, grounded in long tradition rather than holy text, over matters of human life and salvation. Cranach's life trajectory did not neatly coincide with this movement's development. Martin Luther's formal instigation of reform had begun at the end of October 1517 with his official publication of the 95 Theses, supposedly (but probably not actually) nailed onto the doors of the Castle Church, less than ten minutes' walk away. Cranach would have already been 45.

Cranach was an artist who had surrounded himself with learned men, charmed high-ranking patrons, branched out into

1 Lucas Cranach the Elder, *Self-Portrait*, 1531, oil on panel.

several other kinds of business and established himself as a model citizen. He served on the Wittenberg town council twelve times and thrice as mayor.[1] Only on the tail end of these enterprises did Cranach direct his cultural production and his clout as a leading Wittenberg citizen in support of the Reformation. But he was long lived – he passed away on 16 October 1553, at the age of 81 – and trained his sons to carry his work forward: his workshop and style persisted into the seventeenth century under the leadership of his great-grandson, Lucas Cranach III (1586–1645), the son of Augustin Cranach, himself the son of Lucas the Younger.[2] Drawing from considerable experience, starting in his late forties, Lucas Cranach the Elder developed and popularized much of the visual material for Luther's movement, both printed and painted.

On 7 June 1526, Cranach had an even more personal connection to the historic event he witnessed. He had been instrumental in bringing Little Hans's parents together. Katharina von Bora, Luther's wife, had been a nun at the monastery of Marienthron, about three days' wagon-ride away. Before Easter 1523, she had written to Luther, asking him to help her and other nuns to escape the nunnery and join his new faith. Luther had responded to the call; when the nuns' families would not welcome the women back home, he found them stable lives in Wittenberg, through either marriage or employment or both. When Katharina was the only one who had not found a suitable marriage or placement, Cranach took her in. This, however, is not to say she was uncharming. After she moved into Cranach's household, she had many suitors. Though not among them, King Christian of Denmark gifted her with a golden ring during a visit to Wittenberg later that year.

She rejected nearly all the suitors: Luther was one of her only acceptable choices. Estranged from his family, with only twenty guilders to his name, and surrounded by allies like Philipp

Melanchthon, who still thought priests should remain celibate, Luther had been uncertain about agreeing to the union.[3] Cranach probably helped both parties make their decision. The couple married in June 1525, using the King of Denmark's ring. It was a small, discreet ceremony, free from naysayers. Cranach and only two other friends of the couple witnessed the rite.

A year later, Hans Luther's baptism was no ordinary induction of a new child into Christian life. There were other reasons Luther had been skittish about matrimony in 1525: landless farmers and their sympathizers had been leading a series of violent revolts throughout the German-speaking domains of the Holy Roman Empire, a set of conflicts now known as the Peasants' War. Though – in a pamphlet in fact co-published by Cranach that year – Luther had affirmed the authority of worldly princes and distanced himself from the image-breaking and other violence of the revolts, both farmers and princes had come to perceive him as a threat.

In 1529, Luther would write that marriage and a married household were a microcosm of the greater pious order one hoped for in the world.[4] Arriving a year after the peasant battles had died down, Little Hans completed Luther's domestic microcosm. Here was the promise of the movement's stability. With this boy, Luther's household comprised the symbolic kernel of a righteous new sacred order.

Baptism, the anointing of new believers with water, was an essential rite for Christian salvation. Luther had his German manual on the subject printed in 1523 for wide distribution among followers.[5] His particular policies on baptism had strong polemical force at the time. Lutheran followers' belief in infant baptism distinguished them from other religious dissenters from Roman policy: the Anabaptists. It was these lawless Anabaptists, in Luther's opinion, who would in large part foment the insurrection of the peasantry. Anabaptists believed in conscientiously chosen adult baptism. For them, infant baptism was an invention of the Roman Church, found nowhere in the Holy Scripture. Baptism was to be reserved for those who knew they were saved through Christ; people could not merely be born into church membership.

To Luther's mind, by contrast, baptism was not some fallacious swindle invented by a pope, to be subverted so radically. It was a practice strongly supported by ancient Christian tradition, and thus to be upheld. Debates about the afterworldly fate of the unbaptized – introduced by Luther's favoured St Augustine in the fifth century and reflected in later paintings by Cranach – encouraged the practice of immediate baptism. Much as in Roman Church tradition, godparents like Cranach served as proxies, personal guarantors that baptized infants would be brought up as deserving of the Christian rite. With Cranach's promise to oversee this process, Little Hans Luther was baptized as a proper Lutheran Christian in the afternoon of the day of his birth.

At the time of this rite, the City Church had little visual orna-ment. This spareness was also a mark of the new religious era, albeit a contentious one. A little more than four years earlier, in 1522, most of the City Church's old altars had been torn down, their remnants burned. Luther had still been in hiding at the time, in Wartburg Castle in Eisenach. The fortress was a week's wagon-ride away in the direction of Worms, where in May 1521 Luther had been declared an outlaw. In Luther's absence, one of his former dissertation advisors, Andreas Bodenstein of Karlstadt, took charge of preaching at the City Church. In favour of the more extreme factions of reform that had emerged in Luther's wake, Karlstadt encouraged groups of image-destroyers. Though Luther returned to avert what he saw as civic disorder, general scepticism of images persisted. Towards the end of 1524, the last altarpiece was removed, along with an image of the Virgin, to whom the original chapel on the site had been consecrated.

Religious life in Wittenberg would remain relatively calm for the next twenty years, and the church would find new kinds of adornment. The inventor of this new variety of Christian art would be Cranach himself. No other major religious movement and no other single artist have had such a strong relationship with one another, a relationship in which one artist almost single-handedly determines not only a religious community's visual culture, but also how its abstract beliefs *look*.

Cranach's previous societal position set him up well for such a task: not only was he friends with Martin Luther, but he had been court painter to one elector of Saxony or another for much of the century. Cranach was already a community leader. The many business involvements previously mentioned included wine sales, a successful apothecary (he also bought and sold pigments) and co-ownership of one of the city's many printing houses (his was founded to print Luther's first New Testament translation of 1522). Again, by the early 1520s, he had already repeatedly served on Wittenberg's city council.

From here on, though, Cranach's public standing would expand beyond any expectation. With the revolts calmed, with Luther's new Christian order taking shape, Cranach's work would be in such demand that his workshop began to transform itself into something of a proto-factory, producing dozens of versions of the same subject-matter on painted panels for the next several decades. Alongside a steady output of woodcuts, the press Cranach co-owned from about 1522–6 churned out sermon after treatise after public letter after Bible, to be sold at book fairs (or less openly) throughout Europe. After he turned the press over to others, he continued to contribute his and his workshop's designs to illustrations and especially title pages for Reformation publications.[6] This continuous output of printed and painted Lutheran content went on, again, nearly a century after his death. Through this, Cranach established the Reformation brand.

THE ELEVATION OF THE LUTHERAN EVERYDAY

This biography concerns a person for whose existence evidence is largely lacking – except in the art itself. From Cranach's lifetime, more than 1,000 paintings and prints survive, but fewer than sixty references on paper besides contracts (which often prove difficult to connect with one version of a painting rather than another, given the workshop's practice of making multiples). Therefore, this book will of necessity track the artist's life largely through paintings and prints.

The first chapter recounts the trajectory of Cranach's career through tracing his work, first for humanist patrons at the University of Vienna and then as a court artist for the electors of Saxony; it also shows that this background left him particularly well equipped to promote a new standard format for portraiture throughout Northern Europe. The second chapter shows how Cranach's contribution to German humanism and

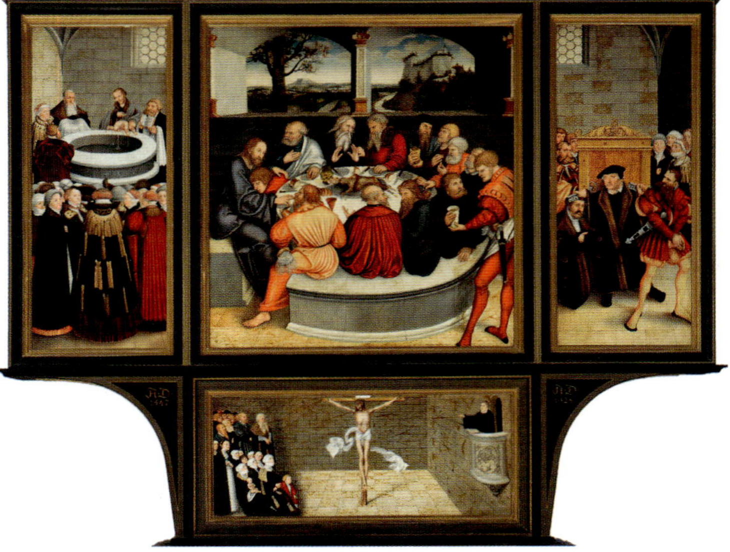

2 Lucas Cranach the Elder and Younger and workshop, *Wittenberg Altarpiece* (front), 1547, oil on panel.

the development of German identity in this period hinged on his repeated – very multiply repeated – treatment of alluring nude women of an eternal pagan past. The third chapter turns towards religious subject-matter, acknowledging Cranach's participation in the pre-Reformation relic industry in Wittenberg but focusing on his major innovations as the founder of a new Christian visuality pointed at divine grace.

In 1547, a year after Luther's death and towards the end of Cranach's stable years in Wittenberg, Cranach would install a large altarpiece in the City Church, one celebrated to this day as a monument of Reformation art; indeed, what Anglophone viewers call the *Wittenberg Altarpiece* is known as the *Reformationsaltar* in German.[7] Cranach finished it not long before the Battle of Mühlberg; poignantly, the day of the battle is the date traditionally given for his dedication of the altarpiece to the Wittenberg congregation.

The Battle of Mühlberg was the most tragic day of the early Reformation. On 24 April 1547, on plains a mere day's ride from

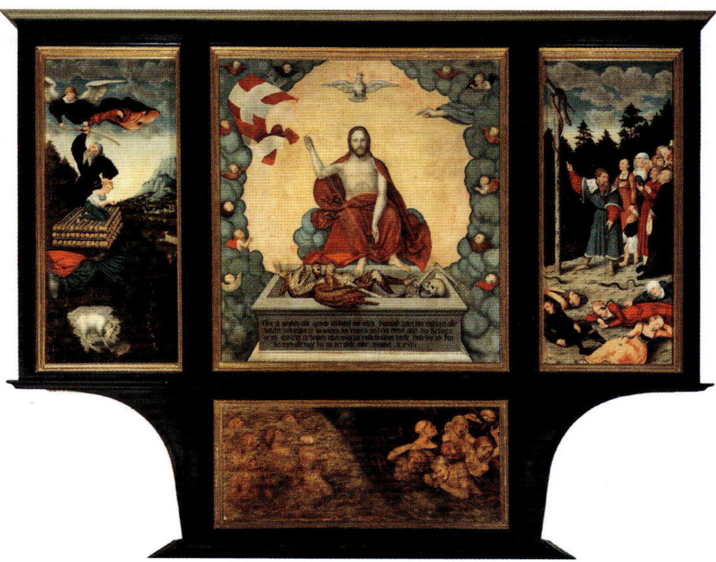

3 Lucas Cranach the Elder and Younger and workshop, *Wittenberg Altarpiece* (back), 1547, oil on panel.

Wittenberg, 7,000 Lutheran soldiers of the Schmalkaldic League died in battle against forces led by the traitorous Albertine Duke Moritz of Saxony. Cranach's beloved patron Johann Friedrich, the Ernestine elector of Saxony and Moritz's cousin, was captured, along with other major Lutheran leaders. Cranach would ultimately leave the workshop to his sons in order to accompany his lordly patron in exile.

Was this great Reformation altarpiece completed as Wittenberg got news of the enemy armies' approach? Did it begin before or after Luther's death in 1546? Was it a memorial? Scholars debate the answers. Documentation from 1546 and 1547 has gone missing from the Wittenberg archives, but it was typical for altars like this to require more than a year in the making. Since much of the altarpiece must have been made after Luther's death, one may assume that the fate of Luther's Reformation in the wake of its founder was very much on Cranach's mind.

The *Wittenberg Altarpiece* is famous for its inner wings, the painted surfaces of the wings that are visible when the altar is open (illus. 2). On first glance, these panels may not look particularly special or worthy of fame. They represent Christian sacraments as everyday scenes: a confession on the right and a baptism on the left. In comparison to, say, Rogier van der Weyden's famous precedent altarpiece depicting Christian rites, with its intricate repetition of complex church architecture, these scenes look plain, even frumpy. In Cranach's altar, the wooden back of the chair in the confession – especially when one considers that painting at this time was done almost entirely on wood – artfully mimics the appearance of an unpainted wood panel, but is therefore almost ostentatiously dull. The blocks of stone on the walls and floor look like blocks of marble but feature little carving or other ornament; the crown glass in the windows has no colour.

It is this lack of frippery that – along with the inclusion of portraits of living worshippers and church leaders – makes these

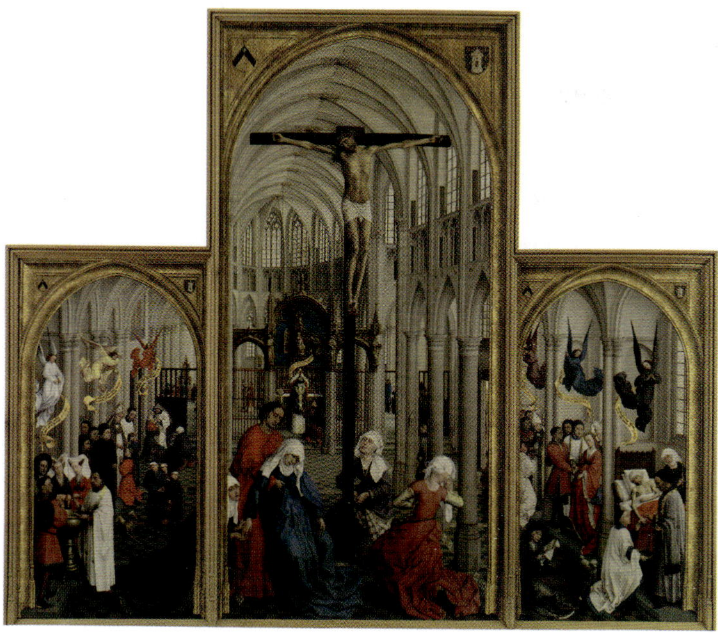

panels so famous. No one would worship the figures on these wings. As Luther would have said, his followers were not supposed to be worshipping images. Though Cranach developed many pictorial strategies to avoid inducing direct worship, this altarpiece show-cases an intriguing artistic tactic. How did one engage with one's neighbour's appearance on an altar?

These are scenes taken from the ordinary religious life of Cranach's community. They are holy rituals, to be sure, but they are nevertheless rituals that every Lutheran would experience. In a culture where altarpieces for centuries had depicted divine scenes of the Holy Family and the saints, such an intrusion of the everyday was remarkable. There on the right panel could be any reasonably well-to-do person confessing sins. On the left, the baptism scene is no nostalgic representation of Hans Luther's baptism, at least not literally, because stodgy Melanchthon is

4 Rogier van der Weyden, *Seven Sacraments*, c. 1445–50, oil on panel.

present. But it could be any other believer's baptism. In the wings of the *Wittenberg Altarpiece* appear not the usual portraits of wealthy donors from the everyday world, given access to a divine realm; we find instead, in the place of that divine realm, the world itself.

These two wings flank a slightly more conventional, though still not very common, altarpiece scene: that of the Last Supper. This scene represents a sacred event from the Christian Bible – Christ's last meal shared with his apostles – and not an everyday occasion or dispensation of Eucharist in the City Church. Christ sits on the left, embracing his beloved apostle John with an intimacy typical of the scene. Judas sits closer to Christ than one might expect, his traditional yellow garb brighter than anything else in the room, his coin-purse swollen to the point of bursting, thrust away from Christ and thus towards the viewer. The landscape outside bears some resemblance to German fortresses perched on cliffsides (often exaggerated by Cranach in his paintings); this is Cranach's only nod in the scene to situating the Last Supper in contemporary Saxony.

To represent the biblical precedent here is a curious choice. Clearly Cranach designed the altarpiece to show the three sacraments honoured by Lutherans since the 1530 Augsburg Confession: baptism, penance and the Eucharist.[8] Thus, the Last Supper stands in for the Eucharist. The Eucharist is the rite during a Christian Mass in which one consumes the body and blood of Christ in the form of bread and wine that has undergone complex spiritual alteration. This rite has long been considered central to Christian faith, and during the early decades of the Reformation occasioned serious debate. (Luther believed that the bread and wine were not mere metaphors for Christ, like some reformers did, nor wholly transformed into the literal flesh and blood of Christ, as the Roman Church held, but that the bread and wine were 'consubstantial' with Christ's flesh and blood, both bread and flesh, wine and blood at once.)

One of the important parts of this debate for Lutherans perhaps appears in this image. Should ordinary people, laypeople, be allowed to receive the Eucharist in both forms, in both bread and wine? For hundreds of years, and somewhat more recently bolstered by the decree of the Thirteenth Session of the Council of Constance in 1415, the position of the Roman Church had been to provide the Eucharist to the laity in the form of bread alone, restricting wine for the clergy's consumption. Lutherans insisted instead on following early Church practice and administering the Eucharist in both kinds. Admittedly, many depictions of the Last Supper in general emphasize the presence of both bread and wine at the biblical meal. However, Lutheran depictions of the Last Supper tend to place special emphasis on the presence of a jug-bearing servant filling a disciple's mug.

Why did Cranach direct his workshop to depict this foundational Eucharistic image rather than the present-day Eucharistic rite? Perhaps there was still some concern for propriety. For decades by 1547, donors had infiltrated the wings of European altarpieces, even appearing on central panels' corners and sides and bottoms; this precedent surely laid the ground for Cranach's depiction of everyday life on these wings. But through all the precedents, the central panel of a triptych altarpiece was still the place reserved for the Christian cult image, the image that, even if it did not function as an idol, focused proper viewer worship. Even bold Cranach may not have been bold enough to put a picture of a weekly church event in the place where, in his youth, a cult statue would have stood.[9]

No one in the congregation would have missed, however, the fact that the apostle receiving wine from the servant had the face of a young Martin Luther. This was not the long-ailing Luther who had died the previous year in Eisleben, but one rather more like Cranach's 1521 image of Luther as 'Junker Jörg'. This character, an aristocrat with a stylish beard, served as

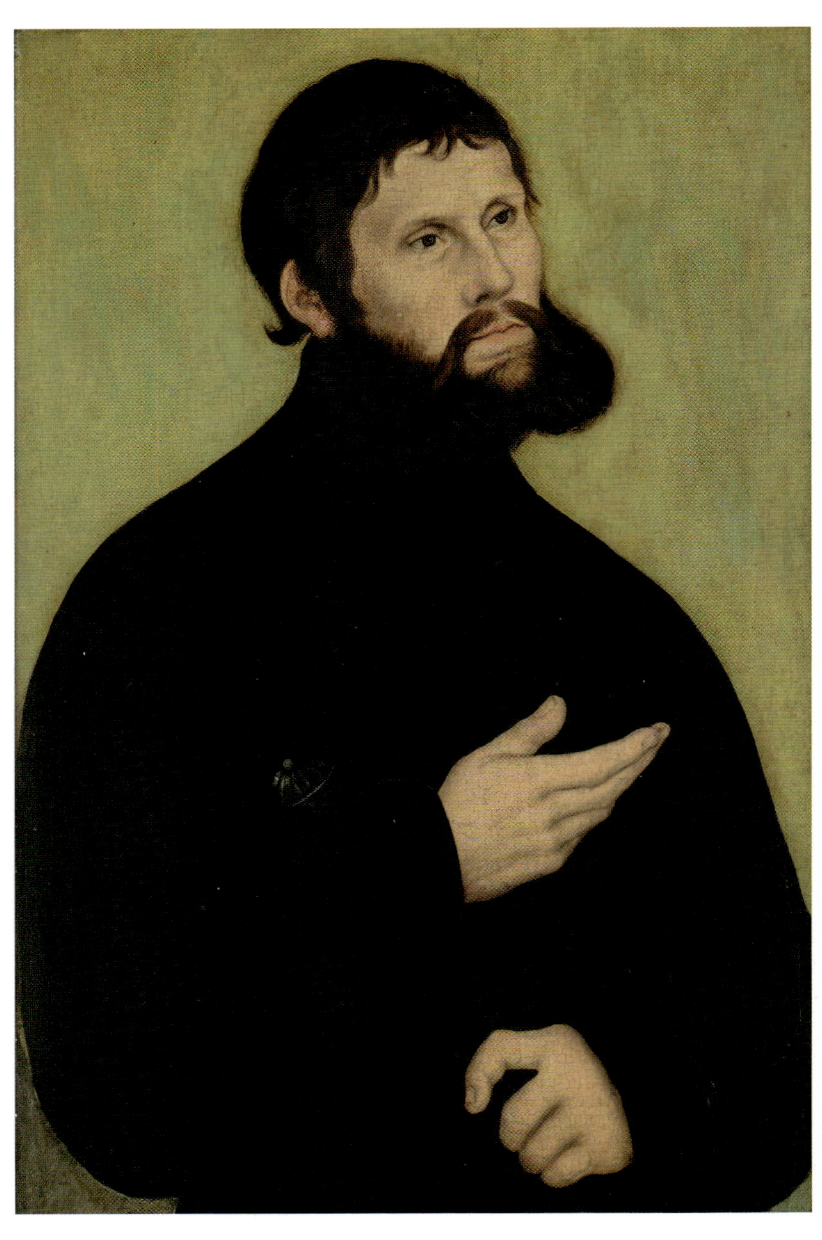

5 Lucas Cranach the Elder, *Martin Luther as Junker Jörg*, 1521–2, oil and tempera on panel.

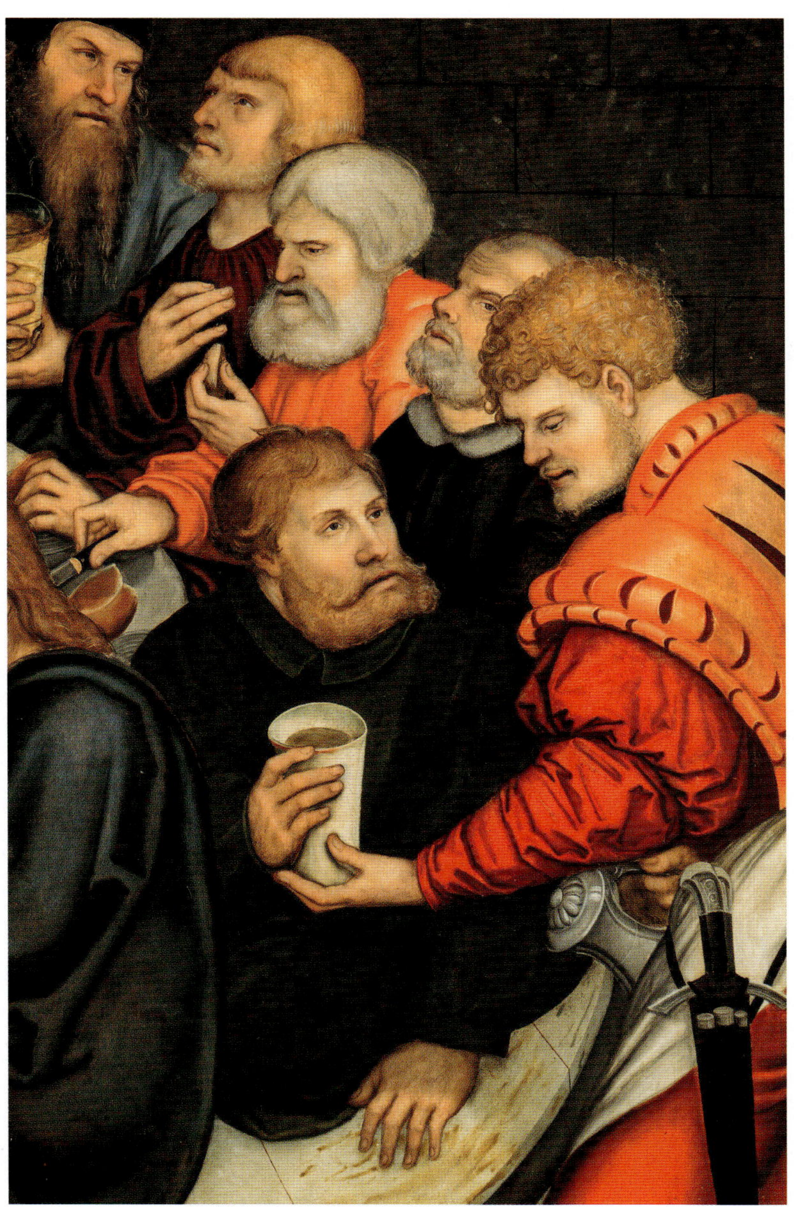

6 Martin Luther as Junker Jörg in the Last Supper, detail of the central panel in illus. 2.

Luther's disguise during his months hiding at Wartburg Castle. This portrait must have dated to the early years of Cranach's friendship with the professor and former monk. The reiteration here is subtle: the hair in the *Wittenberg Altarpiece* panel is lighter than in most extant versions of the Junker Jörg portrait. But the hands are in the same position, albeit filled with a mug of wine and braced against the supper table's altar-like stone or even marble bench. This suggestion of a portrait would have made, in 1547, a less literal memorial than the death mask and other rapidly circulating images (which Cranach's workshop produced) of the reformer on his deathbed. But it also stood for a famous moment in the history of the Reformation, popularized by Cranach, that would endure in the community's sacred memory: the first moment of brave, open defiance of the corrupt previous Church.

## GODFATHER CRANACH AND THE EVERYDAY IN SACRED TIME

One of the most intriguing gifts Godfather Cranach bestowed upon the young Reformation is the predella of this altarpiece. A predella consists of the lowermost panel or panels of an altarpiece, the parts closest to the altar proper and thus closest to prospective viewers. Typically, a predella depicts events in the life of the person on whom an altarpiece is focused. This person could be Christ himself, or his mother, Mary, or a saint. Often predellas feature more than one scene, deployed in a horizontal band of small panels at the bottom of the altarpiece. From an artist's point of view, this was the part of the altarpiece where one might dare to try out new iconography or compositions, or represent more unusual scenes.

In the wake of his friend's death, Cranach took full advantage of the opportunity to invent a new scene that included the late

Luther. At the predella's centre, larger than anyone else present, appears Christ, stoically suffering the Crucifixion. On the right, Luther's mouth may be closed, but his *adlocutio* oratorical gesture, borrowed from the emperors of Greco-Roman antiquity, and his position in the pulpit imply the act of preaching. Indeed, here Cranach's great friend preaches so vigorously that Christ's long perizoma whorls upon the gust. It is as if Luther's words have summoned this familiar version of Christ on the cross, known as *Christus Victor*, Christ in victory over death. On the left, the congregation witnesses this multisensory event: apparition, sermon and perhaps even a breeze that blows only in sacred time.

Cranach made this altarpiece for them, for that pious, contemplative rather than idolatrous group so neatly divided between grown men and everyone else. The altarpiece's literal dedicatee – the Wittenberg congregation – is thus also the 'subject' of Cranach's altarpiece. He depicted the Eucharist, baptism and confession as the great events of *their* lives, as renewed Christians on the Lutheran path.

In doing so, Cranach created the most radically immanent altarpiece in European art history. Here the simple divinity of everyday ritual took the place of Scripture's unreachable sacred history; here each believer was a Christian protagonist. Granted,

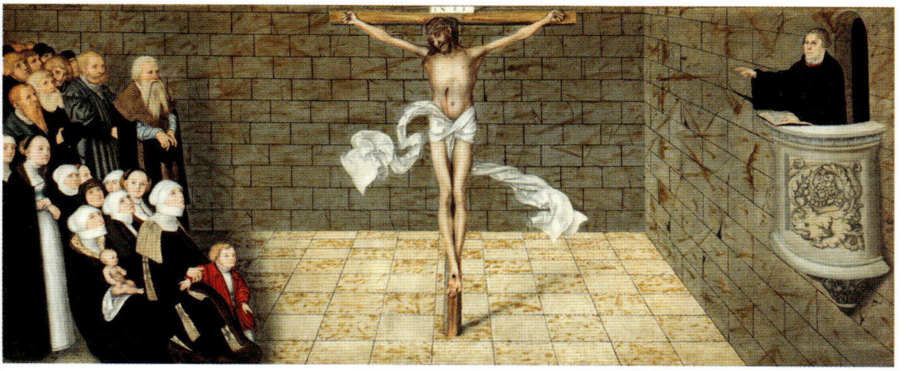

7 Martin Luther preaches to the Wittenberg community, detail of the predella in illus. 2.

in the central panel, Cranach honoured the mystical act by which Christ himself became immanent in humble bread and wine, opening the world to the very possibility of such immanence. But everywhere else in the altar's open state, Cranach honoured the holiness of ordinary people and ordinary life, not in the distant lifetime of one saint or another, but in the present, the here and now.

He honoured this everyday life as sacred just as it was most threatened. The Lutherans of Wittenberg were outnumbered by their detractors, both in terms of Christians of the world and in the more literal terms of mercenary armies. Though the Ernestine electors of Saxony had plenty of income from mining – to this day, their lands are known as the 'Silver Road' – they relied not only on funding armies of their own but also on diplomatic manoeuvring and trade agreements to preserve the freedom of Lutheran worship. When the elector's cousin Moritz of Saxony openly turned on his fellow Lutherans in October 1546, half a year after Luther had passed away, the political balance in German-speaking lands shifted in favour of the Holy Roman Emperor, who had aligned with the Roman Church against the Lutherans. The congregation of Wittenberg had cause for alarm.

I suspect, however, that Cranach's intriguing decisions to elevate Wittenberg life in his altarpiece were left unchanged by such threats. Judas in the Last Supper scene is no portrait of the traitorous Moritz, even though broadsides slandering him as a Judas were rampant by the winter of 1546–7. While Moritz did have a long, thin face and butterscotch-coloured beard, Judas's brow in the central panel is wrong. Perhaps the impression, in the altarpiece, that Christ is directly feeding Judas is an indirect allegory of the capitulation Wittenberg had been forced to give to its new master, who took over as elector that very day in Mühlberg. Regardless, Cranach must have in large part stuck to his hopes for the altar and its congregation.

This altarpiece suggests that, whatever conflicts came, Cranach possessed a spiritual security born out of confidence in the everyday divine itself. By depicting Lutheran rites in all their simplicity on an altarpiece, he elevated ordinary practice to the status of sacred history. It is one thing to feel as though one's rituals and rites temporarily elevate one to a place alongside divine figures like Christ. It is another thing to be so sure of this that one makes one's own congregation, constituted by its rituals, the subject of a monumental altarpiece.

Representing the sermon – not quite a sacrament but rather a guide to the all-important Word of God – on the predella of the *Wittenberg Altarpiece*, Cranach broke away from the plainness of the main panels. Mild divergence of style was not unusual for predellas, which often featured looser brushwork, often applied by assistants rather than the master of the workshop. Here the looseness is most visible in the stonemasonry. Cranach or an assistant painted the walls not in discrete blocks, as in the main panels of the altarpiece, but instead as a background of brush-stroke-striated marble with lines placed atop it, so that marble veins continue across multiple notionally separate blocks. These implausible veins extend the power of the victorious whorl of Christ's garment.

That dramatic representation of Christ's crucial sacrifice, emerging out of loose brushstrokes in the lowliest and smallest panel of the altarpiece, is Cranach's humble acknowledgement of his role. In a place and time famous for scepticism of images and outright destruction of altarpieces and sculptures, Cranach advertised his art. Unlike other reformers of Christianity, Martin Luther encouraged his followers to use pictures, whether mental images or material ones. Surely Luther was thinking of his painter friend, or perhaps was even inspired by his art, when he wrote in late 1524 that he wanted 'the whole Bible to be painted on houses'. And perhaps all these years later, in 1546–7, Cranach thought of how his late friend had gone on to write: 'For whether I want it or not, when I hear of Christ, an image of a man hanging on a cross takes form in my heart, just as the reflection of my face naturally appears in the water . . . Why should it be a sin to have [that image] in my eyes?'[10]

In the early sixteenth century, a godparent was not only the sponsor of a child's baptism. A godparent would also guide a child spiritually in the case of a parent's death. Cranach would serve as a godfather not just for young Hans Luther, but in many ways also for Luther's broader offspring: Lutheranism itself. Here at the crux of Lutheranism's survival, with Luther gone, with Witten-berg under attack or already fallen, Cranach painted the image of Christ at the moment He guaranteed human deliverance. Godfather Cranach presented the Christ of the Reformation not on a hill in West Asia, but as the salvation ensured by the presence of a man on a cross in an everyday congregation's heart.

# ONE

# The Cranach Brand Emerges

When people wrote about Cranach during his life, they usually called him 'Lucas Painter' ('Lucas Maler' in German). This was not a nickname based on his work alone. Cranach was the son of Hans Maler, who may or may not himself have been a painter. The surname 'Maler' was not uncommon.

Lucas seems to have started using the name 'Cranach' around the age of thirty, when he was working in Vienna. Perhaps the move from a generic descriptor to a toponymic indicates his ambition or indeed success as an artist who had transcended his local context.[1] The name comes from his hometown of Kronach, now much smaller, but then a small city near Coburg in Upper Franconia, under the jurisdiction of the archbishop of Bamberg. (The spelling of place names and of most other names and words was very flexible in the sixteenth century.) A couple of days' ride northeast from Bamberg, Kronach lay between that city and Wittenberg. In the years of struggle over religious confession in the late sixteenth and early seventeenth centuries, Kronach would mark the northernmost stretch of Roman Church territory over and against Lutheran Saxony in the north. Though Cranach occasionally worked with patrons faithful to the Roman Church, his mature life lay on the Lutheran side of that confessional border.

Little is certain about Cranach's life in Kronach, besides the fact that he was born there in 1472, probably on 4 October.[2]

Almost no information survives about his mother, who may have been named Barbara. She and some of his at least seven siblings may have perished in a plague epidemic. Cranach apprenticed with his father, though not much evidence remains about Hans Maler or the nature of his workshop. Hans had some dealings with noble families in Bamberg; Cranach inherited money owed from them after his father's death.[3] But besides these references, there are almost no clues about Hans Maler's life. Perhaps he was originally Bavarian, perhaps Hungarian; perhaps he worked on woodcut designs; perhaps he used the name 'Maler' in lieu of an unattractive original name, 'Sunder' ('sinner'), which often designated a family history of transgression; or perhaps he himself was already so well connected as an artist that his workshop was serving the Saxon Elector Friedrich the Wise in Leipzig from 1491 to 1505.[4]

None of these scholarly speculations is certain. We do not even have artworks to go on; no securely dated work survives from before 1500. The earliest extended record of Cranach's personal life comes from 1556, three years after his death, when a tutor in Lucas Cranach the Younger's household, the theologian Matthias Gunderam, wrote a memorial to the late artist.[5] Gunderam was Cranach's cousin, also from Kronach. From his and other testimony, two generalizations can be made. First, the family was reasonably well off. Second, whether or not Hans Maler was a painter of panels, maps or nothing at all, Cranach grew up trained in a figurative tradition of some sort: Gunderam calls it 'ars graphicam', using a word linked since Greek antiquity to both drawing and painting.

Unlike Albrecht Dürer (1471–1528), the other German artist of comparable fame during Cranach's lifetime, Cranach did not so far as we know exhibit youthful signs of self-awareness as an artist, nor did he make early pilgrimages to faraway artists and lands. Though a myth about his having travelled to the Holy Land in 1493 in the company of Elector Friedrich the Wise persisted into the late twentieth century, this account has been exposed as false.[6] In 1498, already 25 years old, he seems to have left Kronach. He may never have returned as a permanent resident. Or perhaps 1498 marked his *Wanderjahr*; the art historian Dieter Koepplin has argued that Cranach must have trained in a workshop in Bamberg.[7] A year or two of travel was traditional for journeymen, those workshop artisans who had completed their apprenticeship but were not yet master craftsmen.

Still, at least until 1498, Cranach may have stayed with his family, helping to raise his younger siblings after his mother and aunt died in the first half of the 1490s.[8] His early twenties were years of some social struggle for him and his family: they endured an inheritance dispute in 1492, and their civic complaint about a neighbouring family dragged from 1495 to 1498.[9] Cranach himself had to make an official demand for payment in 1501 in nearby Coburg.[10] From time to time Duke Johann of Saxony, brother of and co-ruler with Friedrich the Wise, stayed in the fortress in Coburg, the Veste; it would later become one of his residences. Perhaps if Cranach had business dealings there, he had somehow already come to the attention of the family of his future patrons, the Wettin dukes and electors of Saxony.

## PORTRAITIST OF THE URBAN UNIVERSITY

When we do find certain evidence of Cranach's life and work, the year is 1502, and he has moved to Vienna. Here we can make some guesses about the motivation for Cranach's relocation.

Besides being one of Holy Roman Emperor Maximilian I's favoured seats, Vienna at the turn of the sixteenth century was also one of the most culturally advanced cities in the Holy Roman Empire, rivalled only by Nuremberg. The scholar and poet Conrad Celtis called Vienna 'The Eye of Germany'. Maximilian had been nurturing its university for some time; in 1502, during Cranach's time there, the emperor even founded a new institution, the College of Poets and Mathematicians. At this point, Vienna was arguably the greatest university centre in German-speaking domains.

One thing Vienna may have lacked, despite its lively university environment, was a book illustration specialist. In 1498, taking advantage of the end-of-days mood surrounding the approaching year 1500, Nuremberg's Albrecht Dürer had published an impressive chapbook of half-folio woodcuts of *The Apocalypse*. Dürer's dynamic, imaginative *Apocalypse* became a best-seller and catalysed his subsequent fame. Perhaps Cranach, seeing a parallel opportunity, travelled to Vienna in order to provide his services for the major printer there, Johannes Winterburger. Winterburger largely published the works of Vienna's university professors.

Whatever Cranach's reason for heading to Vienna, the place nurtured what would prove to be a major aspect of his artistic personality: he felt at home with students and scholars. For nearly five decades, till he went into exile in 1550, Cranach thrived in the ambit of a major university. Though he may never have been a university student himself, his cousin Gunderam's 1556 eulogy records that Cranach knew Latin. It has even been suggested that the University of Vienna was not his first taste of institutions of advanced scholarship. It is possible, though again not well substantiated, that he acquired a taste for this scholar-adjacent lifestyle first at the Jagiellonian Polish court with its ties to the university in Krakow, or the Hungarian court in then-Ofen, present-day Budapest, where he had distant relatives.[11] Regardless, it was in Vienna that Cranach honed the social disposition that eventually won him learned patrons and friends like Martin Luther. Especially after Cranach left Vienna in 1505, he would over the years produce depictions of many of his academic friends and acquaintances, as well as more specific visual mementoes of their scholarly exchanges.

Most of these mementoes, beginning in Cranach's Viennese period, were works in a genre that had recently spread beyond the ranks of royalty and the uppermost tiers of the nobility: the portrait. It is important here to underscore the relative newness of portraiture at the turn of the sixteenth century. That is, in Europe, painted portraits had been reserved almost exclusively for emperors and kings and their brides or brides-to-be, with some archdukes thrown in. For non-imperials and non-royals, portraits had only recently come into favour as independent painted works. Portraits previously had been largely the province of tombs, and more rarely components of altarpieces, coins, medals and illustrated texts. Across Europe, in the centuries since Roman antiquity, an independent likeness of a living or even recently dead individual was not something for ordinary people, even very wealthy or otherwise prominent ones.

A few general shifts in European image-making foreshadowed the spread of the portrait into broader society during the fifteenth century. For one thing, effigies of donors and patrons began to appear more frequently in religious paintings. Indeed, these figures increasingly appeared *within* a religious scene, as if within the same realm as holy persons, albeit usually smaller in size, or separated by some architectural or other spatial device. For another thing, miniatures, the paintings in illuminated manuscripts often commissioned for religious purposes among elites, began to have increasingly detailed images of their patrons. And finally, interest in the revival of aspects of ancient European cultures – the rebirth that lends this 'Renaissance' period its name – included reworkings of the format of ancient Roman portrait coins into medals.

Crucially boosting all these changes was the most important change of all: the circulation of printed images. Indeed, Cranach's own printed portraiture in the sixteenth century, as well as that of his contemporary Dürer, would dramatically change the availability of likenesses of living people in everyday visual culture. The *Wittenberg Altarpiece*, for example, was thus part of a Europe-wide trend in producing portraits of the living. The shift from a culture focused on portraying divine figures to a culture focused on documenting worldly reality is one of the major hallmarks of the Renaissance.

Cranach worked upon the crest of this transition. That is, he both invented imagery suitable for particularly Lutheran conceptions of divine figures *and* visually documented an incredible number of real-world figures. This second form of activity is no less important than the first. Based on the hundreds of portraits that have survived both in recorded inventories and in collections, Cranach was the most prolific portraitist of his time and place.[12] He worked with a broad range of sitters within German-speaking lands, from rulers and major theologians to now-unknown legal scholars and merchants.

Cranach's first surviving portraits, from about 1502, are of people affiliated with the University of Vienna. One of these individuals remains relatively well known: Johannes Cuspinian, then 28 or 29 years old, a bit younger than Cranach. Cranach depicted him on the occasion of his marriage to his eighteen-year-old wife Anna, née Putsch. The couple appear in matching bust portraits in three-quarter view, as was becoming traditional for commemorating a marriage.[13] These paintings are ideal examples through which to understand the milieu and historical moment from which Cranach launched his artistic career.

The male sitter, Cuspinian, was already an impressive figure. He had studied in Leipzig and Würzburg before arriving in Vienna as a twenty-year-old poet in 1494. After successfully gaining the attention of Maximilian and being crowned poet laureate – the second poet to receive this accolade from this emperor – he studied medicine at the university while giving lectures on ancient writers. Upon completing his studies, he began also to lecture on medicine, a field which then would have included inquiries into the realms of what we might now call astronomy and natural science. At the same time, he became head physician for the prominent monastery of Klosterneuburg. By 1500, he was university rector, the equivalent of a present-day university chancellor or president, but typically with a shorter term. The next year, 1501, Maximilian appointed Cuspinian the princely superintendent, a representative of imperial interests at the university. Around the time of his marriage, he was named the dean of the medical school. In sum, by the time of this portrait, Cuspinian, not yet thirty, had reached the top ranks of university life and was on good terms with the emperor himself.

In 1502 and 1503, Cuspinian was working on his first editions of poetic and rhetorical texts with the printer Johannes Winterburger. Cranach was contracted to provide illustrations for these humanist projects, that is, projects that sought to recover the knowledge and technical skills of Greco-Roman antiquity as well as to emulate them. Perhaps Cranach and Cuspinian became acquainted in preparation for this project, and thus Cuspinian found his portraitist.

The two men in any case shared something more personal in common: they were both from the eastern part of Franconia, a region now in the north of the state of Bavaria. 'Cuspinianus' was, as was fashionable, a Latinization of the German toponymic surname 'Spießhaymer'; it meant 'Spearville man'. 'Spearville' or 'Spießheim' was a village near Schweinfurt, in present-day Oberspiesheim and Unterspiesheim. Spießheim lay only about 112 kilometres (70 mi.) southwest of Kronach, on the other side of Bamberg but still within its jurisdiction.

Two men from the relative backwaters of the same region, encountering one another in a large city, might not necessarily befriend one another. But being of east Franconian extraction had recently emerged as a point of pride in Viennese scholarly

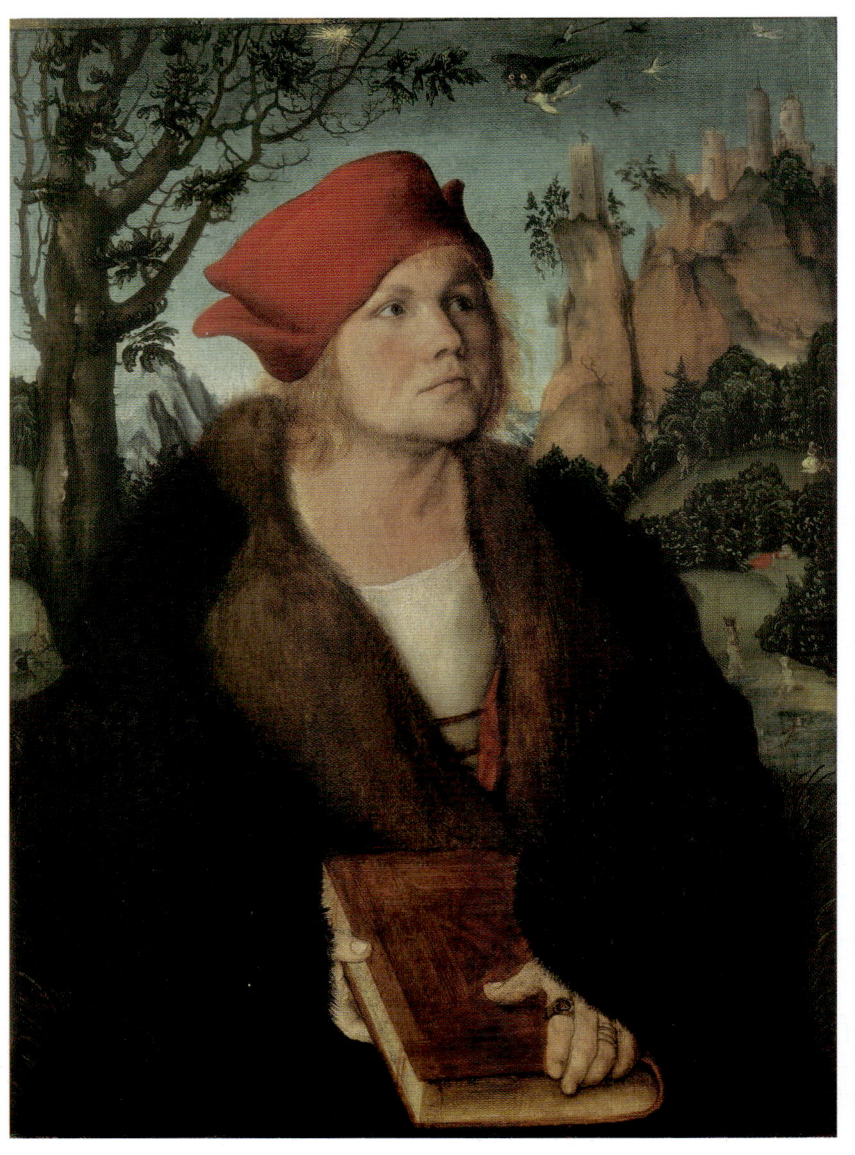

8 Lucas Cranach the Elder, *Johannes Cuspinian*, 1502, oil on panel.

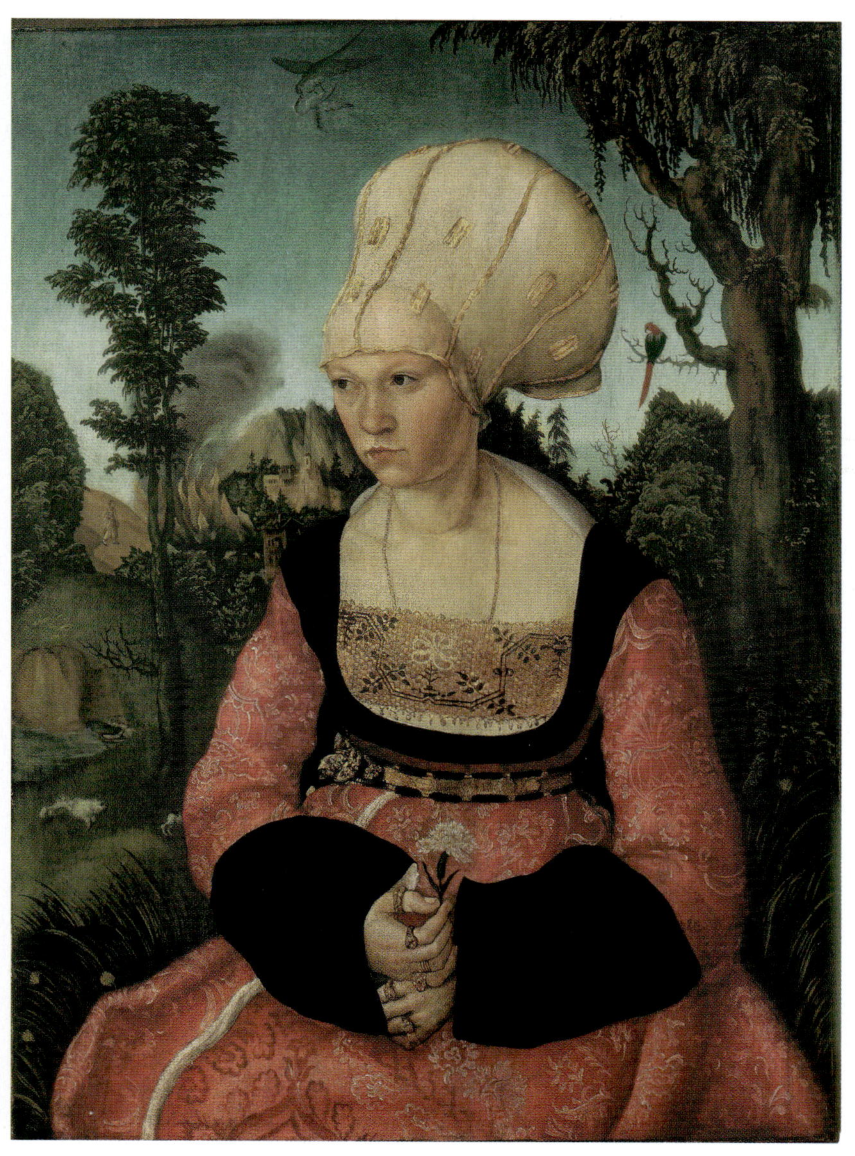

9 Lucas Cranach the Elder, *Anna Cuspinian* [née Putsch], 1502, oil on panel.

circles. The Schweinfurt area was also the birthplace of the most famous scholar at the university, Cuspinian's mentor, Conrad Celtis, the first recipient of Maximilian's poetic laurels. Celtis had been invited to Vienna by the emperor in 1497. He was the one who helped the emperor found the College of Poets and Mathematicians in the year of Cranach's Cuspinian portrait.

The importance of east Franconia here does not end with the fact that Cranach and Cuspinian were both from the same place as the university luminary Celtis. Celtis's larger historical project – here his work and Maximilian's imperial interests mutually influenced one another – aimed to develop a German historical and intellectual identity.[14] According to Celtis's account, Germans descended, through much displacement and travail, from the ancient Greeks. In this version of broader pan-European history, Germans thus bypassed the belated Roman culture from which the Italian peoples sprang. That is, Celtis's work established that Germans, far from barbaric, were in fact closer than their rival Italians to more primary and original sources of ancient wisdom.

Celtis's theory rested in part on the belief that Franconians were the descendants of druids who, forced out of Gaul (the ancient name for the lands largely occupied by France), settled to the east, preserving primordial wisdom and practices.[15] Celtis was publishing this claim for the first time in 1502; surely he had discussed it with his colleague and fellow druid-heir Cuspinian. Perhaps Cuspinian's choice of Cranach as his portraitist came from a shared pride in and desire to promote this special heritage.[16]

Cranach here already, as in later life, engaged in the scholarly interests of his sitter. Cranach removes the dean from the university and surrounds him with a forested, rustic landscape, exchanging Cuspinian's literal setting for his idealized intellectual one. This natural backdrop corresponded with Celtis and Cuspinian's vision for a Germanic future in touch with its past, full of druidic harmony with the divinity of nature. Later in life, Cranach would depict the earliest, primordial precedents of such a vision (as one can read in the next chapter).

One should not, however, mistake Cuspinian's portrait as purely pagan. Here the appearance of a star in the sky – too small and in the wrong position to be the sun – recalls a very important star from the Christian New Testament. That is, its distinctive rays and size liken it to depictions of the star of the Epiphany, the star that appeared in the sky over Bethlehem after the birth of Jesus, interpreted by three magi from the east as a sign of the 'king of the Jews' (Matthew 2). This appearance of the star points to Cuspinian's work on ancient Christian texts.

Cuspinian had early in his career given a series of lectures on the hymns of the fourth-century Roman Christian poet Aurelius Prudentius. These lectures were indeed the project for which the printer Winterburger contracted Cranach to provide woodcut illustrations in 1502–3. The final hymn in the Prudentius book took up the subject of the Epiphany. In this hymn, he describes the star of the Epiphany as the original light source. Having existed before the world, and lingering in eternity, this originary star lends its primal light to other heavenly bodies – including the sun! – and can be seen even in the brightest daylight.

Prudentius urges his readers to look into the sky and locate this star for themselves, just as the magi did centuries before. This suggestion accounts for one of the oddities of this double marriage portrait, which would probably have been arranged as a diptych. Though Anna looks faithfully at where her husband would have been in the hinged diptych – as one might expect from a newlywed – Cuspinian's eyes are directed upwards. It is true that he is not looking directly at the star. However, it would have been awkward to portray both the star and a forward-facing sitter looking up at it. Instead of attempting to solve this problem, Cranach has chosen to enable viewers to obey Prudentius's exhortation. Here the star appears so that any viewer might see it if they looked into the sky, as Cuspinian did. Cuspinian is modelling a humanist gaze that is ready to receive inspiration from the earliest source of all, the first light.

The presence of the star is just one erudite detail in this iconographically rich portrait. Art historians have plausibly elaborated many of the meanings contained here.[17] The encounter between the melancholy owl and its natural enemies, diurnal birds; the bathing women; the figures atop the fortress on the hilltop – all these would have had significances for the initiated literary crowd of Cuspinian's circles. This catalogue of details is matched in the imagery of the portrait of his bride, Anna. Here, a woman facing a town in flames, entangled birds and a parrot over Anna's shoulder all hint at similarly complex meanings. While in some cases this iconography is still clear today – as when the star of the origin of light accompanies the diurnal birds' attack on the night owl, signalling the triumph of the good and the defeat of melancholy – much of the symbolism remains open to further interpretation.

For the purpose of tracking Cranach's development, it is important to remember that the selection of iconography was almost always a collaborative venture. In making reference to a Prudentius poem Cuspinian had edited, Cranach would possibly have been following directions, or at the very least, heavily consulting the sitter. Scholarly clients wanted their portraits to display erudition and wit, and to have inside references that appealed to their inner circle. This trend explains the iconographical density of not only Cranach's portraiture but also that of Dürer, Hans Holbein the Younger and many others less well known at this time. In the first years of the sixteenth century, Cranach still lacked particularly lofty or steady patronage. He probably enjoyed a learned reference on his own, but he also employed it to please Cuspinian, who was an imperial favourite and thus the kind of patron who might further Cranach's career.

Cranach may have also come up with another simpler and more material way of participating in Vienna's erudite culture. In these panels and several others from these years, scholarship influenced not just his iconography, but also his format. Many panels from this period of Cranach's career have almost the same ratio of height to width: 4:3. The proportions seem to be deliberate, no accident of carpentry, nor a standard workshop setting. Cranach was using different kinds of wood and different painterly techniques across these projects. He was not merely painting on standard panels he had bought wholesale – or if he was, he was having them cut down to a very special size.

To be a humanist scholar in Vienna in 1500 was to be aware of the recent discoveries, rediscoveries and pseudo-discoveries of ancient Greek numerological thought by Florentine scholars. Much of this interest in numerology and natural mathematical proportion grew popular through the mid-fifteenth-century theoretical writings of the polymath Leon Battista Alberti, and later and more specifically through the work of the scholar Marsilio Ficino on Plato's texts.[18] The most important ancient Greek mathematician for these writers was Pythagoras, who established certain primal significances for certain numbers. Besides the work on the triangle for which he is famous today, Pythagoras was said to have discovered the perfect, even divine, ratios for tuning musical instruments. These primal harmonies were then extended by scholars like Alberti into the realm of architecture and, by extension, vision and visual art.

Cranach's university patrons in Vienna would have been keenly interested in the antique meanings given to proportion. Following these interests or perhaps stoking them himself, he may have intentionally requested from carpenters the proportions of an ideal Pythagorean ratio.[19] It may be that Cranach believed in the natural harmony of such ratios himself, or at least in their market appeal. Or perhaps an influential patron like Cuspinian specifically requested the format, and, boosting the trend, Cranach then offered this harmonious option to his other clients.

To connect the dimensions of a painted panel with humanist interest in the mathematico-mystical inclinations of the time may seem implausible or superficial compared with the detail and textual specificity of Prudentius's star. But Cranach's engagement with scholarly practice, amid his many academic clients and friends, would be pervasive and profound for his whole life.

## WITTENBERG AND THE WETTINS: A LIFELONG POST AT COURT

At some point in the years when Cranach was working for Cuspinian and others at the University of Vienna, responding to or stoking their antiquarian humanist ideas in paint, he came to the attention of the wealthy elector of Saxony, Friedrich III of the House of Wettin. Conrad Celtis himself might have been the link: the older scholar knew Friedrich. The elector's coffers were running full in the wake of the second great 'silver rush', or *Berggeschrey*, in his territories towards the late fifteenth century. Prosperous as Friedrich was, he already had a court painter, Jacopo de' Barbari. Still, he wrote to Cranach in 1504, inviting him to Wittenberg, too. One possibility is that Friedrich, aware of Maximilian's milieu and its promotion of German identity, wanted a proper German to work for him, too, instead of or along with the Venetian Jacopo.

Another possibility has to do with the increasing importance of visual art to court culture as Saxony thrived under Friedrich's rule. Perhaps Friedrich needed more work than an ageing Barbari was willing or able to take on. Friedrich wanted a court artist who would work beyond panel paintings and prints. Electoral Saxony's artist would oversee the production and design of caparisons

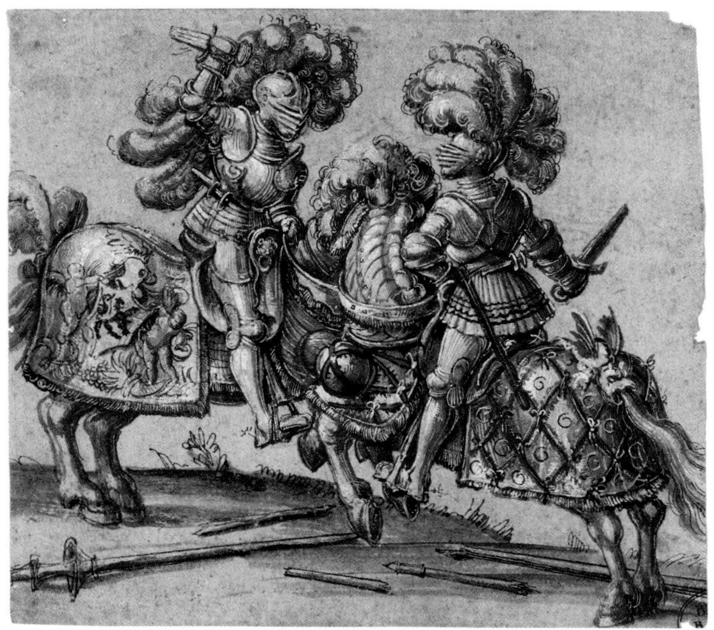

(horse-coverings) for jousts, courtly attire, festival costumes and masks, coats of arms, medals, coins, feast-day decorations, hunting paraphernalia and interior decoration (which included supervising the whitewashing of walls, dreaming up carpet patterns and chandeliers and executing massive paintings on textile – for multiple residences). Furthermore, Friedrich would ask his artist to act as a diplomat, furnishing gifts for, as well as personally socializing with, important foreign rulers and nobles, including the emperor himself.[20] Decades later, under the electorship of Friedrich's nephew Johann Friedrich, Cranach himself would oversee both defensive and offensive military assistance, including bastion design, on-site documentation of battles, standard-bearer flags and even the provision of varnish for weapons.[21]

Cranach would perform marvellously in every courtly capacity. In return, he was paid one hundred guilder a year, plus additional

10 Lucas Cranach the Elder, *Turnier-Zweikampf, c.* 1509, pen on paper.
This drawing is one fine surviving document of the mostly ephemeral labours of a court artist of Cranach's stature at this time.

expenses for individual projects and whatever he earned from working for other patrons. He also had separate funds for basic expenses such as clothing, horses, food and lodging.

It is difficult to convey the impressiveness of this salary in twenty-first-century terms, due to the very different values that commodities and labour costs possessed in the early sixteenth century. Such comparisons are furthermore difficult across different cities and states. It is still worth noting that one hundred guilder (*Gulden*) comprised the same salary that Nuremberg-based Dürer, more renowned than Cranach even at the time, agreed to receive from the Emperor Maximilian years later, in 1518, and would receive as a yearly pension for the duration of his life.[22] One hundred guilder per year was a payment proffered by only the loftiest patrons to the very best artists.

With a steady and ample income, Cranach formed his own workshop in 1505. To Wittenberg, whose university had been founded only in 1502 by Friedrich, Cranach brought along the

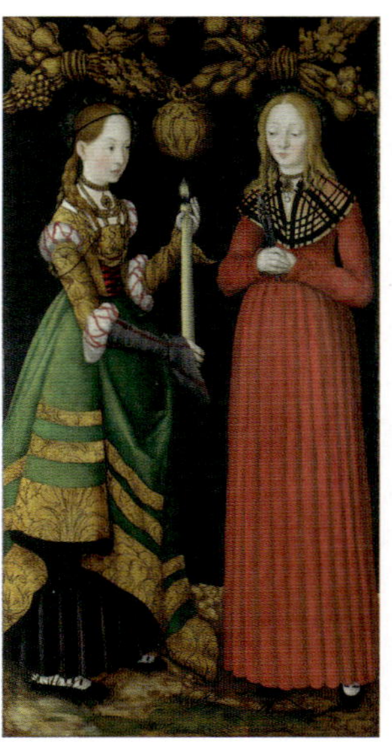
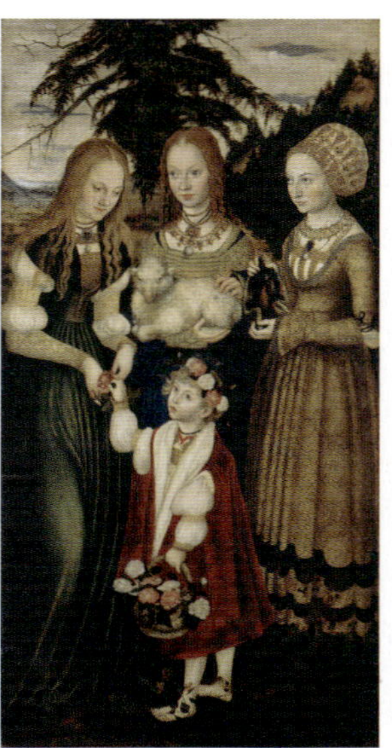
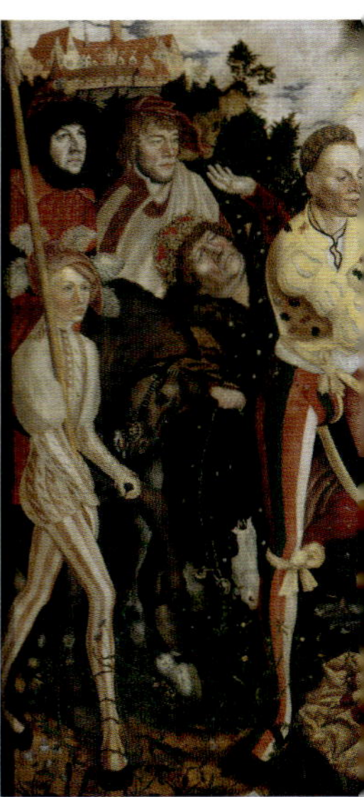

weight of his humanist experience in longer-established Vienna. Appropriately, the earliest surviving artistic monument commissioned by the elector, the 1506 *Altar of St Catherine*, was devoted to the patron saint of scholars and educators, Catherine of Alexandria.

There are several reasons to call this altarpiece a monument. Size is the first: it is the largest surviving work on painted panel Cranach had completed to this point. More than 1.2 metres (4 ft) tall and almost 2.7 metres (9 ft) wide, the altarpiece when open would have commanded the apse of the transeptless, modest but attractive Castle Church of the elector's Wittenberg residence. The church, begun in the 1490s, may have housed the altarpiece even before construction was complete.

Another impressive feature is the comprehensive iconographic programme. Trios and duos of female saints adorn all four surfaces on the wings, both open and shut: on the inner wings appear Dorothea, Agnes and Kunigunde on the left, and Barbara,

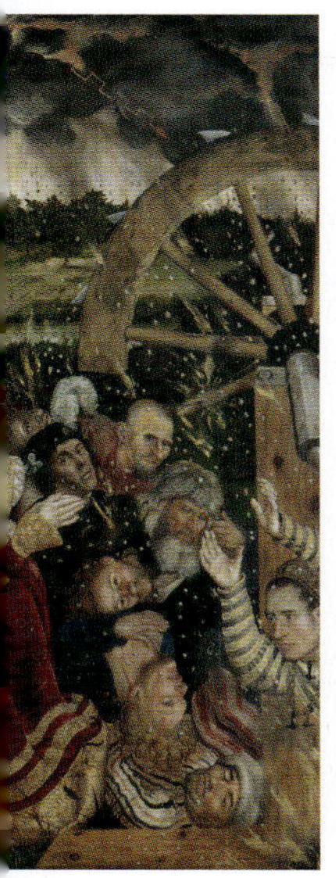
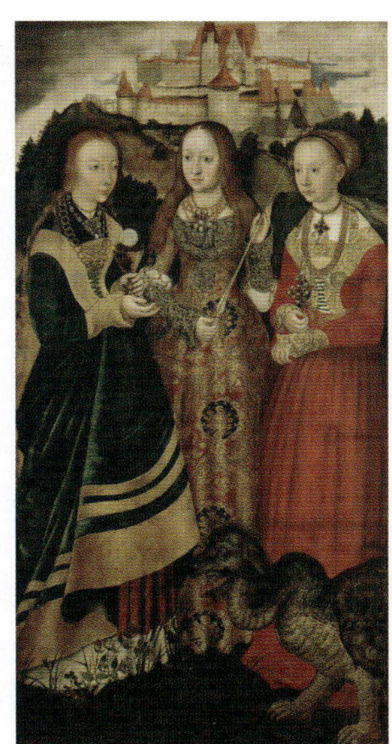
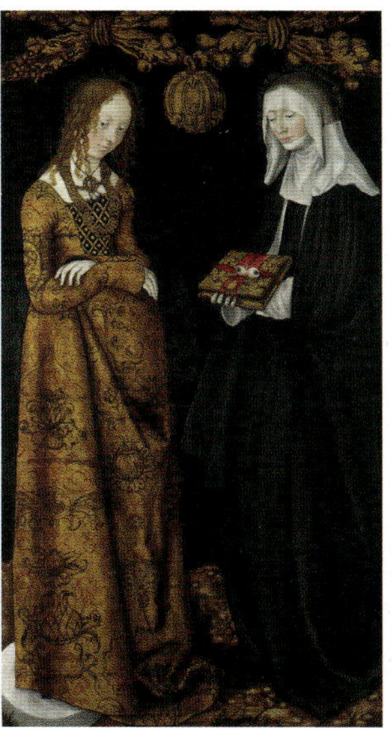

11 Lucas Cranach the Elder, *Altar of St Catherine* (open), 1506, oil on panel.

Ursula and Margaret on the right; on the outer wings, visible when the altarpiece was closed, we find Genevieve and Apollonia of Alexandria on the left and Christina of Bolsena and Ottilia on the right. St Catherine of Alexandria kneels in the middle of the hectic central panel. Most of these women were in the special category of saint known as 'virgin martyrs', a designation reserved for those murdered because of a Christian commitment to chastity. However, some of them, like Kunigunde, the wife of Holy Roman Emperor Henry II, were not virgin martyrs, and some virgin martyrs frequently included at the time, like Agatha, are here excluded. Indeed, there is no obvious single category that fits all these female saints.

Given this broad female iconography, Cranach and his patron may have intended to direct the altarpiece towards female viewers more generally. Imagery about women, especially imagery providing models for the proper roles of women, was part of German and more broadly European visual culture of this time, from cathedral jamb statues of the wise and foolish virgins to, more recently, print series featuring iconic images of famous women from both pagan history and the Bible. There was even a special kind of large altarpiece now called 'Virgo inter virgines', 'The Virgin among the virgins', featuring the Virgin Mary amid virgin saints. The general point of such images was to provide moral examples.

Why would Elector Friedrich have gone to his new court artist and commissioned a similar altarpiece, with an emphasis on female models of piety, for the Castle Church? There are no conclusive answers to this question. One might suppose a woman of the house had been recently married or deceased. The most likely candidate would be Sophia of Mecklenburg, the elector's sister-in-law, who had passed away in 1503. But a separate memorial commission for her is already known from 1505, an altarpiece for the Marienkirche in Torgau, though scholars are not certain whether it or any of its component panels survive.

One candidate for a dedicatee about whom records are sparse is the unmarried elector's long-term companion, with whom Friedrich had three children who survived into adulthood. In a record of one of Martin Luther's conversations, this companion is referred to as 'the Watzler woman', 'die Watzlerin', but otherwise goes unnamed; Friedrich's last testament of 1525 refers to her as the mother of his sons. Later sources from the eighteenth century name the woman 'Anna Weller', but there are no extant documents from her lifetime that confirm this name.

In 1506, Cranach completed what one might today understand as a 'romantic' woodcut of a young noble couple riding in the countryside, sharing a single horse and accompanied by a pair of dogs. In some copies of the print, considered to be from the second 'state' or version of the woodblock, there are, as here, two coats of arms suspended above the lovers in the blank sky. These are the arms of the Saxon electorate, crossed red swords on a field divided by black and silver, and those of the Saxony proper, a green bend coronated, or crancelin, across bars of sable and gold. (Woodcuts rendered heraldic elements in black and white, though in some prints these could be hand-coloured for sale.) The image itself comes from a long graphic tradition depicting lovers on a hunt, a visual tradition that, as Dieter Koepplin has shown, could have different moral applications depending on what kind of text accompanied the image.[23]

The moral valence here was meant to be positive. In rare copies of this version of the woodcut, a love poem in rhyming couplets appears printed below the image, with a brief couplet above serving as superscript or title.[24] The superscript reads: 'A jolt to my heart, be undaunted and stout:/The one I desire is the one I've caught.'[25] Below, the verses make an allegorical poem about a hunter's chase for a hind or female deer, signed with the

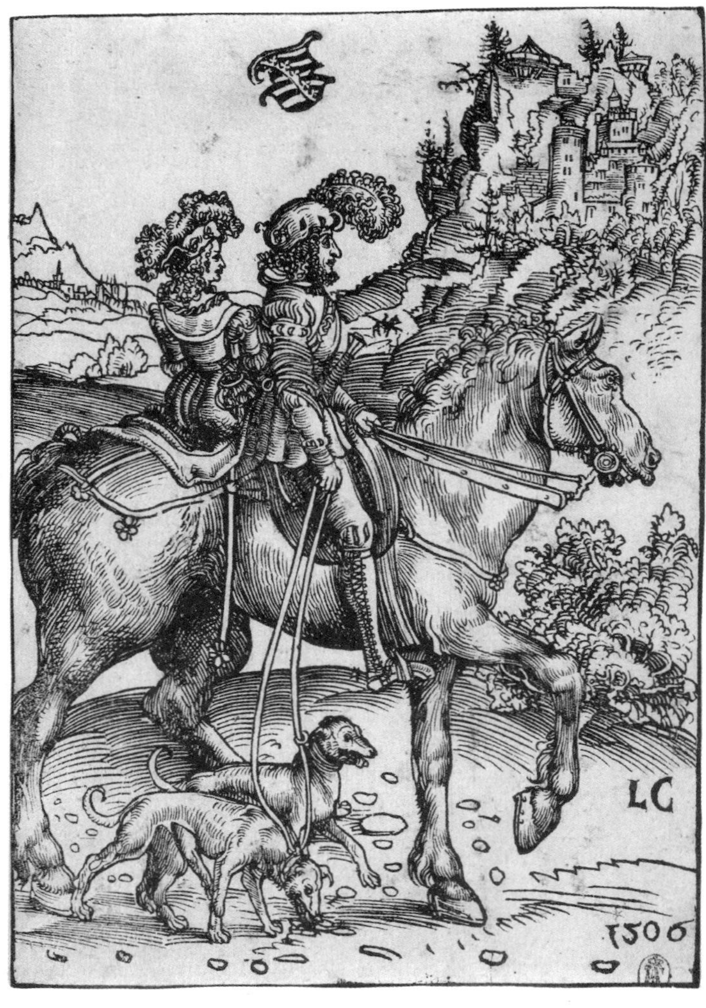

letters C.M.O. This poem, which includes a reference to the ancient Roman Empire, might remind some Anglophone readers of Thomas Wyatt's (1503–1542) later sonnet known as 'Whoso List to Hunt', first published posthumously in 1557. Almost certainly, C.M.O. was aware of the original Petrarchan sonnet

12 Lucas Cranach the Elder, *Gentleman and Lady Riding to the Hunt*, 1506, woodcut.

(now known as Sonnet 190) that inspired Wyatt. Petrarch's Sonnet 190 had appeared not only in various printed Italian editions from Venice but in a Latin edition of Petrarch's collected works published north of the Alps, in Basel, in 1496.

Unlike in either Petrarch's original or, later, Wyatt's famous response to it, C.M.O.'s lyric 'I', the speaker of the 26-line poem, successfully acquires the hind he has hunted. In Petrarch, the speaker notes that the deer has been declared free by 'Caesar' and therefore remains free; in Wyatt, the deer *belongs* to Caesar, and indeed this possession is often interpreted as a reference to Anne Boleyn's having been taken by Henry VIII (rather than by Wyatt). In C.M.O.'s version, however, the hind 'has willingly fallen into my [the speaker's] net'.[26] The 'Roman Empire'

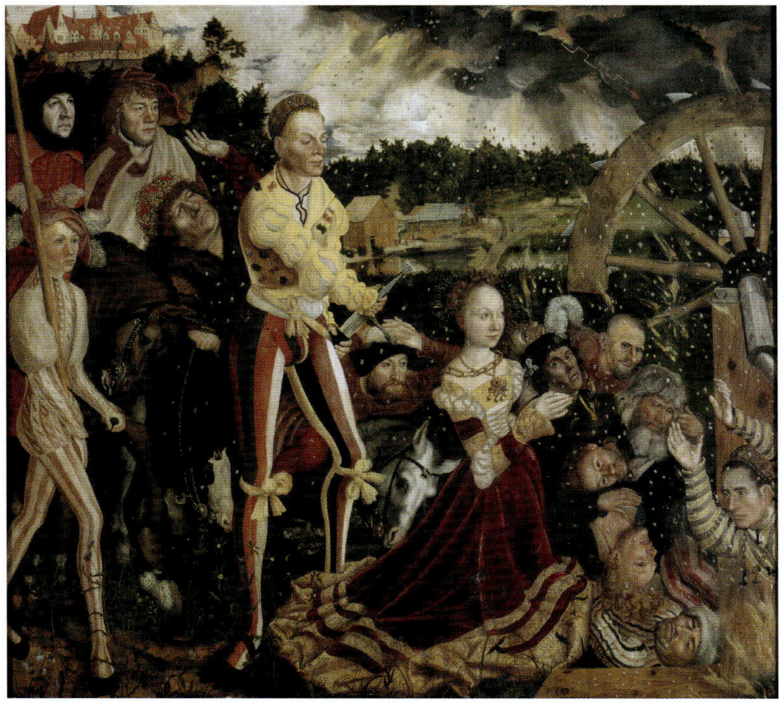

13 *Martyrdom of St Catherine*, central panel of illus. 11.

is mentioned only to declare that this particular hind has no equal in it – and perhaps also to remind a learned reader of the Petrarchan reference to Caesar's hind.

By 1506, Friedrich would have similarly already won his companion to his side. Since Friedrich's oldest child must have been born at least a few years before 1506, one may assume that his long-term relationship with the mother of his children was already well established. Though woodcuts tended to be aimed at a more general audience, it seems possible that this image, with the Saxon coat of arms, was at least inspired by Friedrich's relationship with his companion.

It is thus also possible to speculate that she may have provided in some way a partial motive for the commissioning of the *Altar of St Catherine*. One can imagine that an elector's live-in mistress might have had to endure not only Christian scorn but also the by-products of political pressure on the elector, who was supposed to have married within his station (and never did). Certainly the serenity shown by Cranach's St Catherine of Alexandria at the scene of her final beheading provided an excellent model for such endurance.

Whether or not this altarpiece had anything to do with Friedrich's long-term companion, it is important to note again that its iconography was not strictly devoted to virgin saints, and any association with 'the Watzler woman' cannot be disproven on the basis of sexual activity. At the heart of the altarpiece, Cranach gives us St Catherine amid multiple legendary trials within a very original, unusual composition. The various trials depicted all occur in a popular tract describing the lives of saints, the *Golden Legend*. The vignettes here include the burning of the fifty learned grammarians and rhetoricians Catherine debated and persuaded to Christianity (though they were martyred, they suffered no harm); the attempted breaking of her body between four iron wheels fitted with razors (an angel broke the wheels instead); and her beheading (here impending, but finally effective). Much of the rest of her story in the *Golden Legend*, not depicted here, has to do with her high rate of conversion of the pagans around her and with her overcoming obstacles schemed up by the emperor.

Given the larger group of women around long-suffering Catherine, there is still a third context at Friedrich's court for which the altarpiece was appropriate. When the elector had Cranach catalogue his sizable collection of relics, a task he completed by 1509, the first section focused on women saints in general. These saints are not labelled as women, however, but as 'virgins and widows', the two saintly categories for women. Not only do all the women of the *Catherine* altarpiece fit this category, but they also, save for St Genevieve, are explicitly mentioned in Cranach's inventory within that opening section. Admittedly, Friedrich's relic collection was so comprehensive that there were few well-known saints from whom he lacked a trace. Nevertheless, it is possible that the altarpiece's iconography connects with relics present in Wittenberg.

This discussion of the various contexts for the grand female-oriented altarpiece should not obscure the primary and most obvious relevance of the commission. St Catherine of Alexandria was the patron saint of scholars, and for good reason. During her disputation with the fifty grammarians and rhetoricians of the Roman Empire, she not only vanquished them all intellectually with her logic, but also specifically alluded to the role of knowledge in appreciation of the true Christian God. Instead of valuing the works of humankind alone, Catherine recommended, humans should appreciate the God-fashioned cosmos and acquire knowledge of it.

From 1507 on, the Castle Church was the official church of the university, which by the end of Cranach's life would indeed be an established centre of study of God's cosmos. If the foregoing speculations about the reasons for a major woman-themed commission for this church have any merit, what we have here is a major early altarpiece that may have combined the personal investments of the elector with his public institutional ones. Cranach was already uniting everyday life with a sense of long-term cultural legacy.


## PORTRAITS OF ELECTORS

Cranach's portraiture comes into its own in Wittenberg. Though the allusions and learning of a university environment endure in other areas of his oeuvre, his Wittenberg portraits shift emphasis. Here, Cranach reduces the density of his symbolism and at the same time increases his skill in achieving a realistic likeness.

Cranach's earliest surviving proper portraits from the court at Wittenberg (as opposed to paintings in which real people appear as donors or as part of the action) are not of Elector Friedrich the Wise himself but of his brother Johann, known as the Steadfast, and Johann's son Johann Friedrich, later known as the Magnanimous. Because Friedrich's children with his partner were not considered legitimate, these men would become his two successors. In 1509, when these panels were painted, Johann Friedrich would have been five or six years old. His father, Johann, would have proven himself already as his brother's close advisor and confidant, at times almost a co-ruler.

Though these paintings are early in Cranach's long career as a portraitist, they show him already as a master. Unlike in the symbol-saturated earlier images from Vienna, Cranach here balances a fascination with textures of hair, ornament and facial modelling with a sensitivity to the dynamics of composition (where figures appear on the panel, and in what proportion to it). Both figures dominate the space around them and overwhelm the viewer with finery and emotive presence rather than with

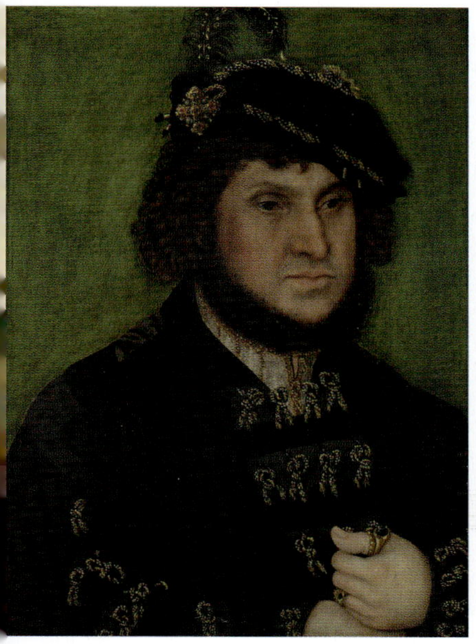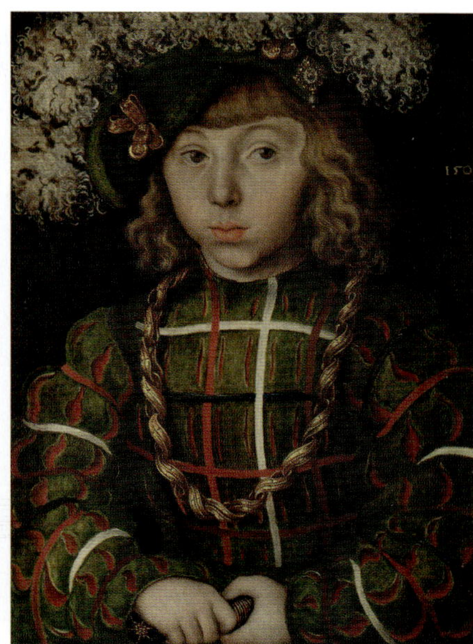

insignia. As was typical, the pair's identifying coats of arms appear on the reverse of each other's panels.

Given that Johann's coat of arms appears on the reverse of the painting featuring his son, and vice versa, and that these coats of arms do not seem to be later additions, one might deduce that these two paintings were in fact intended to go together early on. This iconographic evidence is corroborated by other material similarities reported in conservation studies of the object (the panels were made in the same way from the same wood, for example). Still, the pairing is unusual for a few reasons.

First of all, the two figures do not possess any compositional symmetry, only a symmetry of colour achieved by the reversed use of green and black for figure and ground in each panel. The colours do not exactly match, though both greens use a mixture of verdigris with other pigments. Rather than symmetry, Cranach plays with imbalance: the pairing of a traditional three-quarter

14, 15 Lucas Cranach the Elder, *Johann the Steadfast* and *Johann Friedrich the Magnanimous*, 1509, oil on panel (diptych).

bust of Johann with the more frontal half-length rendering of his son – who is proportionally huge – jars the eye and creates a sense of different proximities to different sitters. Second of all, diptychs featuring two real-life sitters usually depict a husband and wife together (as in the Cuspinian portraits). Here, Johann Friedrich appears in the right-hand position of the missing wife – his mother, who died less than a fortnight after he was born.

Finally, the gazes of father and son do not obviously complement each other. It is relatively typical for the male figure in a heterosexual couple portrait not to look at his partner figure (as in Cuspinian's portrait). In the case of a devotional diptych, pairing a divine figure like the Virgin Mary and a worshipper, it is standard for a divine figure on the left-hand side of a diptych to appear as if no other panel were attached. However, the right-hand figure of a diptych – whether worshipper or wife – ought to be looking devotedly towards their left-hand complement. Johann Friedrich, appearing elevated above his father, does not. Instead, he looks slightly upward and to the right, as if looking past the viewer at something more interesting.

It is this last oddity that gives viewers a clue as to how these paired panels may have functioned. When the two panels were hinged together, perhaps they were displayed to emphasize the father's portrait, with the other panel serving as a cover. In other words, the reverse of the son's portrait, with his father's coat of arms, would be visible when the diptych was in a closed position. When a viewer opened the diptych to look upon the father, with the covering panel slightly open, the son might appear to be gazing directly at the viewer. Both panels were already in their frames when painted, so Cranach may even have planned them to work this way. If we thus opened up the diptych to look at Johann, we would find Johann Friedrich on the inside cover. Here he would seem closer to us, almost as if in his father's lap, which would explain his largeness and elevation within the frame. This effect would disappear the more one opened the diptych, but such objects were often displayed at an angle.

Whatever the intended mode of display, both portraits possess a drama and detail that would invite a viewer to look at them face to face, and closely. Johann's black coat has bands of grey, at least one of which has curved, feathery patterns not unlike what one would now call a paisley, perhaps early evidence of the influence of Persian buta (or boteh) ornaments. Johann here participates in long-standing European courtly preference for clothing with reference to fashions from cultures to the east of the continent.

Cranach balances many kinds of fineness across the panel. The twisting bands of Johann's hat and the knots decorating the front of his coat are interwoven with gold and small pearls. The brushstrokes here suggest a speedy making, the highlights dynamic rather than systematic, the gold's sheen rendered by thick yellow bits of impasto. But Johann's face displays a different painterly virtuosity. Though his beard and curls frame his features, leaving them exposed to view, they are finely painted, giving the impression of individual follicles. The modelling of the face proper reflects both Cranach's confident agility and his care for detail. The stubble is smooth shadow rather than prickle, but it still enhances the softness of the lips. Cranach used white highlights, especially in the brow, to give his patron's face a healthy sheen, then allowed the red of the caruncle (the inner corner of the eye) to bleed delicately up into the white. This slight reddening of the eyes, combined with his downcast gaze, may reflect a trace of the widower's mourning for the absent wife in the facing panel.

Little Johann Friedrich looks out quizzically from that panel with equally busy, more colourful attire. His green doublet is patterned with a thin-banded tartan of red, white and blue; its red lining is visible through the frequent slashes. Between these slashes and the bunching up of the sleeves at the bands, Cranach has created the sense that this six-year-old is bursting with growth and potential energy. The ornaments on Johann Friedrich's cap may not signify any worldly allegiances in particular; though the rightmost of the three visible ornaments may have an enamel on it, the pattern does not correspond to any known coat of arms. But the gold and the size of these ornaments, along with the heavy golden chain with links too large for a child's frame, point ahead to his significant responsibilities, as yet unknowable in 1509, in the future of Christendom.

This diptych is an early example of Cranach's mastery of the portrait genre. Surviving portraits attributed by scholarly consensus primarily to Cranach, rather than to members of his workshop or to copyists, number upwards of 250.[27] This father–son pairing marks a turning point in Cranach's career. In 1508, Friedrich sent Cranach to work for Maximilian I on the latter's sojourn in the Low Countries. Cranach painted the emperor and his heir, Charles V, though neither painting survives. We know about this trip because it was mentioned in the formal oration of a University of Wittenberg scholar, Christoph Scheurl, in 1509, an oration in which Scheurl likens Cranach, alongside his contemporary Dürer, to the great painters of antiquity.

After this moment, the number of surviving paintings grows in general, and we begin to find panels that have a touch of the Cranach style but are attributed by scholars primarily to members of Cranach's workshop or to a follower. Cranach's workshop had become the cultural heart of a thriving electorate. It was expanding to include other well-trained painters, and its output of painted panels more than doubled from the first decade of the sixteenth century to the second. By 1513, Cranach had begun purchasing his own pigments in massive enough quantities to record in contracts that he used his own store rather than purchasing supplies from other merchants.[28] This suggests that he had securely established his apothecary by then. His practice was growing in all directions.

Among the most majestic examples of Cranach's portraiture in this period of bloom are Cranach's 1514 double life-size portrait of Friedrich III's cousin Heinrich (now historically known as Heinrich IV), also of the House of Wettin, and his wife, Katharina von Mecklenburg. Again, documentation is lacking, though there is an invoice for certain works executed for Heinrich's wedding in 1512.[29] This invoice is often taken to correspond at least in part to these two panels, despite the two-year discrepancy. Even if this invoice is for these panels, a two-year lag should not necessarily be taken to mean that Cranach worked slowly. The impression of quick facture present in the 1509 portrait of Johann the Constant corroborates several comments by peers, including Scheurl, about Cranach's speed. These comments had a positive value, a marvelling at virtuosity, that might not be intuited by a twenty-first-century reader; 'that was dashed off quickly' does not always sound like praise. But Cranach was proud enough of his swiftness to have had 'pictor celerrimus' ('fastest/very fast painter') carved as his epitaph.

Swiftly painted or not, the full-length portraits of Heinrich and Katharina exhibit many qualities that would become recognizable as part of a Cranach 'brand' or style. The first is the ground on which the figures stand, which, if one dares the anachronism, may be characterized as a 'moonscape'. (These paintings antedate the earliest detailed images of the surface of the moon, Galileo's, by nearly a century.) This is one way of describing the panels' bare, greyish-clayey strip of foreground, topped here and there with pebbles of the same hue. This strip, often just broad enough to support the stance of a full-length figure, is accompanied by a plain black background. The result is that the figure itself, with its plausible modelling and colours, stands out as all the more lifelike and alive.

*Overleaf:* 16, 17 Lucas Cranach the Elder, *Katharina von Mecklenburg* and *Heinrich the Pious*, 1514, oil and gold leaf on panel.

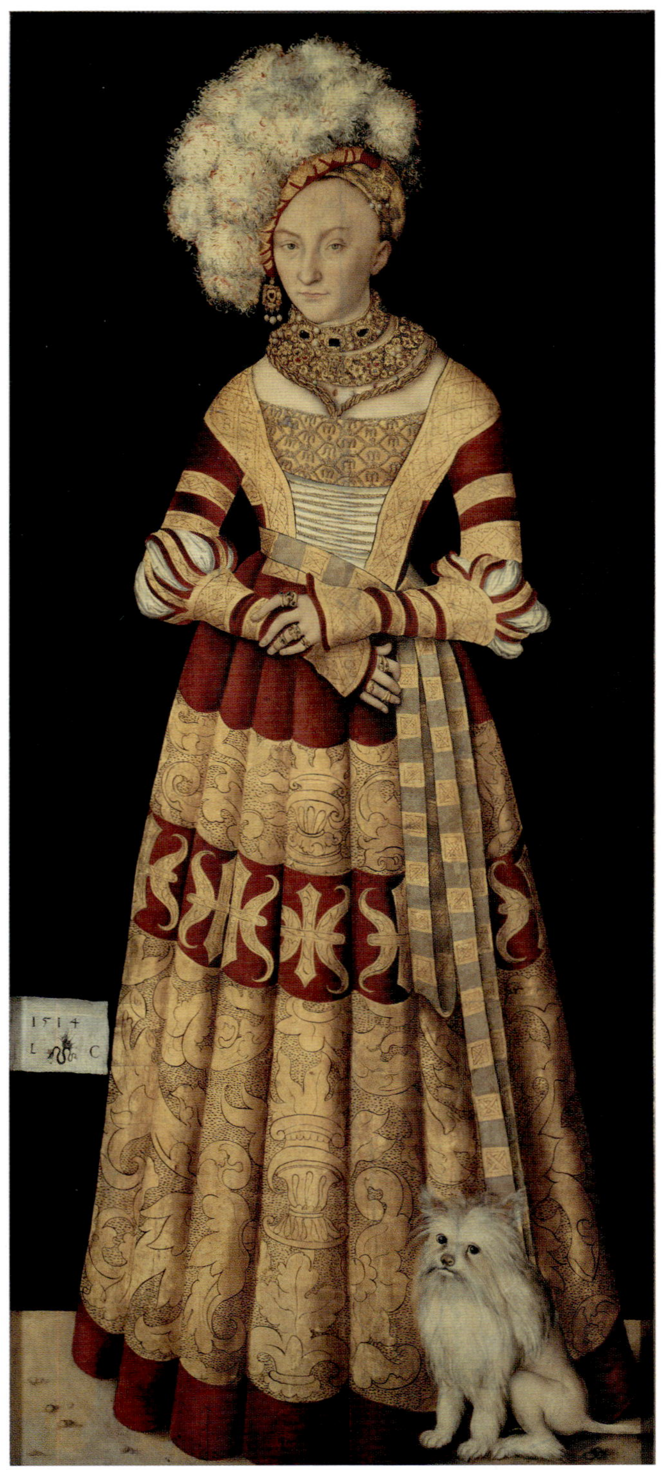

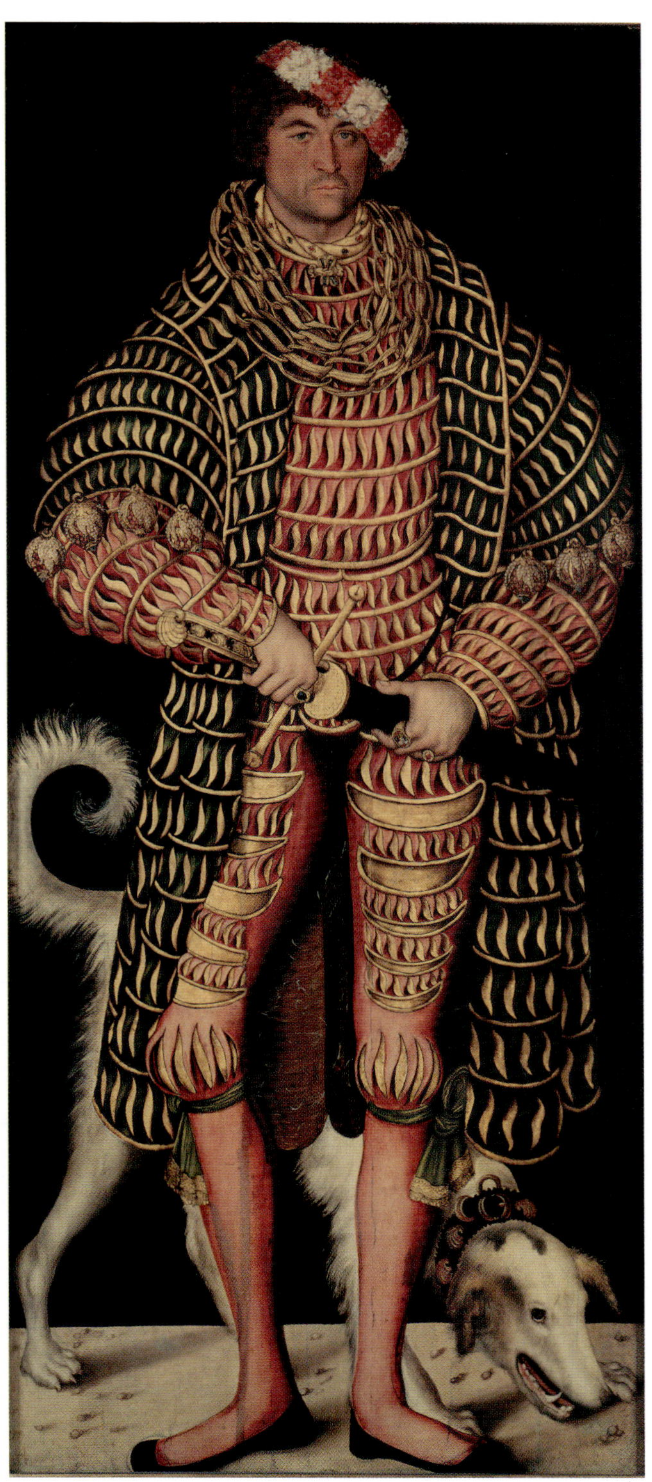

Cranach first deployed a moonscape, or something like it, in the context of his earliest paintings of nudes, which will be discussed in the next chapter. The use of a strip of ground itself seems to derive – like other aspects of his paintings of naked women – from a Botticellian *Venus* painting similar to the famous *Birth of Venus*, either one such painting now in the Gemäldegalerie in Berlin or another like it. The Berlin Botticelli *Venus* in turn seems to derive from ancient statues of Venus in a 'modest' pose, the so-called Venus *pudica*. Cranach's moonscape seems to be a cross between the plain pedestal of an ancient Mediterranean statue and the open soil depicted in Northern European altarpieces with isolated full-length figures like saints. Where a stone figure gets a bare stone plinth, a living figure gets a plinth of bare earthly matter. This black-backed dead moonscape will appear over and over again when Cranach wishes to emphasize an isolated full-length figure and endow it, by contrast, with life.

The second quality that made this double portrait so Cranachian was the signature. Right around the time of his career turning point, in 1508, Friedrich the Wise bestowed Cranach with an officially recognized emblem: a winged snake with a ring in its mouth. In more recent heraldry parlance, this creature is known as an amphithere, a double-beast (double because a creature of both land and air). In Cranach's time, the creature may have been more familiar as a jaculus, mentioned by Pliny in his *Natural History*, Lucan in the *Pharsalia*, or Isidore of Seville in the *Etymologies*. Some scholars have thought that the snake might have appeared as a symbol of Kronos (or Cronus/Κρόνος), the ancient Greek ancestor god and Titan – understood also from time immemorial as Chronos, the god of time – whose name may have punned with 'Kronach'. Many of the humanists around Cranach and throughout German-speaking lands sought to render their name in Greco-Latinate terms. Yet there is no other evidence of Kronach's being related to Kronos in the period. The ring in the serpent's mouth remains unexplained except perhaps as a reference to the electoral rings of the rulers Cranach served. The signature retains some mystery as a humanist hieroglyphic.

Whatever it meant exactly, the use of this symbol, often painted along with the initials L. C. and the year, as in Katharina's portrait here, merged the authority of antiquity with that of more continuous European practices. Though Cranach does not seem to have used the symbol as a coat of arms, ordinary citizens were permitted to fashion their own, and the amphithere would have been associated with heraldic devices that would have marked such civic legitimacy. The symbol also looked like a maker's mark or trademark, a symbol that appeared on goods destined for the market in order to distinguish one maker's ware from another's. In Katharina's portrait, Cranach's symbol, with its associations with late medieval European civic legitimacy, appeared on a cartellino, a small white piece of paper. Ancient Greek and Roman artists had developed the tactic of signing one's work with a figurative cartellino, including on mosaics. When cartellini appeared in late-fifteenth and early-sixteenth-century Italian imagery, and from there in prints circulating northward in the period, the little piece of paper usually curled or showed creasing or tearing, as it often did in ancient imagery. These curls and creases and tears enhanced the Renaissance cartellino's participation in the ancient artistic gimmickry later known as *trompe l'oeil* ('trick-the-eye'). Cranach nods to this trope, giving tonal value to the edges of the paper. And thus, here, medieval German civic visuality meets the visual play of the ancient Mediterranean.

This brings us to the third hallmark of the mature Cranach brand visible in this image: a stylistic plurality within individual works. The faces of the figures are modelled with great sensitivity and produce a sense of depth, while the dressed bodies often flatten, focusing on pattern and texture of fabric. If one were expecting a consistent style, the paintings would feel discordant, divided, as if different parts of a big workshop had not bothered to confer before doing things each their own way.

Another way to look at it, though, is to say that the paintings balance themselves. The drama of personality in the faces matches the drama of material and iconographic wealth displayed in the clothes. The different styles in these different passages in the paintings are the ones best suited to their parts in a painting's internal drama as a whole. Over and over again in Cranach portraits from this point onwards – and in some of the other kinds of painting, too – the identity conferred by material possessions and iconographies of rank complements, by visual contrast, the kind of identity conferred by human interiority and expression.

But as much as these paired portraits of Heinrich and Katharina are the epitome of Cranach production in the decades to come, they are extremely unusual in format. Surviving full-length portraits from this period of anyone besides kings and emperors are rare. This commission on the part of the younger brother of a duke, Georg, who himself oversaw only half an electorate, is rather bold for 1514. (Georg and Friedrich split rule of Saxony following an arrangement made by their grandfather in the fifteenth century.) The double portrait's boldness recalls the bastard Admiral Philip of Burgundy's 1516 portrait as Neptune – with the Low Countries personified as his bride Amphitrite – by Jan Gossart, though Cranach's effort shows more restraint than Philip's bawdy court would have encouraged.[30] Such restraint recalls in turn Jan van Eyck's *Arnolfini Portrait*, though the life-size scale of Cranach's paired portraits, advertising the public roles of two members of the ruling class, differentiates them from the private contemplation inspired by the smaller format of the merchant couple's portrait. In any case, paired full-length wedding portraits may have been a genre the examples of which largely failed to survive: a genre Philip of Burgundy and Gossart subverted, and a genre Cranach helped propagate.

The two gold-bedecked figures in this diptych would turn out to be key figures of the Reformation. Katharina's late 1520s correspondence with Johann Friedrich, with whom she was friendly, suggests that she had a role in persuading her husband, Heinrich, to convert to Luther's cause. Around that time, Heinrich came to odds with his older brother, Georg, who was a staunch defender of the Roman Church. Upon Georg's death in 1539, Heinrich took over and officially promoted Lutheranism in the Saxon lands on his side of the family; the resulting confessional unification of Saxony earned him the moniker 'Heinrich the Pious' ('der Fromm'). Here, of course, he is a young man, and Luther had not yet made his intervention in the city of Wittenberg. But portraits of him by Cranach or Cranach's workshop trace his appearance for the rest of his life.

## THE CRANACH STANDARD AND ITS INFLUENCE

This sense of a Reformation life captured at several stages through the portraiture of a single artist is for no one more extensive than for that little boy weighed down by gold chains in the 1509 diptych with his father. Young Johann Friedrich, the elector's nephew, was thirteen when Luther first publicized his 95 Theses critiquing the corruption of the Roman Church. The men who would become the closest advisors to Luther and who helped Luther develop his form of Christianity were doing so within Johann Friedrich's direct social ambit during his own formative years, and under his military and financial protection as a mature adult. If Friedrich gave Luther sanctuary against assassination attempts at a crucial stage, in the wake of the 1521 Diet of Worms, it was Johann Friedrich who oversaw the practical institution of the Reformation itself, supporting surveys of countryside parishes and protecting a transregional community of Lutheran thinkers. Cranach was the visual witness of this protectorship,

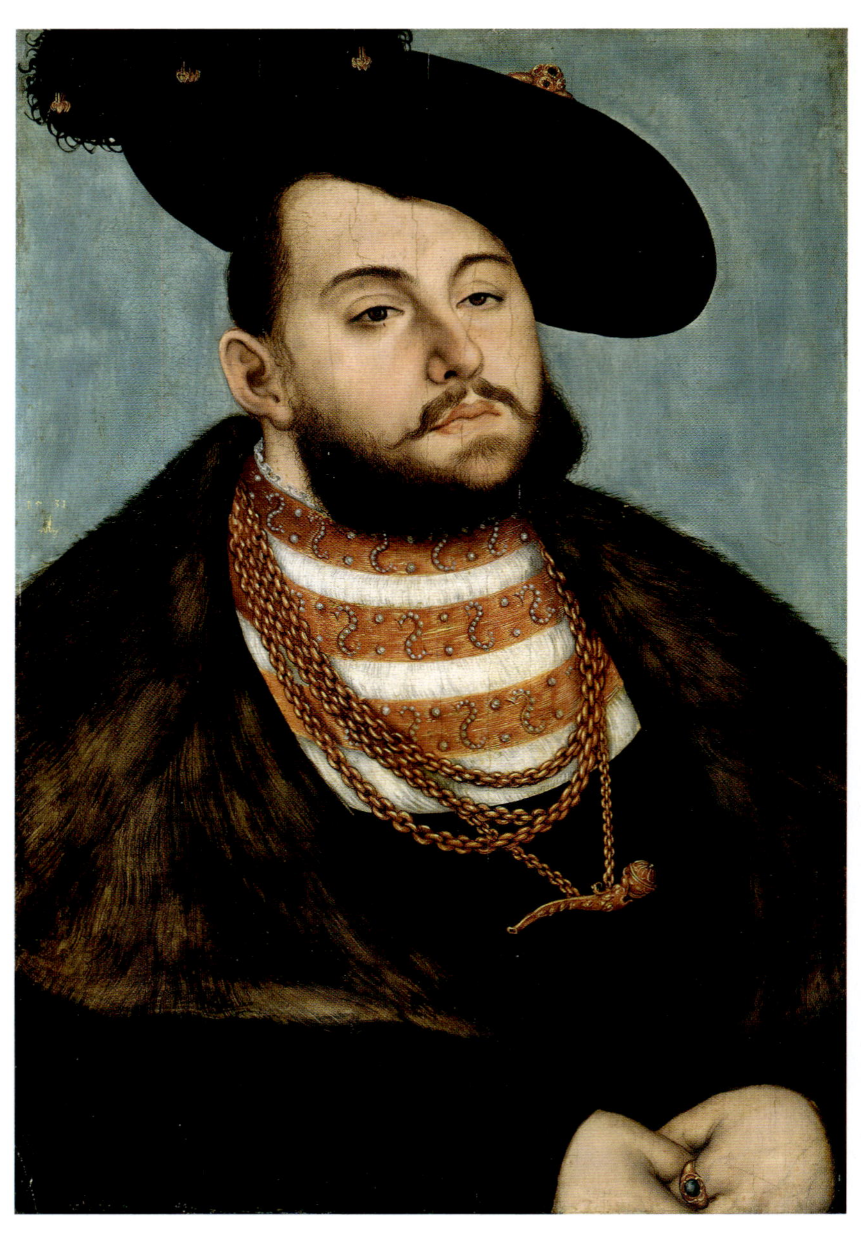

18 Lucas Cranach the Elder, *Johann Friedrich the Magnanimous*, 1531, oil on panel.

the promulgator of its propaganda and, in the future elector's last years, a close companion.

In a portrait of 1531 in the Louvre, a 28-year-old Johann Friedrich looks out past the viewer, more equanimously than he did as a child. Soon to become the elector of Saxony, he is holding onto an electoral ring, perhaps the same one Johann wore on his thumb in 1509. There is other stylistic continuity across decades: though the design is slightly different, the family's love for gold with pearl ornaments also remains. From beneath the great fur shoulders of his cloak emerge guards or bands of golden thread across a broad chest decorated with *passementerie*, or elaborate trimmings, including pearls. These guards appear reddish with gold glints.

But in fact they were not painted with gold at all. Here Cranach was imitating a common technique of applying gold leaf known as 'water-gilding' that used a red-clay pigment called 'bole'. Painters across Europe had been using this technique for centuries. The red bole served as a mordant, a kind of adhesive, for gold leaf to be affixed to the panel. By painting thin lines of lead-tin yellow over red (probably Cranach's most typical red glaze, based on red mercuric sulphide), Cranach was simulating the effect of the traditional method without employing actual gold.[31] Viewers accustomed to the old-fashioned gold-dominated religious paintings that appeared in their local churches – paintings in which the red bole would have been showing in places as the panels aged – would have recognized the conceit.

The fact that Cranach did not use actual gold leaf for this portrait does not mean he was stingy or short on funds. From early on, he and other sixteenth-century painters throughout Europe would have been influenced by changes in taste heralded by the theories of Leon Battista Alberti (the same Florentine polymath who helped spread the importance of Pythagorean or pseudo-Pythagorean numerology). Alberti's manual on painting circulated widely, and the ideas therein even more widely. One of Alberti's precepts was to esteem painterly technique above expensive materials. So, while Cranach did use gold leaf for certain special commissions throughout his career (as in the portraits of Heinrich and Katharina), he often chose to simulate the presence of gold through virtuosic artifice instead. The fact that this particular strategy echoed traditional medieval painting techniques made it perfect for the elector and the sophisticated viewers of his portrait: those gold bands combined painterly imitation with allusion to familiar, traditional art. Bridging new tastes with the old would be perhaps the Cranach workshop's most successful long-standing practice.

Comparing this image with Cranach's earlier portraits and paintings, though, yields an unexpected observation. For all its sophistication, it is less lifelike, for example, than the figures of the *Altar of St Catherine*. Cranach has modelled Johann Friedrich's face with nuance, conveying its softness and sensitivity; the child's bow-shaped lips have persisted into adulthood (Cranach was especially mindful of this part of the future elector's face: the panel's age has made a thinning correction to the lip visible). No doubt damage to the panel has compromised the success of the fur mantel and the darkest parts of the beard. But overall, this figure is stylized and flat in comparison to the earlier work.

Part of the reason for this relative stylization is that by 1531, the Cranach brand had been established for a couple of decades. The intriguing mark of the serpent – which appears here over Johann Friedrich's shoulder beneath the year – had become a literal trademark, a sign of quality. For the workshop was no longer bound to produce only what was commissioned. Authorized by the winged-serpent mark, Cranach's panels were sold for the open market from the workshop, or perhaps at fairs in Leipzig. In this context, buyers and viewers would expect a representation of the elector-to-be, verified as made by the Wettins' own highly esteemed court painter – a certified Cranach, one might say – to have a certain formula: a softly modelled face, finely rendered fancy material like fur or velvet, and little else besides the winged serpent seal. But here 'formula' is less a negative critique than a positive innovation. Cranach was building a community of admirers for the Wettin family and the elector-to-be, and community-building demanded a consistent, identifiable – perhaps even non-Italian and thus less plastically modelled – style by which a community might recognize itself.

Despite Cranach's particular style, his continued development and reinforcement of what constituted 'a Cranach' paralleled the simultaneous development and reinforcement of standard expectations for portraiture in Europe in general. The three-quarter bust view with the sitter staring out at the viewer had become the rule. But Cranach's portraits of the future elector and other Wittenberg luminaries of this time may have inspired a still more specific code. Putting a modelled face atop a mass of body clothed in luxury materials, devoid of almost all other symbolism, on a blue backdrop with a monograph and the year – this would become the norm for a certain kind of Northern European portrait: that of the merchants of the Hanseatic League.

The Hanseatic League was a long-standing economic union of Northern European merchants operating within and across larger political boundaries, mostly along coastlines from London to present-day St Petersburg. After centuries of growth and a fifteenth-century peak, their territories were shrinking by the early sixteenth century, particularly but not only because the Swedish Empire had come to dominate the Baltic Sea and local German princes – like the elector of Saxony – had become more active in managing their own region's trade. Nevertheless, they remained a significant, wealthy and influential presence in every major northern coastal town in Europe from the Low Countries eastward.

The most notable surviving portraits of Hansa merchants come from Hans Holbein the Younger's workshop in London; the German painter began to associate with the denizens of the Steelyard colony of merchants there in the early 1530s. Holbein's paintings of the merchants generally presented them in three-quarter view, with finery, against a flat blue background, with the year and age of the sitter written in gold letters and numbers floating upon that background. A well-preserved example of this format is Holbein's portrait of Hermann von Wedigh (1532) in the Metropolitan Museum of Art.

It is true that Dürer also produced some surviving portraits that adhere to this convention, most notably those of Nurembergers Hieronymus Holzschuher and Jakob Muffel (both 1526) in Berlin's Gemäldegalerie. But it is Cranach who, starting in at least 1524, establishes the standard. His portrait of Christian II of Denmark of that year, now in the Veste Coburg, may have been one of several models Hansa merchants saw and then desired for themselves. Cranach went on to paint several other rulers in this way, including Margrave Casimir of Brandenburg and (more than once) Johann Friedrich's uncle Friedrich the Wise in the years following his death in 1525. Cranach also experimented with other background colours, particularly various greens. But it is the plain blue that increasingly marks the portraiture of these decades.[32]

Most significantly of all, blue becomes the background colour for the Cranach workshop's portraits of Martin Luther and, in the years following their marriage, Katharina von Bora. With that association well established, by 1530, blue becomes well near the only backdrop for Saxon electoral portraiture. The 1531 painting of Johann Friedrich in the Louvre is a masterful rendition of a formula that would endure for years to come. (See, for example, the double portrait of Johann Friedrich and his wife Sibylle of Cleves two years later, made after they had become Elector and

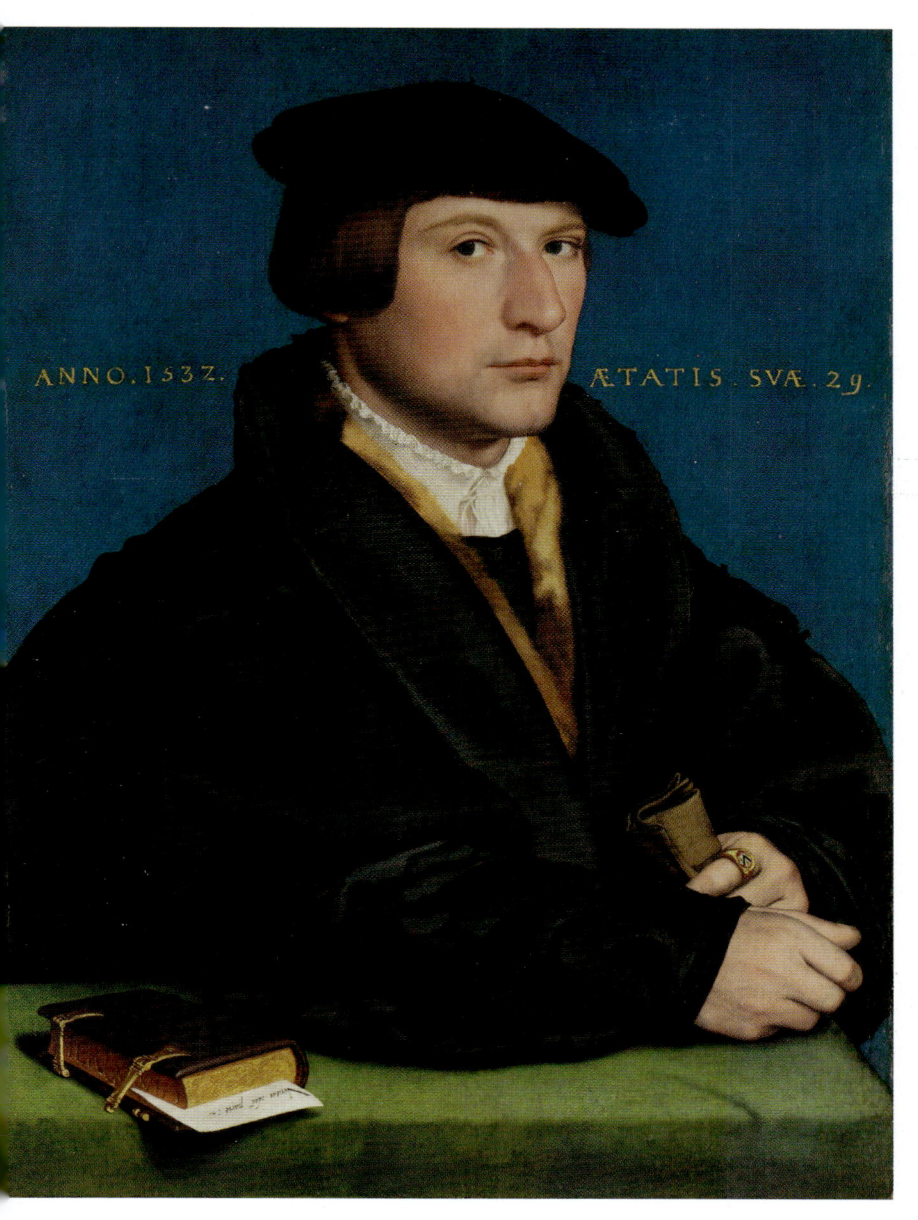


19 Hans Holbein the Younger, *Hermann von Wedigh III*, 1532, oil on panel.

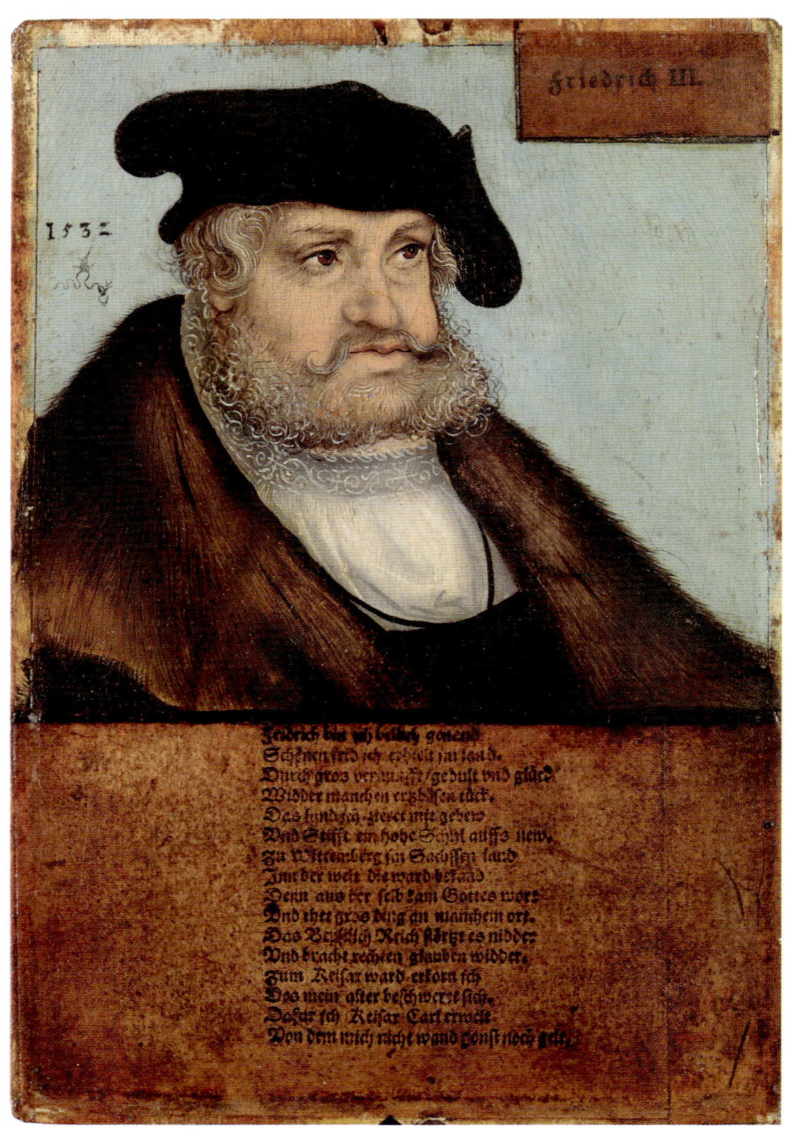



20 Lucas Cranach the Elder and workshop, *Friedrich III, the Wise, Elector of Saxony*, 1533, oil on panel.

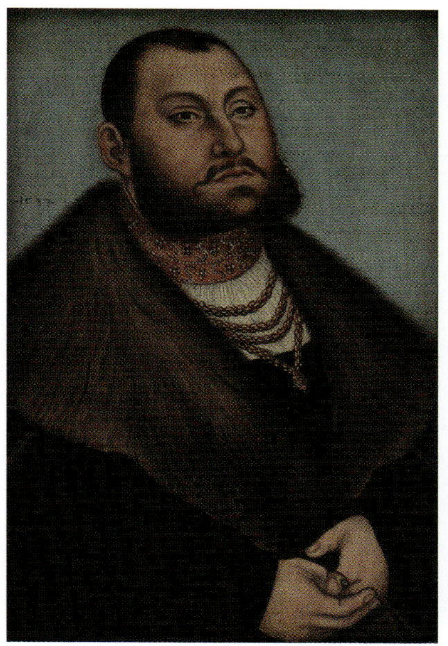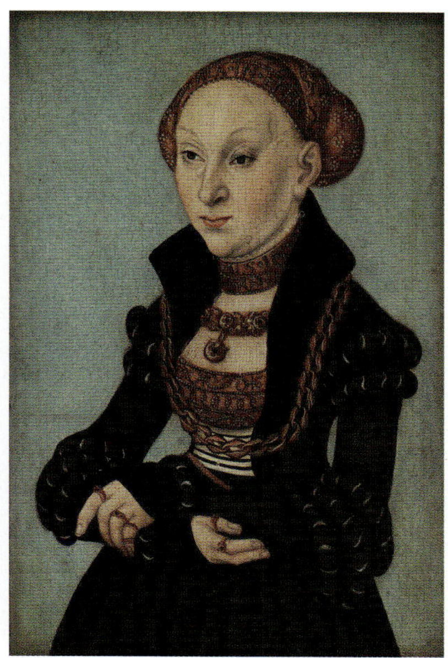

Electress.) This formula then spread across Northern Europe, aided by the circulation of printed portraits, to become a norm for northern Renaissance portraiture in the 1530s.

The 1531 Louvre painting's distinction from others in its series is the future elector's odd pendant, which takes the form of a boatswain's whistle shaped like a grotesque boar or fish swallowing a sphere. This whistle appears only once elsewhere in surviving portraits of the elector, in a painting from the late 1520s now in a private collection.[33] Such whistles were widely used at the time, but largely by captains and, indeed, boatswains. Saxony was a landlocked state known for mining and Church reform; it was not particularly known for seafaring, despite profitable trade along the River Elbe. Though pendants like these often signalled membership in an elite society (like the Order of the Golden Fleece), no known society used a boatswain's whistle as its emblem. So why is Johann Friedrich wearing this pendant?

21, 22 Lucas Cranach the Elder, *Johann Friedrich* and *Sibylle of Cleves*, 1533, oil on panel.

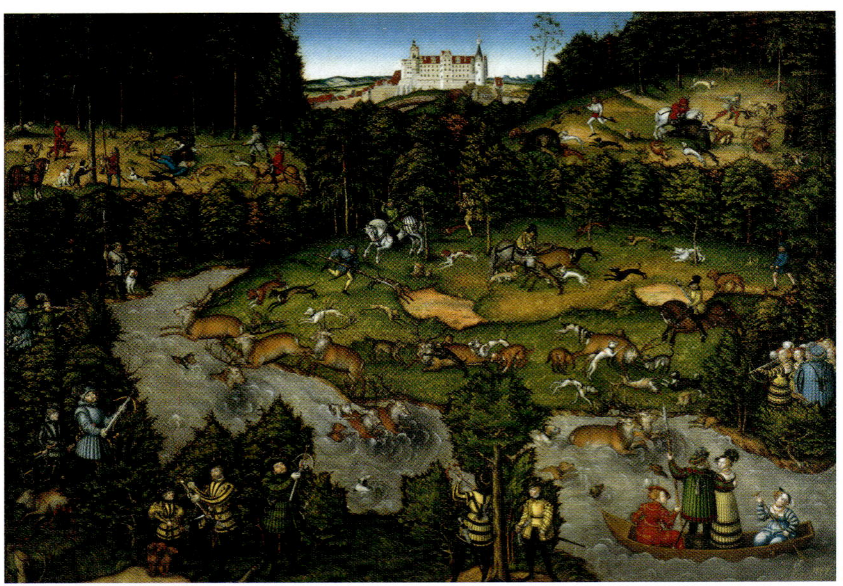

As with so much of the iconography of this time, one cannot answer this question with certainty; so much material culture and evidence has been lost. One might speculate that Johann Friedrich was actively working to strengthen his electorate's ties to the seafaring Hanseatic League, and vice versa. There are other attestations to such a connection. In the 1520s, ceramic oven tiles bearing portrait roundels of the most famous reformers in Wittenberg were circulating through Hanseatic territories on the Baltic Sea. After Johann Friedrich became elector in 1532, portrait tiles of him and his wife – as political figures aligned with Lutheranism – grew equally popular in Hansa lands as far west as London.[34] The silhouettes on these roundels were based on Cranach workshop blue-background versions. The Reformation movement pushed across the continent in printed words and images, to be sure, but also in the homes of northern merchants, heated by their massive ceramic-tiled ovens.

23 Lucas Cranach the Elder, *Hunting near Hartenfels Castle*, 1540, oil on wood, transferred to masonite. Large hunting scenes were another means by which Cranach promoted rulers' diplomatic might. Borrowing from the luxury

The Cranach brand empowered not only Luther's reform, but also the increasingly mighty Saxon rulers who stood behind that reform. Cranach's visuals, transmitted via prints and oven tiles, were everywhere from London to Riga. No wonder Hanseatic merchants craved portraiture according to the Cranach workshop formula.

Back at court in Wittenberg, though, other kinds of art grew even more popular. Watched over by St Catherine, the thriving university encouraged an ever-broader taste for the humanist reawakening of Greco-Roman antiquity. The next chapter examines precisely how Cranach developed and responded to this taste, proliferating images of alluring naked women and altering the field of German painting itself.

tapestry tradition, Cranach used the trope to include members of court and even elites never known to have joined Johann Friedrich in a hunt – that is, sometimes these pictures were socially aspirational.

# TWO

# The Mythographer of Women: A German Renaissance

By the end of the first decade of the sixteenth century, Cranach became known beyond portraiture for paintings of classical antiquity that emphasized nude female bodies. These paintings bolstered a Renaissance European sense of a shared inheritance of the Greco-Roman past, of participating in a long-lost set of cultural touchstones that were now again at the heart of educated European identity. Europeans hoped that by recovering this lost past they might recover their authentic selves; Cranach's works, rendering the motifs of antiquity in direct yet evocative forms, fed this hope. Albrecht Dürer's innovations and adoption of Italian humanist values did much to shift German visual orientation towards classical antiquity. Cranach and his long-term standardization and repetition of classical tropes broadened and advertised a German humanist community.

In conceiving these paintings, Cranach was not just emulating the content of Italianate humanist painting, but also adapting technical strategies he had first seen in Italian art. When Cranach painted the portraits of Heinrich and Katharina of Saxony in 1514, he was translating a 1490s Tuscan painting trend into an idiom for full-length courtly portraiture. The proper Tuscan way to do it, seen earlier from the Botticelli workshop as well as from Lorenzo di Credi, was to set a warm-fleshed Venus figure posed in the antique *pudica* or 'modest' position – with her hands at

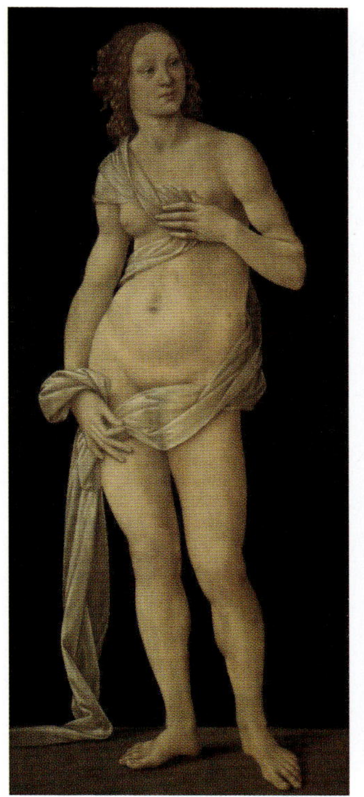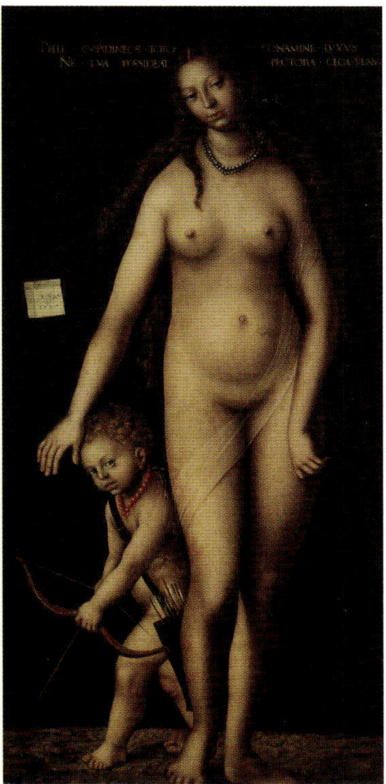

least moving in the direction of covering the genitals – against a bare black background. Again, the simultaneous unfathomability and flatness of that black surface heightened the tactility and thus availability of the well-modelled female figure.

The appeal of this strategy for depicting the isolated female nude persisted for decades, and not only in Cranach's workshop. The prosperous and learned Duke of Mantua, Gianfrancesco II Gonzaga, sent just such a version, painted by the northern Italian Lorenzo Costa, to the king of France, Francis I, in 1518. It is possible that this same duke was in fact responsible for exposing Cranach to this particular Italian style. Cranach's patron Friedrich the Wise of Saxony had mentioned to Gianfrancesco in a letter

24 Lorenzo di Credi, *Venus*, 1493, oil on canvas.
25 Lucas Cranach the Elder, *Venus and Cupid*, 1509, oil on panel, transferred to canvas.

of 1507 that he, Friedrich, was interested in his Italian paintings, and was willing to exchange German paintings of the same quality.[1]

But Cranach's earliest surviving painting to take up this trope already shows his own sensitive transformation of the subject-matter. This life-sized painting, dated 1509, depicts not just Venus but her son Cupid.[2] In the middle left, Cranach draws upon his old trick of signing on a cartellino, here a small piece of paper, unfolded, slightly crumpled and set skew in space so as to appear real. He had already used such pieces of paper to sign earlier works, but now the splotchy delicacy of ink on a flimsy surface has a special sensory role. Amid the date and the artist's initials, rendered in the human-ist majuscule he would have admired with his university friends in Vienna, appeared his new signature serpent, which Friedrich had given him as an official mark the previous year. Here the serpent is very lightly 'drawn' as if with silverpoint (a pencil-like medium of the time) on the paper. Floating in black paint near the smooth, soft gradients of Venus's skin, the snake appears as if also on a kind of skin, tattoo-like. The easily damaged cartellino both calls attention to the vulnerability of Venus's skin and, marked, stands in for a claim on that bare skin.

Indeed, one great difference between Cranach and his Italian counterparts is the extent to which the viewer can claim all of Venus's body. Cranach's Venus covers neither breasts nor pubic region, though her left hand retains the curl of fingers that might have been used to cover the latter. A transparent scarf or sash wraps from upper hip to opposite lower thigh. This scarf, rather than concealing anything, invites the viewer to imagine again a play of textures, this time a contrast between fabric and skin. The sliding downward motion implied by the scarf's loose wrapping enacts a striptease. It is as if the goddess has been undressing before us.

Another difference from the Italian paintings of the nude against a black background is the presence of Venus's son, Cupid.

One might think the presence of a child would interrupt the sense of sexual invitation. But Venus is precisely *not* resting her hand in motherly fashion on her child's forehead. At most, his forehead and/or forelocks graze the back of her thumb. She is posed as if she might rein him in but has not yet. And of course this is not any mother and son (let alone a Madonna and Child, of which it is an erotic counterpart).

This is the personification of love standing with her offspring, the personification of desire. As Cupid or Eros, the god of erotic love, this mischievous boy embodies the same seductive power possessed by an image of a nude. Garlanded with a bright coral necklace – an exotic material intended to prevent illness and redolent of Venus's mythical watery origins – Cupid looks directly at the viewer, arrow ready between his fingers on his bow. He is a threat. His name is embedded early in the inscription towards the top of the painting, which details the nature of that threat:

> *Pelle cupidineos toto conamine luxus*
> *Ne tua possideat pectora ceca venus*
> Banish [your] erotic debaucheries with all [your] effort
> So that Venus doesn't take over your blinded heart

Of course, Cranach's sensuous rendering of flesh and the stark availability of the female figure belie this moral admonition. As Joseph Koerner observed of roughly contemporary depictions by Hans Baldung of nude women in 'witchcraft' contexts, here the viewer becomes complicit, by viewing, in the same sinfulness the picture warns against.[3]

In this early surviving nude, there is one more quality worth remarking that enhances the allure of the female figure: her distracted gaze. Heavy-lidded, her eyes move off to the side – echoing and amplifying the gaze of many Tuscan examples – allowing the viewer to look at her without her looking back. She is available not only to touch, but also to sight, without resistance. Her hard nipples point by contrast directly at the viewer in a way that may seem not comical, but rather enticing, to a man attracted to women (the usual viewer of Cranach's non-religious paintings). The pointing nipples and the heavy eyelids, alongside the flush on her cheeks and reddened lips, indicate that this particular female body is aroused. Such arousal is described here in the passive voice precisely because there is no depicted agent causing it. Venus is aroused and available. Cranach invites the viewer to insert himself into the agentive role. In other words, the visual conceit here is that the viewer is the one who has aroused her and made her available, or at least will be able to take advantage of that state.

This motif of Venus and Cupid as archer against a black background repeats in seven other surviving variants by Cranach and his workshop in his lifetime, ending around 1537. There are even more surviving variants if one includes images featuring Cupid with a honeycomb. And if one counts surviving images of nude or partially nude frontally available women against a black or largely black background, including Lucretia and Charity, the number increases to 56.[4] These paintings themselves spawned many further imitations from painters outside the workshop. The once-Tuscan strategy of isolating luminous, sensuous flesh on a dark, stark surface becomes another hallmark of the Cranach brand, and by extension of German Renaissance painting.

## THE HONEYTHIEF AND THE GENTLEMEN'S CLUB OF LETTERS

Most of Cranach's paintings with nude women were destined for private enjoyment in the homes of humanist scholars. This was not a passive market: sometimes those scholars themselves participated in developing the context and content for a female nude. The best example for this participatory art-making is one of Cranach's more popular nude subjects, *Venus with Cupid as Honey Thief.* Though Cranach made some versions of this painting in the stark moonscape style, the subject-matter more commonly survives with a typical Cranachian pastoral or rural background. Also known as *Cupid Complaining to Venus*, the example here, one of two in the National Gallery in London, bears the date of 1529.[5] Most of Cranach's dated paintings of this subject appear within two years of this date.

The subject comes from a poem then attributed to Theocritus, Idyll 19, or 'Κηριοκλέπτης' (Keriokleptes), 'Honeythief'. The pseudo-Theocritan poem runs as follows:

A bad bee once stung the thief Eros
while he was stripping honey from a hive, and his hands'
fingertips prickled. He was hurting and blew on his hand
and stomped the ground and jumped; to Aphrodite
he showed the injury and complained about how small
a beast the bee is and how much pain it causes.
His mother laughed: but you, aren't you the same as bees,
being so small, though you cause so much pain?[6]

This poem more or less describes the scene in the painting. The evidence of small Cupid's thievery is in his hand; the sources of his hurt crawl upon him; though no swelling from a sting is visible, his open mouth, upper lip pulled in a grimace, suggests outcry; unchildlike eye wrinkles express his pain. Venus, on the other hand, looks wryly out at the viewer, as if having just delivered her rather comfortless observation not to her son, but to the painting's audience.

The switch from Eros and Aphrodite to Cupid and Venus, from ancient Greek to Latin, implies an intermediate step in the panel. Indeed, the text that appears posted on a tabula to the tree against which Venus leans is not the Greek of Pseudo-Theocritus's idyll but Latin, and is condensed from eight lines to four. Where do these lines come from?

Pablo Pérez d'Ors has uncovered much of the delightful context for the creation of this group of paintings.[7] Pseudo-Theocritus's poem (or a similar version of it) was available to the humanists of Cranach's circle in a Greek edition that had come out from the much-admired Aldine Press in Venice in 1496. By the 1520s, chief among Cranach's local humanists – besides Luther himself – was Luther's primary ally in reform, his linguistic and theological consultant, Philipp Melanchthon. Once a child prodigy in Greek studies, Melanchthon took the post of professor of Greek at the University of Wittenberg in 1518, at age 21. In a letter of 2 June 1526 from Melanchthon to his fellow Lutheran scholar Joachim Camerarius, Melanchthon asked his friend to have the Aldine edition of Theocritus and other ancient Greek poets sent to him, so that he could 'interpret them'.[8] This meant Melanchthon wanted to translate the verses from ancient Greek into Latin.

At this point in Wittenberg and elsewhere in Europe, proficiency in ancient Greek was desirable among scholars, due to Melanchthon's influence locally as well as to longer-term humanist trends. But such proficiency was not a given. Furthermore, Theocritus's works offered a particular challenge: he wrote in the Doric dialect, which differed in many forms and vowels from the Attic dialect of, say, Plato, as well as from the Koine Greek of the Septuagint Old Testament – the kinds of ancient Greek through which humanists and scholars then (and now) learned the language.

Melanchthon's request of Camerarius thus takes on a playful swagger. The former-prodigy Greek professor was eager to tangle with difficult forms of ancient Greek lyric. But he also wanted a nerdy philological romp with his friends. The resulting Latin translations of the poem first came out in a collection called

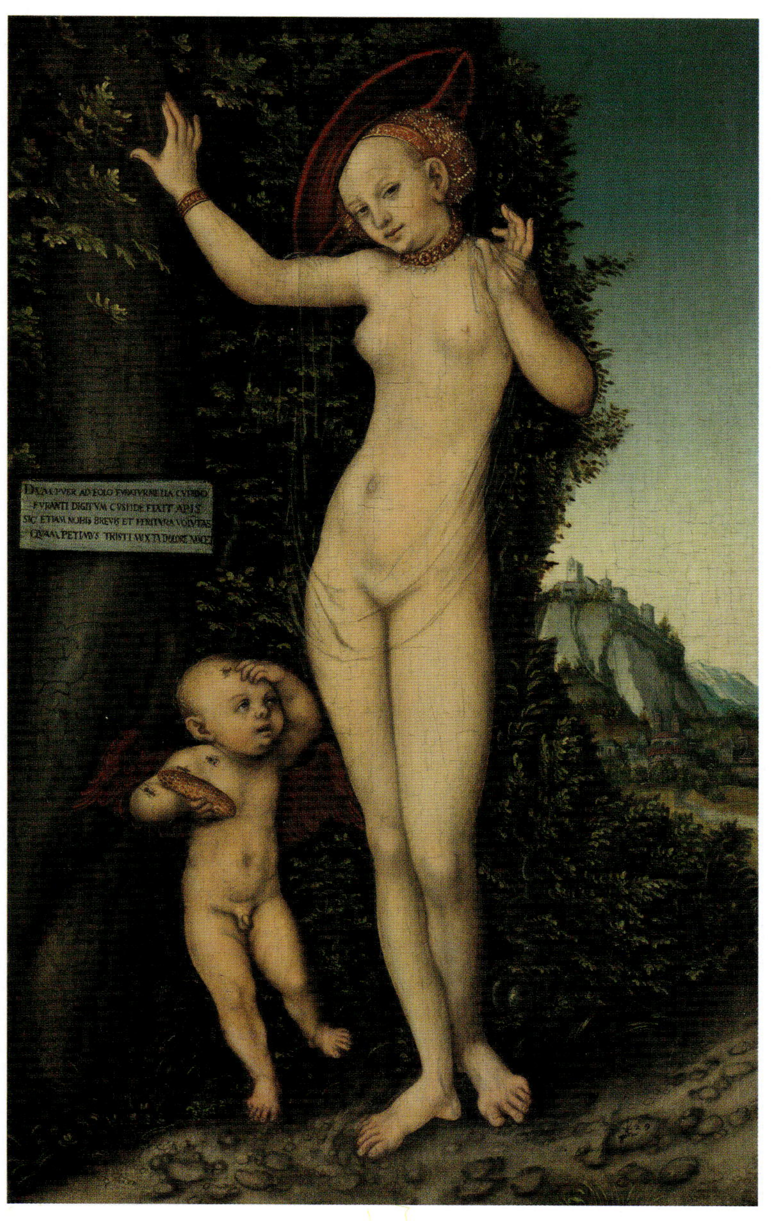

26 Lucas Cranach the Elder and workshop, *Venus with Cupid as Honey Thief*, 1529, oil on panel.

*Farrago aliquot epigrammatum* (Medley of Some Epigrams) in January 1528: versions appear from Melanchthon, Camerarius and their friend Caspar Ursinus Velius, court historian to the Holy Roman Emperor's brother Archduke Ferdinand I in Vienna.[9] By late 1528, two other scholars joined these three in publishing their differing versions of Idyll 19 in a collection of Latin translations entitled *Epigrammata Graeca veterum elegantissima* (The Finest Greek Epigrams of the Ancients).[10] Though some present-day art historians, including Dieter Koepplin, have surmised that there must be a now-lost earlier painting of *Venus with Cupid as Honey Thief*, the dating on the only surviving painting prior to 1528 is suspect.[11] It seems plausible that Cranach produced paintings of this theme in a pastoral setting not in anticipation of but in response to the scholars having circulated the Theocritus in Greek among themselves and come up with their own renderings of Idyll 19 in Latin.

Yet none of the scholars' published translations is like the Latin interpretation of Theocritus's idyll that appears on the painted panels. The panel version is not really a translation at all. Instead, the panels bear a clever four-line digest of the longer poem. The presumptive author of this quatrain is Georg Sabinus, Melanchthon's student and future husband of Melanchthon's daughter. Sabinus would have been nineteen years old in January 1528, when a very similar version of the quatrain was first published in a different section of the *Farrago* collection, near other poems by 'Georgius', as 'On Amor Honeythief'. The quatrain on the panel reads:

> *dum puer alveolo furatur mella Cupido*
> > *furanti digitum cuspide fixit apis*
> *sic etiam nobis brevis et peritura volu*[p]*tas*
> > *quam petimus tristi mixta dolore nocet.*

> While the boy Cupid thieves honey from the hive
>   a bee has stabbed the thiever's finger with its sting.
> So indeed, brief and dangerous for us, the pleasure
>   we seek, mixed with sad pain, does harm.[12]

Sabinus has elided Pseudo-Theocritus's discrepancy in scale between small cause (bee) and large effect (pain); there is no mention of Cupid's similarity to the bees in being a small cause of great pain. Instead, Sabinus skips to the real point, so to speak, for a living audience: just as Eros's acquisition of honey earned him a bee-sting, erotic pleasure is itself painful.

Sabinus's goal is to address that audience directly: in this variation on 'Amor Honeythief', there is a more direct relationship between the person 'speaking' the lines and the listeners. In the second half of Sabinus's quatrain, the verbs and pronouns are in the first-person plural: 'we', 'us'. The original poem is mostly in the third person. (Even the second-person 'you' from the mouth of Venus in the Theocritan original does not easily apply to the audience: there, she is clearly addressing Cupid.) By shifting to a pronoun that includes the reader, Sabinus moves away from recreating the ancient tale and towards applying it to the real present.

This move may help explain one mystery: why would Cranach have popularized the variant quatrain written by one of Melanchthon's teenaged students rather than an authentic translation from antiquity by one of the great humanists of Melanchthon's circle? There is no evidence of direct connection between Cranach and Sabinus. The version on the panels indeed differs in the second line from the 1528 version published under 'Georgius': among other things, the version attributed to the nineteen-year-old lacks the play on *cupido* and *cuspide*, 'Cupid' and 'cusp' or 'edge', instead offering a cliché from Ovid, the 'busy bee'.[13] Otherwise, both the *Farrago* quatrain and the version in the panels borrow bits and pieces from the multiple translations that appeared dozens of pages earlier.[14] This borrowing would have been a normal aspect of humanist play, as well as something one might expect of a nineteen-year-old student.

The fact that Melanchthon published Sabinus's digest of the idyll, and perhaps passed on an improved version of it to Cranach, signals that the young student had a special place in Melanchthon's club of scholars in 1528. Did Melanchthon help Sabinus with the quatrain? Did Melanchthon's suggestions produce the wittier version that appears on the panels? It is possible. There has been some scholarly discussion of Melanchthon's secretly writing work attributed to his protégés, though in the case of Sabinus the discussion seems based on a misunderstanding.[15] In any case, by the time Sabinus was ten years older, married unhappily to Melanchthon's teenage daughter – who would often flee to Melanchthon's house with their children – Sabinus emended his version of the quatrain. In the first edition of his own collected poetry, the 1538 *Poemata*, his 'Amor Κηριοκλέπτης' (Love the Honeythief) exactly resembles the version in Cranach's paintings.[16] This change suggests that Sabinus was aware of at least one of the panels. In this 1538 context, one might today read a bitter, toxic-masculine note into a poem about how pleasure was always mixed with pain: not long after Sabinus's wedding to the then barely fourteen-year-old daughter of his former professor, the quatrain appears between a poem decrying 'Lecturers and Tyrants' and one unironically likening Sabinus himself to the mythical horse Pegasus.

Whoever authored the version of 'Amor Κηριοκλέπτης' that Cranach painted in the years following 1528, and however its personal meaning may have evolved, the point here is that this painting and Cranach's other paintings like it had a backstory in the social scene of German humanists. There happens to be relatively well-documented evidence for the particulars of this example, but it is hardly unique. Though Cranach's mythological nudes still make an intriguing, learned impression today, in the early sixteenth century they also signalled that their owner was in the know, invested in what the biggest regional scholars had been discussing lately in their private and public correspondence.[17]

In Cranach's interpretation of the honeythief motif, the direct warning unique to Sabinus's quatrain – 'the pleasure we seek . . . does harm' – is not uttered by the figures in it. Venus always looks the viewer in the eye, but her mouth never opens. Rather, this warning becomes a pastoral or rural variant of the warning in illus. 25. The viewer is again complicit in the sinfulness against which the picture warns. Cranach presents Venus's body in frontal contrapposto, contrasting her available, curving flesh with the flattened backdrop of leaves. Yet she gestures at her son's example as he is stung by the honeybees. Here Cupid himself stands in for the viewer caught in the trap of Venus's allure. Cranach collapses warning with the predicament warned against; this painting similarly features the collapse of desire ('eros') with its consequences. In other words, this painting repeats the push and pull of danger and desire common to many of Cranach's nudes at yet another level.

It also places danger and desire not in a dreamy, anchorless moonscape setting, but in the forest: at a remove from, but within sight of, civilization. This pastoral setting was appropriate for Theocritus, who was known as a bucolic poet. It was also particularly appropriate to a subject-matter, eroticism, that lay at the edges of civilized behaviour.

Cranach had begun to develop this landscape idiom already in Vienna, as we saw in the Cuspinian portraits. Its particular expression had also become a hallmark of his workshop: a clifftop citadel in the remote background, resembling cliffs nearby along the River Elbe; other less grand architectural forms tucked below; the foreground on a hill above that middleground, obscuring much of it with a backdrop of foliage and a tree trunk. At the bottom appears a smooth path of pebbled stones reminiscent of the moonscape.

As Cranach encouraged increasing demand for his recognizable paintings of these popular subjects, he had to come up with formulas that allowed his workshop to keep up with the demand. Looking more closely at the Cranachian landscape formula in these pastoral *Venus with Cupid as Honey Thief* panels, we can appreciate the efficiency of his large workshop's method from the late 1520s onwards. First, the basic composition would be sketched out onto a prepared wood panel. A corner area would be laid out in lighter blue-greens to convey the far distance, mountains and sky and town, often with a fortress perched on a high precipice. Meanwhile, to the left, the area of the figures would often be left blank, in 'reserve'. Filling in the rest of the space between the distant mountains and valleys of more densely populated civilization would be the backdrop previously mentioned, a thick, green-black wall of foliage ribbed with a tree trunk or two. It is this wall of leaves that most gives away the workshop's practice: the leaf-wall often unapologetically follows the outlines of the figures themselves, as in our example and most other pastoral subjects by Cranach. In cases in which the surface of a panel is worked on by multiple hands – one artist specializing in the figures, often the 'master' of a workshop, and others specializing in different aspects of the landscape – this formula of dividing figures from background simplifies the division of labour.

Cranach was not alone in developing such workshop practices, which he had partly inherited from painting trade traditions. But rather than concealing the collaborative nature of his panels, the way Flemish painters (who even more frequently divided artistic labour between landscape and figure specialists) often tried to do at this time, Cranach exploited the high contrast between sectors of his panel. The dynamic relationship between figure, foliate backdrop and distant blue landscape became a proud feature of much of Cranach's output, especially but not only his images featuring nudes.

## THE PRIMAL FORMS OF GERMANKIND

At this point in his career, Cranach's use of the nude female figure does not always centre eroticism and its perils. Some of his most intriguing paintings are those that place undressed figures in woodland scenes. The standard title for these works, *The Silver Age*, has come into some dispute.[18] In the sixteenth century, patrons and makers and admirers of paintings often referred to them by their subject-matter, but no one, including the artists, bestowed standard names or titles on the works. Titles of paintings like this one are conventions that have built up over time. So, despite debate about what is actually depicted here, art historians often conventionally refer to Cranach's images of naked humans in the forest as depictions of the Silver Age.

What was the Silver Age? Among Cranach's associates, the most salient source from the late 1520s into the 1530s – when he and his workshop made these images – was Hesiod, whose *Works and Days* had been made available throughout Europe in the original ancient Greek in 1495 by the Aldine Press, the same Venetian press of Manutius that produced the Theocritus edition. According to Hesiod in this text, the Silver Age was the second of the five major eras or 'ages' of humankind.[19] In this age, humans had to labour for the first time (previously, during the Golden Age, the planet provided people with everything they needed naturally, with no effort on their part). Childhood lasted a very long time: Hesiod specified that a child would live for one hundred years alongside their caring mother, a 'big baby'.[20] Unfortunately, this infantile quality persisted. As adults, unlike their Golden Age predecessors, Silver Age humans would not last very long once out of their mother's care, since they could

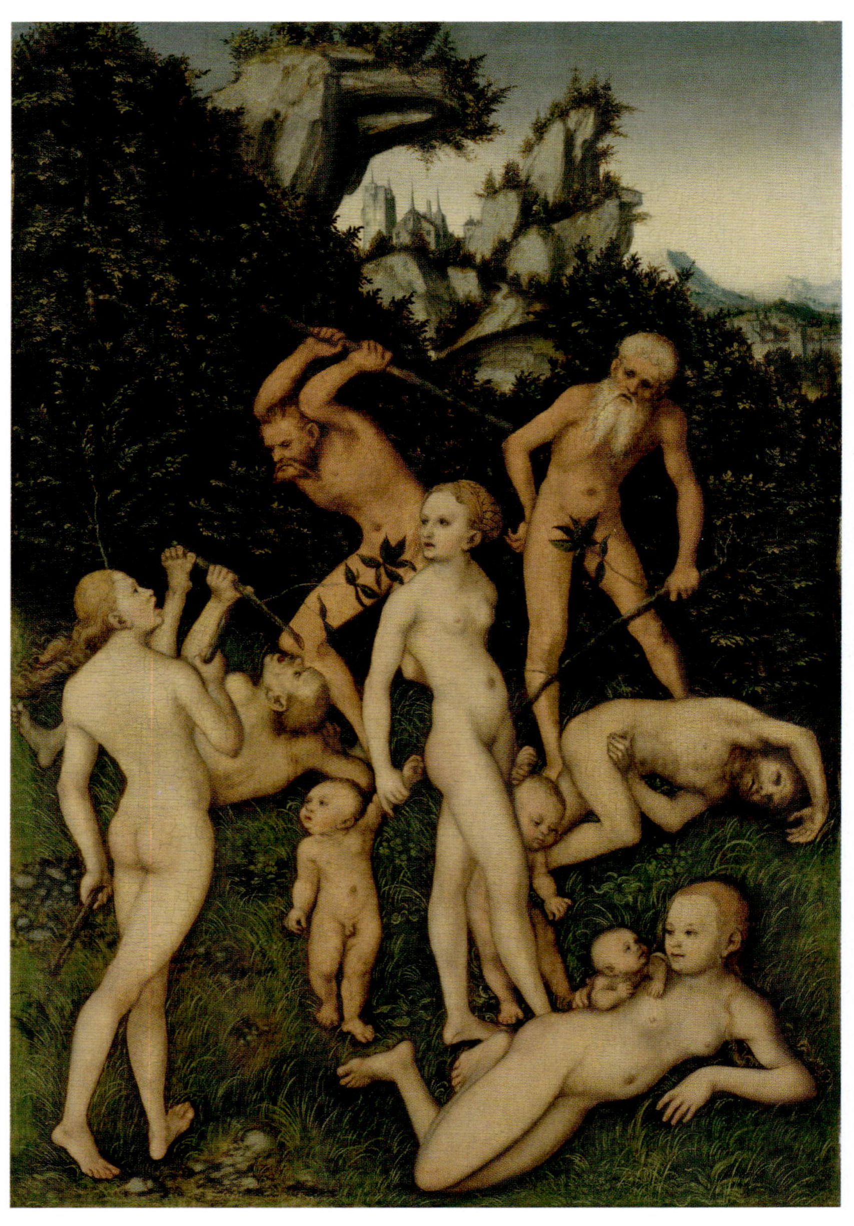

27 Lucas Cranach the Elder and workshop, *The Silver Age*, c. 1527–30, oil on panel.

not keep from doing violent and inappropriate things to one another.

Hesiod's description very much fits the foreground of this image and of Cranach's other renditions of naked people in some conflict in a pastoral setting. The images feature women who appear peaceful and caring with multiple children; occasionally, the women's expressions are not placid, but horrified by the violence around them. This might be the case here in the first *Silver Age*, now in London: one of the two upright women looks askance at the other, who has her mouth wide open and grips a stick of the sort used by the violent upright men in the middleground. If this woman on the left is indeed aggressive, rather than condemning the male violence she faces, she is an anomaly amid the surviving paintings of this type. The paintings otherwise separate male and female thoroughly, with men cast in the role of foolish big-baby aggressors and the women as caretakers of smaller male children. Such a separation is in keeping with Hesiod's differentiation of gender in *Works and Days* as well as with the expected viewership of Cranach's portable panel paintings (as opposed to those made for altarpieces and communal religious spaces). The doomed people of the Silver Age and the audience for these paintings are all men by default; women are separate figures providing care.

The only exception to this separation in Cranach's surviving *Silver Age* panels is in an example in Moscow (illus. 28).[21] In this image, a human man, upright, grabs a woman from the clutches of another male, whose hairy bottom and knee suggest that he is a satyr. This woman's relation to the two men is ambiguous. Does her left arm, outstretched towards the human, reach for him or ward him off? Is her right hand, draped over the satyr's curly head, in the middle of a companionable gesture affirming her bond with the satyr, a gesture made awkward by the conflict, or has her hand simply landed there as she attempts to get back on her feet? Does she perhaps, as would be understandable, wish to be free of both antagonists? Whatever the case may be, she is notion-ally if not literally separate from these men, an object of their desire and violence, not an agent.

The Silver Age paintings also differentiate the forms of men from those of women, beyond mere genital distinction. The men are darker, the women paler, though sometimes men who have already been defeated in brawling take on a paler, and thus more feminine, hue. In other words, darker skin tone here seems to index brutishness. Most significantly, the men's poses are often original inventions by Cranach, or, in their group frenzy, borrow from the imagery of ancient sarcophagi friezes depicting battle scenes. They tend to constitute the middleground, their bodies blocked by the women's forms, almost never obscuring them.

By contrast, the women – even when in the middleground – generally appear unblocked and thus directly available to the viewer; their poses allude to well-known stand-alone ancient statues, whose forms were known broadly from prints, casts and circulating drawings. (The statues proper may have originally come from group figural contexts but were isolated both by their long years of ruin and by Renaissance display practices, in which these statues were only sometimes deployed alongside other dis-crete statues.) The standard poses include the Venus *pudica* mentioned above, but also: the simple Cnidian Venus in con-trapposto; the Venus Callipyge (known for the S-shaped curve of the rear of the body, as in the leftmost figure in illus. 27); the Venus Crouching (as in the leftmost figure of illus. 28); the Nymph *alla spina* (seated, one ankle crossed over the knee of the other leg, one hand on the foot of the crossing leg); the Venus Binding Her Sandal (a kind of standing variant of the *alla spina*); the reclin-ing draped statue then known as Cleopatra but now called *Ariadne* in the Vatican collections; and even adaptations of what is now known as the Apollo Citharoedus but was at the time used for representations of female figures by many artists.[22] These figures

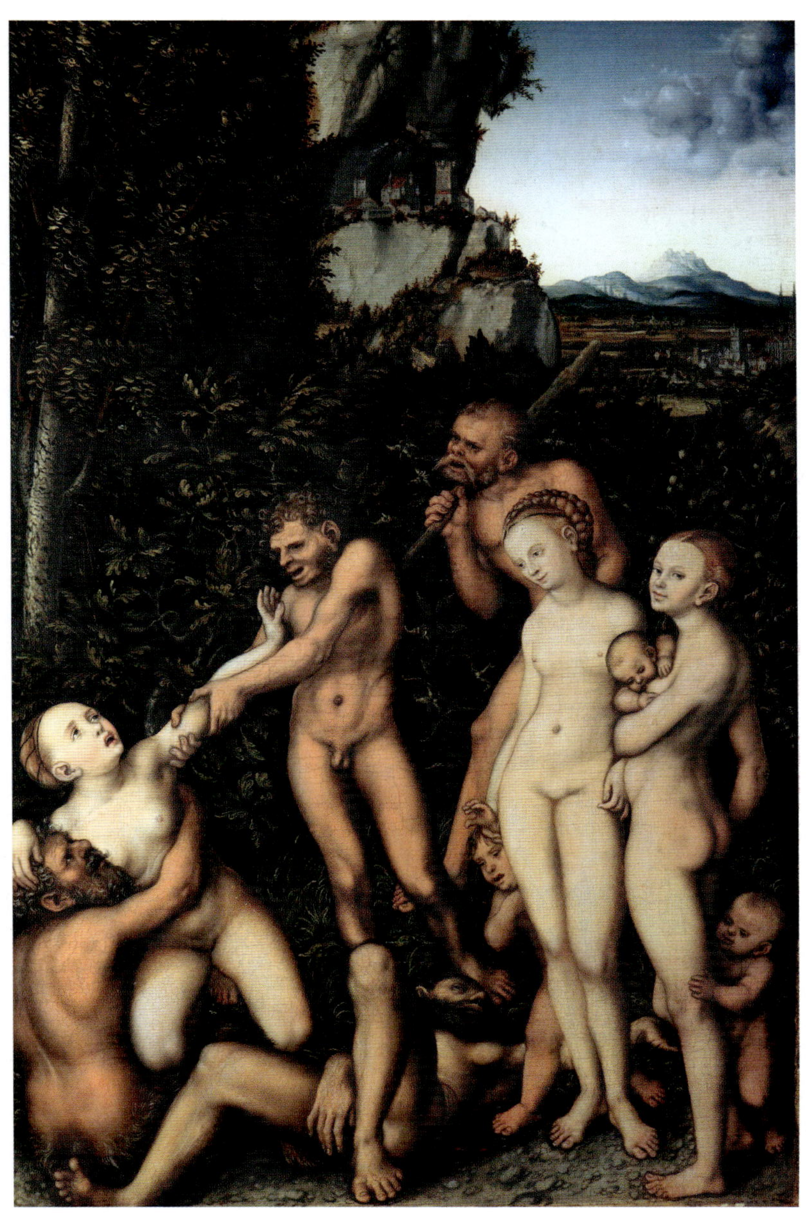

28 Lucas Cranach the Elder and workshop, *The Silver Age*, 1530, oil on panel.

would have been recognizable to much of Cranach's learned clientele, affirming humanists' familiarity with visual as well as textual remnants of antiquity. For those less learned, these female nudes would also provide a kind of survey course in ancient Greek statuary of women. The recombination and redeployment of archetypal ancient Greek female forms on these panels resemble those in Maarten van Heemskerck's sketches of nude statuary as displayed in the Medici Palazzo Madama's courtyard in Rome.

That courtyard, though, places the statues in a colonnaded setting that honours antiquity, that perhaps even aspires to a rebirth of the vanished ancient culture from which the statues came. Cranach instead places these female forms as living humans in the living forest on the outskirts of towns and fortresses dominated by German architecture of his time. Why are women posed like ancient Greek statues in this forest? To make sense of this, one must first understand what the German forest would have meant to Cranach and his learned clients. It was a kind of 'forest primeval', an ancient or even timeless forest inhabited by

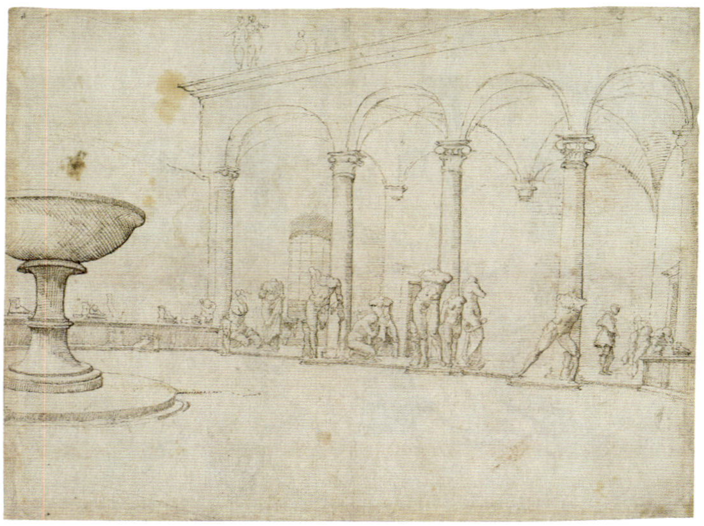

29 Maarten van Heemskerck, *Garden Courtyard in the Palazzo Madama with Antique Sculptures*, 1532–6, brown ink on paper.

beings known as 'wild men'.[23] Wild men, proliferating in German tapestry and church carving from at least the fourteenth century onwards, typically had hairy bodies and wielded clubs or tree branches in their violent encounters with one another and other forest beings. They were willing to kill for what they wanted, especially other men for the sake of obtaining women.[24] Though Cranach has mostly subtracted the hair from his wild men's bodies, the rest of their iconography fits. This is their forest.

Cranach here has brought the local German tradition of wild men together with the ancient Greek theory of the Silver Age. He claims that the stage of human development described by Hesiod is the same primordial state of human existence that everyday Germans have known about for centuries, preserved deep in the German forest. Just as in the context of the Cuspinian portraits, Cranach painted these Silver Age pictures with a native pride in the emerging sense of Germany as a concept with its own deep history that reached into antiquity.

To build his case, Cranach did not depict the women of the forest the way his contemporaries did, as hairy and stout as the men.[25] In keeping with Hesiod's positive characterization of the female caretakers of the Silver Age, Cranach used positive models of female bodies from antiquity. By the late 1520s, these bodies' poses would already be familiar to Cranach's patrons not only from imagery circulating from Italy, but also from Cranach's *own* repertoire of female nudes from antiquity, from *Venus* to *Lucretia* (illus 30).

This assimilation of classical myth and local lore might work in two directions. These are primeval German women, taking on the standard ancient models of beauty prized in Greece of old. Their faces resemble those in Cranach's portraits of women from Saxon courts. Cranach here is reinforcing and at times creating a stereotype of German beauty that would endure: pale, blonde, long-limbed.[26] Indeed, these adaptations of ancient Greek

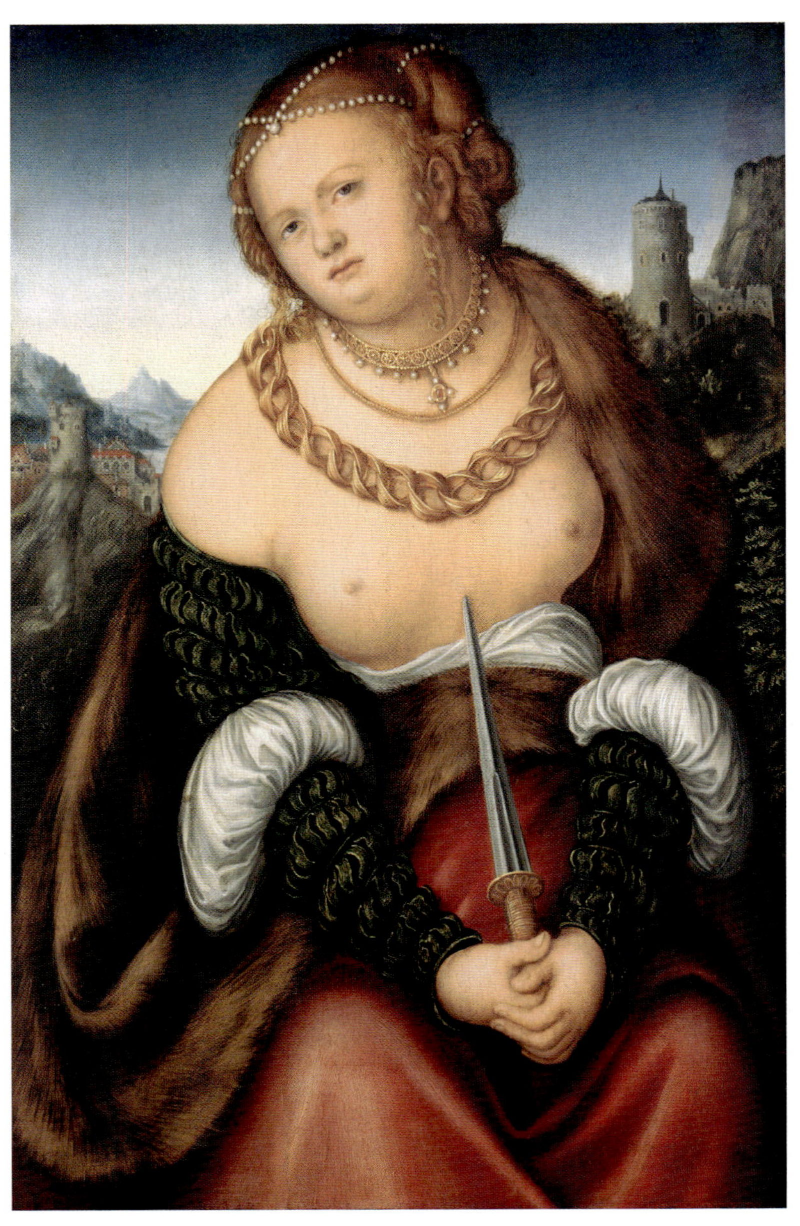

30 Lucas Cranach the Elder, *The Suicide of Lucretia*, c. 1518, oil on panel.

figure-types accommodate typical fifteenth-century features of depicted female bodies in Germany and the Low Countries: smaller breasts than a Greek Venus, a more jutting, rounded belly and overall leaner, more attenuated bodies. These are 'typical' German bodies put in ancient Greek poses. By situating these women alongside the wild men of the German forest of the Silver Age, Cranach claims the primordial authority of ancient Greece's archetypal forms for German flesh.

There was one German claim to great heritage from antiquity that was already particularly well known in humanist circles around Europe: the Nymph of the Fountain. Twelve variant paintings of this subject attributed to Cranach and/or his workshop survive today, and other copies abound. The paintings depict not just any nymph near a fountain, but a particular remnant of antiquity attested in fifteenth-century archaeological records somewhere near the banks of the River Danube. Dürer had portrayed this nymph beside her ancient inscription already around 1514.[27] Here is the inscription recorded on the fountain:

> *Huius nympha loci, sacri custodia fontis,*
> > *Dormio, dum blandae sentio murmur aquae.*
> *Parce meum, quisquis tangis cava marmora, somnum*
> > *Rumpere. Sive bibas sive lavere tace.*

The nymph of this place, guardian of the sacred fountain,
> I sleep as long as I feel the alluring water's murmur.
Refrain, whoever you are touching my rounded marbles
> from interrupting my
> > Sleep. Whether you'd drink or bathe, keep quiet.

These lines appeared in a compilation of antique inscriptions in the late fifteenth century collected by the Italian humanist Michael Fabricius, a prior in the Carmelite cloister in Reggio Emilia.

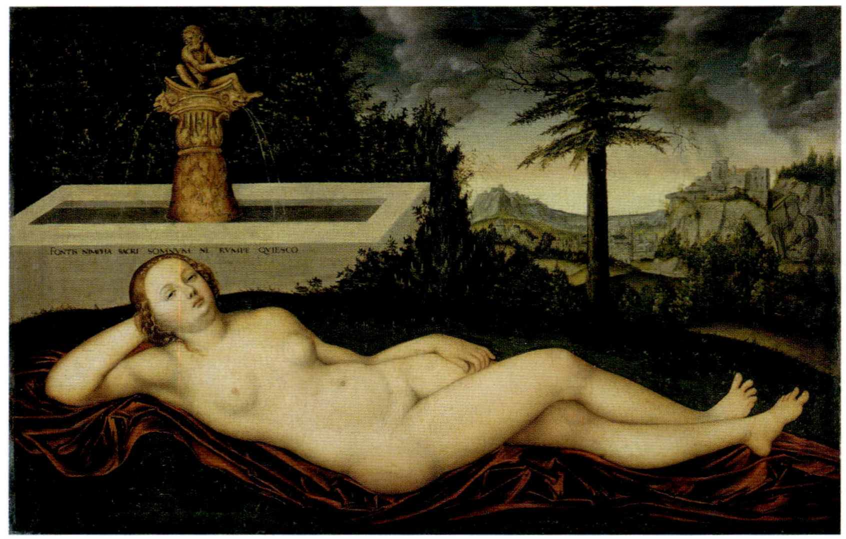


We now know that this inscription probably never existed as an actual remnant of antiquity. Fabricius had taken the lines not from travel accounts of the River Danube but from a fifteenth-century neo-Latin poet, Campani, who composed them in Rome, riffing on classical pastoral poetry.[28] However, once Fabricius published these lines claiming that they were from an inscription found on a tablet 'upon the banks of the Danube' next to a sleeping nymph, the claim proliferated as fact in further compilations and publications. One such version, for example, made its way into a compilation of inscriptions collected by Bonifacius Amerbach in Basel from around 1514–19.[29] However Cranach and his German friends became familiar with the account of the ancient German nymph who spoke in a Latin inscription, they in a sense took false bait in their earnest efforts to compete with Italian claims to antiquity. As Christopher S. Wood has pointed out, 'The Danubian location was remote enough [from central Italy] that no one would bother to check – that was part of the

31 Lucas Cranach the Elder, *The Nymph of the Fountain*, 1518, oil on panel.

joke' that Fabricius played when he turned a contemporary poem into an obscure inscription.[30] But for these humanists, the ground of knowledge was not verifiable archaeological discovery but rather the intellectual amplification of traditional precedents, the celebration of ancient chains of transmission for their own sake. Given this theory of knowledge, these lines of poetry were as authentic as any other.

The repercussions of the joke-turned-serious echoed into the visual world, not just along the banks of the Danube and in Wittenberg. These lines became associated with actual surviving ancient statues of sleeping women, who in turn became associated with the nymph. The most famous of these was the reclining statue of Cleopatra/Ariadne mentioned previously, but there were others, now lost. These statues inspired, among other things, a woodcut illustration of a nude woman in the 1499 *Hypnerotomachia Poliphili*, a widely circulating fictional account of a young man's travel through a dreamworld of classical themes, objects and symbols.[31] It was most likely this version of the antique

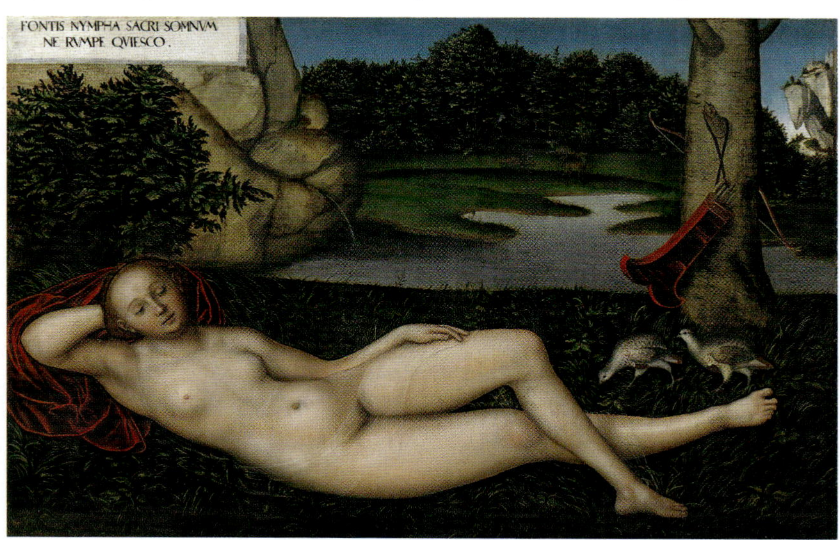


32 Lucas Cranach the Elder, *The Nymph of the Fountain*, c. 1534, oil on panel.

reclining female nude, or another sketch of a lost nude antique sculpture, that inspired Dürer's drawing and (at least initially) Cranach's multiple panels.

Unlike Dürer's drawing, Cranach's earliest surviving dated version of 1518 (illus. 31) resembles a more famous painting almost twice its size: Giorgione and Titian's *Sleeping Nude* of about 1508–10.[32] Both images show a nude upon fine, virtuosically rumpled drapery, stretching left to right from head to toe in the foreground, on a deserted pastoral hill distant from the background's traces of civilization. Dürer's version more directly resembles the *Hypnerotomachia* image, with a German-style fountain inscribed with Roman majuscule letters added behind the nude. In a sense, Cranach synthesizes these precedents from Giorgione/Titian and Dürer, providing his nymph with an inscribed fountain. Cranach's fountain, though, is a pastiche of antique forms both Greek and German: the nozzles are stylized ram-like heads set at the upper corners of a compound Greek column surmounted

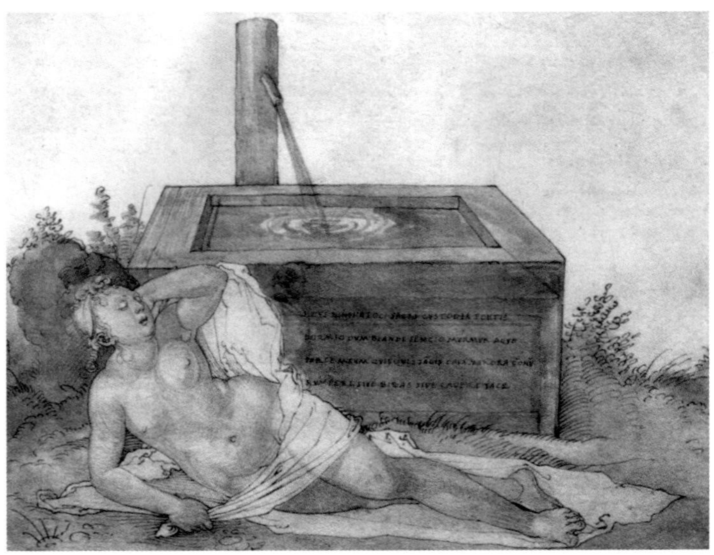

33 Albrecht Dürer, *The Nymph of the Fountain*, c. 1514, ink on paper.

by a German wild man, who, posed like the Roman sculpture Spinario, clutches a torn stick and stares out at the viewer with finely picked painted highlights on his notionally brass eyes.

Wood has written about how these panels by Cranach 'reconvert' the female nude statue into a living being.[33] Indeed they do, and the living being involved is not just any life form, but the guardian of her particular place. Again, here, the German forest claims an archetypal classical form of female life as its own. Though Titian would also endow well-known sculptures with life in, for example, his *Bacchanal of the Andrians* (1523–26), he and Giorgione could not make such a regional cultural claim. Cranach's paintings present his viewers with the nymph from the banks of the Danube, who never existed, whose supposed ancient inscription was nevertheless documented more thoroughly than any actual German remnant of the classical past.

Given that the *huius nympha loci* verses faked by Fabricius were so widespread, it is a bit surprising that Cranach's versions of the nymph all share a different inscription.[34] 'Fontis nympha sacri somnum ne rumpe quiesco,' says each nymph: 'As nymph of the sacred fountain, I ask you not to disturb my sleep.' This elegant hexameter, condensing Campani's poem, does not appear in any published texts of Cranach's time; it is attested only in these paintings. It omits the features the painting can better render visually – the temptation of the water, the tactility of the stone – and it lifts the restrictions upon what the viewer would want to do if they happened upon this scene: confronted with this real, live woman, the viewer might imagine more than drinking and bathing. Would they act like the classical satyr who might assault the nymph, or like the cultured human following the inscription's injunction? The monostich is impeccable in its adherence to the expectations of classical Latin verse. It suspensefully mismatches natural word-stress and meter in the first half of the line, then resolves stress and syllabics in the second half's assured command;

the caesura or expected break in a line of hexameter falls exactly between the nymph's self-description and that command. Some Wittenberg humanist knew what the nymph was supposed to say, and said it better for the purposes of a painting.

As with Cranach's image of *Venus with Cupid as Honey Thief*, Cranach's primary goal was not to accurately represent an ancient artwork, or even to generate imaginative fodder for a humanist to daydream about what that ancient work was really like. These paintings are what Wood called 'fictions', objects that encouraged the proliferation of storytelling by which humanists like Cranach and his friends so often authenticated themselves and one another.

What story of the nymph do these paintings tell, in the end? Fascinatingly, Cranach's nymph is never actually asleep. She has already been awakened. It seems that the viewer is the one who woke her up; the stand-in for his forbidden presence is the ejaculatory jet of water, whether from a man-made nozzle or directly from a rocky cleft, that almost always (though not in the 1518 example in illus. 31) pours in a location vertically aligned on the panel with her genitals. In some of the panels, like ours, the nymph looks directly back at the intruding viewer. Her drooping eyelids are inviting, but, coupled with the command of the inscription, mean danger. Cranach shows the nymph of the deepest river of the German forest both prepared for and forbidding erotic interaction with the learned male viewer.

As in all ancient stories of erotic encounter most popular in the Renaissance, the woman resists the man. Especially in a Christian or 'moralized' context, the man is warned of her danger. But resistance and warning are futile: the story is told, the painting is painted. She has already been awakened from the 'sleep' of art and antiquity and brought to life. In a predicament familiar from the nudes discussed so far in this chapter, the painting enacts the same transgression it disavows.

In the 1518 version, a beautifully painted pine tree, reminiscent of Cranach's landscape backdrops from his years along the Danube in Vienna, interrupts the usual upper-right-hand quadrant of background. This is not the kind of compartmentalized workshop-assisted painting that becomes normal for Cranach in the 1520s. He is adding a personal touch, a souvenir of *his* Danube, to alert us that the fountain to which the nymph belongs is also a local fountain. Of course, the wild man there stares. The energy of the erotic paradox of dangerous desire matches the untapped power of the nymph of the fountain, enduring in the timeless forest. Though 'nation' did not mean the same thing it does in the twenty-first century, the idea of German-ness was just at this time coalescing into a political and collective identity. These are paintings of German classical antiquity, and she is the first national nude.

## JUDGEMENT AND THE MECHANICS OF THE FOUNTAIN OF YOUTH

In one of Cranach's most popular subjects, the painter reflexively stages the scene of his work's display: a man peruses the forms of naked women. As is typical of the subject-matter, Cranach's more than a dozen depictions of the Judgement of Paris almost always take place at the moment of judgement, the juncture at which Paris must choose the most beautiful goddess of the three naked before him: Juno, Athena and Venus.[35] The moment is uncomfortable. In this example from New York as in other Cranach versions, Paris's expression reflects the befuddlement of a mortal choosing among eternal beings who also happen to be attractive naked women. He is half-reclining, half-seated – all but sprawled – on a semi-natural block of riverbank stone that becomes a kind of anti-throne as the gods loom over him.

Paris's story is and was well known. The version Cranach was probably most familiar with was the one transmitted through

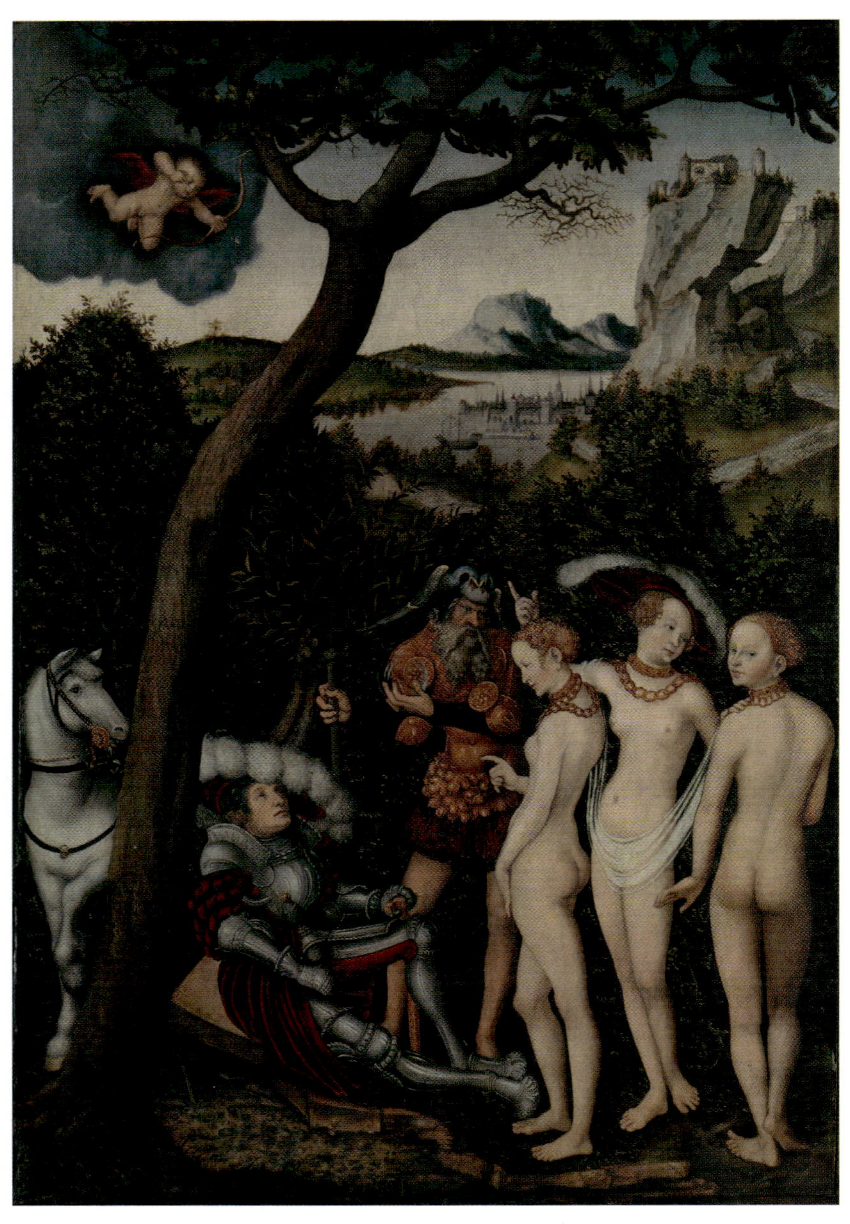

34 Lucas Cranach the Elder, *The Judgment of Paris*, 1528, oil on panel.

medieval romances of Troy.[36] Details from Guido delle Colonne's late thirteenth-century *Historia destructionis Troiae* ([Hi]Story of the Destruction of Troy) may be responsible, directly or not, for the somewhat unusual presence of Paris's horse tied to a tree, and the nakedness of all three goddesses as they submit to judgement.

In the medieval sources Paris's predicament remains the same as that alluded to in Homer's *Iliad* (24.25–30). Because Zeus/Jupiter feared the repercussions of assigning an apple labelled 'most beautiful' to any one of the goddesses present on Olympus (including his wife), he sent his messenger Hermes/Mercury down to the human Paris, a prince of Troy living in pastoral exile as a shepherd, to ask him to resolve the dispute. The romances provide further details about each goddess's attempt to convince Paris: Hera/Juno offered to give him rulership of Europe and Asia; Athena offered to give him all of human knowledge and skill in war; and Aphrodite/Venus offered him the most beautiful mortal woman alive, Helen of Sparta.

Cranach's paintings present the next moment: Paris is about to make the 'wrong' choice. Most viewers of these paintings would have known that Paris does what all Cranach nudes warn against – that is, he gives in to desire and acts based on lust. Paris chooses Venus, who personifies his own desire. Since her reward, the woman he desires (Helen of Sparta), happens to be a rival king's wife, the Trojan war ensues. It reminds viewers, yet again, why succumbing to lust is bad and would be the likeliest moral of the story, given Cranach's audience. This moral of course would not just be Cranach's. Among other sources, the Greek scholar Nikolaus Marschalk had lectured students at the University of Wittenberg in 1503 that the right choice for Paris would have been to seek knowledge and wisdom, but even a life of action (aligned with Hera/Juno) would have been more acceptable than choosing pleasure. The woodcut from the printed version of this address was used in a university textbook the next year.[37]

The biggest difficulty with applying this likely moral to the painting is that, here and in most of Cranach's versions, it is almost impossible to tell the different goddesses apart.[38] In what is perhaps the earliest painted example, from circa 1512–14 and now in Fort Worth, Texas, the frontmost goddess has seductively undone her hair from the usual updo.[39] She begins to lower herself towards Paris with extended arm. Of surviving variants, this is the painting that most unambiguously distinguishes Venus in feature from the other two goddesses. But even in the Fort Worth painting there are no other cues.

Such an indifference to the usual symbols or attributes of Greco-Roman divinity is extremely unusual. Even Marcantonio Raimondi's famous contemporary print after Raphael, in which compositional drama overwhelms iconography, shows identifying attributes discreetly strewn by the feet of the three goddesses. Again, if Cranach is exhorting viewers not to be like Paris, to make the right choice, why would he make it so hard to tell what the right choice would be?

Take our New York example. One goddess stands in front of Paris in the *pudica* pose, pointing at him; one points up at Cupid in the sky, wearing a fancy feathered velvet hat; the other looks at the viewer over her shoulder in the Callipyge pose, both upper and lower cheeks reddened. Any of these details could associate a figure with Venus. Though all three women have varying head-dresses and neck adornments, none of these ornaments clearly assign their identity. Mercury still holds the apple, rendered here as a glass sphere. (The replacement of the apple with another spheroid is typical for images of the Judgement of Paris in the period.)

Though Cupid is an attribute of Venus, and so the figure with the broad-brimmed hat who points to him could be the goddess of love, even this identification complicates matters. Earlier versions of the image, including a 1508 woodcut and paintings produced in the 1510s, do not include Cupid shooting an arrow in the sky. By the period of Cranach's advanced output of variants on humanist themes, the late 1520s and 1530s, Cupid, as here, is not even shooting at Paris, nor into the world where Helen waits to fall in love with Paris. Instead, Cupid seems to be aiming at his mother – if the one at whom he aims is in fact Venus – an act that is missing from any version of the story. But this feature is consistent in the later versions of these paintings: Cupid is aiming at one of the goddesses, and if any of them is wearing a fine hat, she is plausibly the one at whom he points his arrow. In the only late version in which there is a clear winner in the competition, a painting from the 1530s now in St Louis, the hat-wearer is the one with her hand on Mercury's ball as Cupid aims at her from overhead.[40]

Barring further archival discoveries buried in humanist viewers' letters to one another, we cannot know for certain why these goddesses are so hard to tell apart, why they are almost always based on a statue of Venus, and why the winner is today clear in only two of the thirteen surviving renditions attributed to the master or his workshop. One explanation emerges from the context of Cranach's other paintings of female nudes: perhaps the panels do not in fact exhort their viewers to choose a wiser course than Paris did. In Cranach's erotic paintings, the viewers have always already succumbed to desire and simultaneously obtained visual access to the body they desire. Perhaps these panels challenge the viewer with the prospect of being less wise than Paris, unable even to see the wisdom of Athena or political power of Juno. They have already chosen desire, and so the desired body is all they can see.

Still, what does it mean that Cupid, god of desire, is targeting his own mother, goddess of love and desire herself? Cranach's audience, largely familiar with Ovid's *Metamorphoses*, would recall the moment in Book X that Venus's accidental playtime injury from her son's arrow caused her to fall in love with the first mortal she saw, Adonis. Perhaps the conceit here is that the goddess looking out of the painting will soon be struck by Cupid's arrow and fall in love with the man gazing at her painted form.

Such a shift might be aided by Hermes/Mercury, the god of transition and change, aligned here with a supposed ancient author of occult and alchemical texts known as Hermes Trismegistus. At first it seems unusual that Cranach has depicted the typically youthful-looking, bare-faced Mercury as a bearded older man. But this version of Mercury makes him recognizable as Trismegistus, whose *Corpus hermeticum* was pored over by the great fifteenth-century Florentine humanists whom Wittenberg scholars so admired. This version of Hermes was depicted as a bearded prophet, as, for example, on the floor of the Siena Duomo in the 1480s. In particular, in the New York painting, the peacocks on Hermes'/Mercury's head, feasting on a cracked-open egg or fruit, might well represent a discrete and crucial moment in the process of alchemical transformation: the Peacock's Tail, 'the stage at which the red Philosopher's Stone would emerge from the Egg'.[41] The conjunction (so to speak) with alchemical specifics is uncanny.

In these paintings, Mercury is explicitly Hermes Trismegistus. Now the sphere he carries seems like a paradoxical alembic or other alchemical tool. Paris here – so awkwardly red, his velvet stuffed into his armour – may himself be the red sulphur of a late stage of the Philosopher's Stone, which must be tested with three kinds of fire to fully achieve its powers. Cupid's fire was the most important of these. These arguments may sound like conspiracy theories, but here they are plausible. As Helmut Nickel has shown, the Judgement of Paris had been used elsewhere to diagram alchemical processes. Cranach, who had been running Wittenberg's apothecary for about fifteen years, would certainly have been familiar with the basics of alchemy, even if he usually hired others to run the shop.[42]

But Cranach's Hermes Trismegistus is doing more than just performing the greatest achievement in the age-old lore of alchemy, if he is at all. After all, Cranach delighted in painting red velvet (illus. 64), for which he was well known; what else would he have used to dress Paris? In the realm of painting, the magic of Hermes Trismegistus is certainly having an effect: the transformation of mythical goddess into a mortal's nude object. He is the stand-in for the painter, who first transforms paint into life, and whose colours and forms then transfer affect into a viewer's flesh-and-blood body.[43]

Cranach thematized another mystical transformation of the nude female body in his last famous mythological work, *The Fountain of Youth* (1546). A folk myth in multiple European cultures at least as old as Herodotus, the fountain of youth was supposed to contain 'living water' that rejuvenated those who bathed in it.[44] Painted when Cranach himself was about 74 years old, the panel depicts a de-ageing sequence from left to right. First, old men and younger

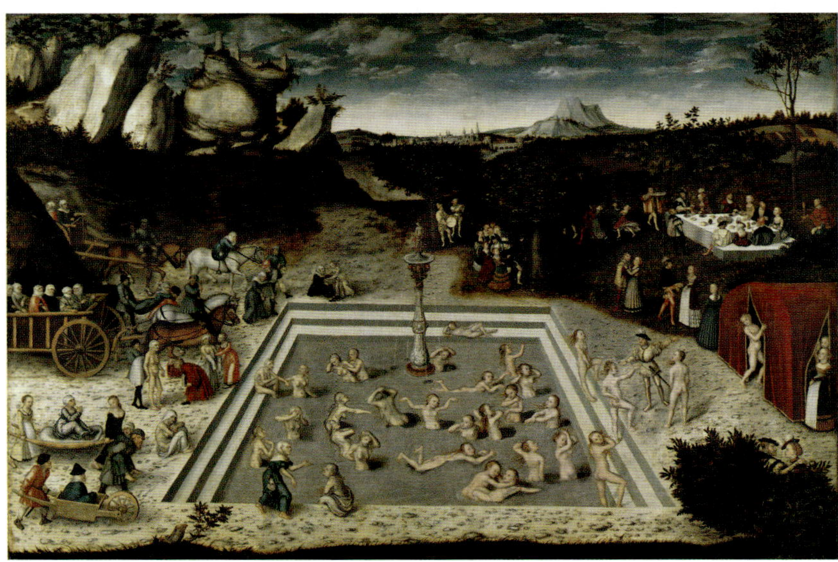

35 Lucas Cranach the Elder and/or Younger, *The Fountain of Youth*, 1546, oil on panel.

women cart, carry and otherwise escort older women across the signature Cranach moonscape to a squarish, shallow grey pool. Next, the older women, having disrobed, wring their hair and wash themselves in the pool's left-hand side. The fountain at the centre of the pool marks a sharp transition: from its jets rightward, younger women cavort (some even in an overtly homoerotic fashion, toward the foreground) and bathe. Finally, at the right of the painting, young women go to changing rooms and emerge to join their courtly male lovers, who are of varying ages, at a banquet beneath a wide-spreading grapevine with flourishing shoots and ripe, bulging grapes.

Many of these elements are standard for the subject-matter from the fourteenth century onwards.[45] Though (unlike their Italian counterparts) German bathhouses of the time were often mixed-gender, representations of the fountain of youth were sometimes gender-segregated, as here.[46] It was apparently a commonplace, one Rabelais rehashes for example in *Pantagruel*, that men had no need for the fountain of youth because they could grow young from exposure to younger women.[47]

By the 1540s, the visual trope of the grotesque ageing woman in particular would have been perhaps just as familiar as that of the classicized female nude to Cranach's audience. Such imagery derived from a different genre: that of 'witch' pictures.[48] (The word 'witch' is here in the first instance put in quotation marks to indicate that the actual figures represented in this genre had little relationship to witchcraft as historically practiced.[49]) The narrow, elongated, downward-pointing dugs of the older women on the left of the pool belong to the standard iconography of this genre, with which Cranach would have been familiar. In fact, Cranach had painted standard witches before, as evil visions associated with melancholy, in the 1530s (see the upper-left corner of illus. 64); in 1545, the year before painting *The Fountain of Youth*, he had also designed a woodcut for his friend Martin Luther's pamphlet *Wider das Bapstum zu Rom vom Teuffel gestifft* (Against the Roman Papacy Founded by the Devil) that featured similar aged, albeit demonic, hags tending to an infant and toddling pope (see its male-demon-heavy title page, illus. 44).[50]

As far as we know from what survives, Cranach did not personally indulge in making erotic witch imagery, which often contrasted youthful nude women with the grotesque older women who presumably inducted the former into their company. This genre was so well developed in German and Swiss visual culture in the early sixteenth century that already in 1518 the Bern-based artist Niklaus Manuel commingled the two female types in one drawn figure now known as a witch.[51] Confounding, perhaps even spiting viewer expectations, Manuel combines at every turn the signs of old age and seduction, collapsing Death and the Maiden: the witch's arm cocked at her hips is bony and sinewy as that of Death himself; her contrapposto clangs her knobbly knees together; the audacious white highlights on her erect nipples point downward at the ends of empty, hanging dugs; her coyly tilted head possesses a direct, inviting stare, but also the lax mouth – and even lolling tongue – common in older people whose jaw muscles have relaxed or who struggle to breathe through their noses.

In *The Fountain of Youth*, by contrast, Cranach does not so much confound as reverse the expectations of the multigenerational witch picture. His painting's structure, though it certainly contains the requisite mockery of the ageing female body, is much more wholesome. Rather than older women corrupting the young, in Cranach's painting winsome maidens help carry and convince older women to purify themselves in this fountain. Their grey skin turns pink-white.

The obvious Christian parallel for the folklore of the fountain of youth – the origins of which are obscured by its long durability across several European cultures – is the purificatory rite of

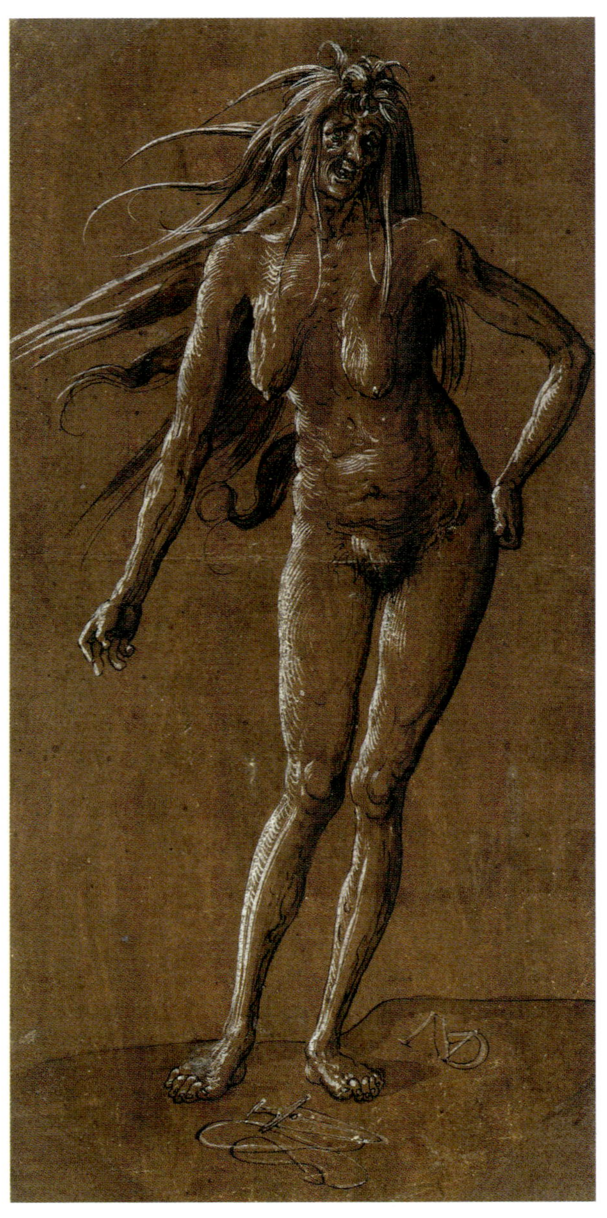

36 Niklaus Manuel Deutsch, *Witch*, 1518, pen, wash and white heightening on red prepared paper.

baptism. The parallel was well discussed in Cranach's time. For example, the future anti-Lutheran Thomas Murner led readers of his 1514 *Badenfahrt* (Bath Tour) through a spiritual bath at the hands of Christ. Later in this text, he discussed the fountain of youth as a metaphor for the act of baptism that renewed the inner purity of a child in even old men.[52] Despite the thoroughly worldly setting of Cranach's image, this Christian resonance would have been a part of the way the viewer understood the painting. The fountain's four jets would have echoed the four rivers of Paradise or Eden, often identified in folklore as the location of the fountain of youth.

But this is not a Christian fountain. Putti or miniature Cupids spew its waters. Above them, topping the column, is a flesh-toned statue of Venus. In fact, it is a *Venus with Cupid as Honey Thief*. This fountain is presided over by that explicitly dangerous form of eros that drives so many of Cranach's mythological nudes.

The main difference between this version of *Venus with Cupid as Honey Thief* and earlier versions by Cranach and his workshop are Cupid's red wings, reminiscent of the red-winged Cupids from the later Judgement of Paris pictures. Indeed, if we scan around the pool, we can recognize other figures in familiar poses on the 'youth' side of the fountain, most prominently the reclining nude from the Nymph of the Fountain pictures. These figures represent the Cranach workshop's nude output of the 1520s and 1530s. This pool does not just produce youthful women; it produces *Cranachs*, Cranach nudes.

On the left-hand side of the pool appears a curious detail. A scholar (perhaps also a medical doctor, since medical training was not so separate at the time), identifiable as such by the massive tome he carries, is examining one of the freshly disrobed older women closely with his spectacles.[53] His focus is on her navel; perhaps, on the level of humour, he is assessing stretchmarks. Her toothless grimace takes on personality beyond caricature from the impatient aversion of her eyes as she submits to inspection.

The scholar looking so carefully at this older figure – studying her transmission history, the navel of her ancient origin and the post-pregnancy marks of her reproductive activity – is a cipher for the humanists' role in Cranach's transformative artistic process. In other words, this figure stands in for the fact that it is through scholarly inspection of the old forms and scholarly transmission that Cranach is able to birth those old forms anew. This *Fountain of Youth* recasts the Renaissance as an erotic allegory of renewed desire for and renewed availability of the dangerous pagan sources.

Cranach's *Fountain of Youth* is therefore also an allegory of the painter's role in a prosperous society rebirthing its own history. The men who enjoy Cranach's reborn classical nudes are rich: at right, we see fine clothes and millinery, a lush love garden and servants bringing in food and drink in well-made vessels. This is the wealth of a society able to access the restored, ever renewable forms of its past. Cranach sold his buyers and friends art as their own German form of immortal beauty. This was the artist's job. His workshop was the fountain.

# THREE

# The Look of Luther's Reformation

he concept of Renaissance or a rediscovery of ancient cultural heritage was one of two central features of Cranach's time and place; the Reformation of the Christian faith was the other. These two epoch-defining projects were connected. Martin Luther and his followers – including Cranach – would have understood their Reformation as the result of rediscovering and reviving Christendom's original practices and creeds. Most early adherents to sects or confessions of Christianity that broke away from the Roman Church in the years following 1517 identified themselves as 'evangelicals'. This word denoted their intended fidelity to the ancient text of the Gospel (ancient Greek 'euangelion', εὐαγγέλιον) rather than to the notionally corrupted Church policies established in the intervening centuries.

As a painter for humanist scholars, one who was also competent in printmaking and ran an efficient, productive workshop, Cranach was central to developing and distributing a visual culture aligned with both Renaissance and Reformation. He had established himself in Wittenberg well before Martin Luther's religious interventions: Cranach moved to Wittenberg in 1504, Luther permanently in 1511. Cranach would have already listened to Luther preaching in Wittenberg's parish church (now known as the City Church or Stadtkirche) about grace and the true nature of salvation in the mid-1510s. Though there are no records of their direct contact prior to 1520, the year of Cranach's first portrait of the reformer, by 1521 Luther was speaking very warmly and intimately of Cranach in his correspondence, and Cranach and Philipp Melanchthon – Luther's sidekick – had become pamphlet collaborators.[1]

It is worth further outlining Luther's Reformation in the most general terms here.[2] It began with his famous 95 Theses, objections to certain, especially monetized, Church practices, above all to the sale and promotion of indulgences. Indulgences were Church-approved reductions of the amount of time believers were required to spend in purgatory, a post-death state of existence between the world and heaven in which believers could be purged of sins. (Technically, the amount of time reduced was applied to believers' penitential practices, that is, to the time and effort spent asking God for forgiveness of sins through prayer and deed; however, many believers understood indulgences to apply primarily to penance done in purgatory.) The Church sold indulgences, often in the form of slips of paper or vellum printed with contractual words, to raise funds for its projects, including, at this time, the construction of St Peter's Basilica in Rome.

On 31 October 1517, Luther wrote to his local archbishop objecting to indulgences, enclosing a set of learned Latin arguments against such practices, the aforementioned 95 Theses, in his correspondence. This text – which was likely never nailed to the doors of the Castle Church that day, despite popular myth – was soon translated into many European vernacular languages and spread widely around Europe over the next couple of years. Meanwhile, Luther extended his preaching against institutionally mediated forms of salvation. Salvation, he believed, could come only from God, through a believer's faith in Jesus: hence the Reformation slogan *sola fide*, 'by faith alone'. In 1525, worshippers in Wittenberg began to practise Luther's recently reformed liturgy (a set of rites and practices for the Christian celebration of the central ritual of Mass, instructions for which Cranach's press had published the preceding year); by 1528, this liturgy was spreading throughout Saxony and other German-speaking lands.[3]

Besides an appeal to the desire not to be exploited, one of the reasons Luther's rejection of the Roman Church became a successful movement was Luther's access to print technology and distribution networks for text and image alike.[4] These local networks had been emerging for several decades, since the invention of the printing press in Europe. The literate population's access to contemporary debates was both more widespread and more trustworthy now that a single more-or-less identical form of a text could spread rapidly and relatively affordably. Once a book, sermon or screed's pages were typeset, by the early sixteenth century a press could reproduce thousands of pages a day. The labour of a typesetter went further than that of even the swiftest and least error-prone scribe.

Cranach was central to the harnessing of print technology to the Reformation. By 1522 he co-owned an active press geared almost entirely to printing Lutheran tracts, and published at least 36 different editions of such texts for the next three years. A remark of Luther's in a 1525 letter that 'Lucas's' press was not busy and so would have been free to publish Luther's small treatise written on the occasion of the marriage of Wolfgang Reissenbusch of Liechtemberg suggests one of the reasons Cranach, in a city like Wittenberg with at least ten different active printing presses in the 1520s, might have abandoned this venture and focused on his other work in print.[5] From that point on, working with other printers, Cranach continued to serve as the main designer of Reformation prints both for loose distribution and for book and Bible illustration. Cranach had been working as a print designer long before he met Luther: recall that he was employed by Johannes Winterburger, the Viennese publisher of Conrad Celtis, when he painted Johannes Cuspinian.[6] Most of Cranach's print output was in the woodcut medium, a relief technique in which woodcarvers cut away negative space on the block, leaving lines on its surface raised for inking. Already by around 1502 Cranach's woodcuts of the Crucifixion appear tipped into missals circulating at this time in German-speaking and Polish lands.[7] Here and there he continued to produce illustrations for standard Christian liturgical and other texts as well as printed illustrations for more worldly verse, like the 1506 signed and dated *Gentleman and Lady Riding to the Hunt* from Chapter One (illus. 12).

Cranach's woodcut idiom balanced the traditional simplicity of the medium with confidently applied techniques for creating the illusion of space through gradients of dark and light on the surface of a page. Unlike Albrecht Dürer from 1498 on, Cranach still used large open expanses of carved-out woodblock for a blank sky, while using relatively short, arcing hatching to give value to the figures of humans and animals as well as natural landscape features and built settlements. Though perhaps some of the effect can be attributed to the woodblock carvers Cranach worked with – it was typical for painters like him to provide drawn designs for blocks that would then be worked by block-carving specialists – the lion's share must come from Cranach's thoughtful design process. There is an easy confidence in the distinction between thick dark outlines and the finer slivers of wood that model the forms outlined. He was adroit indeed in the *ars graphicam*.

## PRINTING FOR BELIEVERS: RELICS BEFORE REFORM

Printing whole illustrated books required significant investment upfront – in woodblock carving, paper and printer labour – and Cranach did not have that kind of support for independent projects in Vienna.[8] But in Wittenberg, Cranach's extraordinarily wealthy employer Friedrich the Wise commissioned a major printed work from Cranach and his workshop that participated in the same monetization of Christian practices Martin Luther would later decry. This project is known as the *Wittenberger Heiltums-buch* or *Heiligthumsbuch* (Book of Relics), completed in 1509.[9] The genre of Heiltumsbuch was a Northern European phenomenon, related to earlier forms of representing a collection of relics in painted form; a Heiltumsbuch translated these visual inventories to the form of a codex.[10]

What would Luther have objected to here? At this point, relics – remnants of saints and other holy figures as well as objects associated with these figures and holy events – were not just held to be miraculous; they were also often associated with official indulgences. In other words, praying in front of a particular relic would grant the believer a remission of a certain number of days or years from penance. Now, there is no direct evidence that if people prayed with mere printed images of the relics, they believed they would be granted the indulgence associated with those relics. But the gaining of an indulgence from an image is likely to have been a common function of other religious prints, such as, for example, Cranach's woodcut of the Annunciation, which survives in Berlin (in this impression only) with its accompanying text guaranteeing 80,000 years of indulgence.[11] Unlike indulgence-granting prints such as this *Annunciation*, individual objects depicted in Cranach's *Heiltumsbuch* do not come accompanied by individual indulgence designations for users of the book. Instead, as in this example, the text focuses on the individual relic fragments or *partickeln* and their origins in the body or clothing of a given saint (illus. 37).

The focus on individual pieces and their saints of origin confirms that this Heiltumsbuch, like others, was used to promote the relic pilgrimage industry. This was Europe's most profitable tourism sector at the time. The Saxon elector's book advertised at its

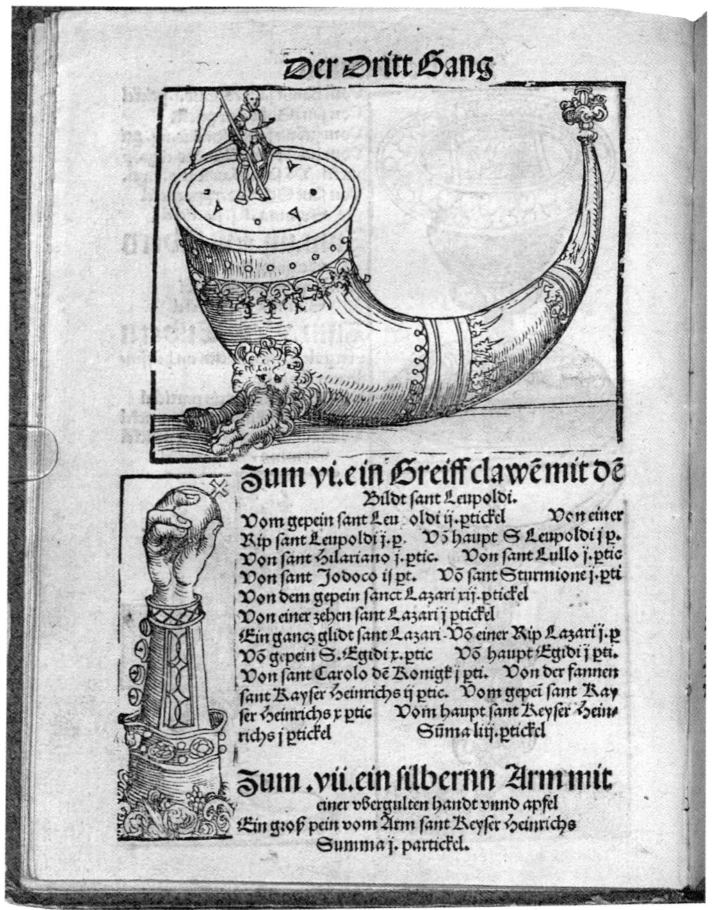


beginning and end the total days of indulgence that a comprehensive visit to the collection could yield and (in the introductory text) the holy personages who had authorized these indulgences.[12] If a believer brought the hefty catalogue along on their visit, or studied it well and used the common mnemonic techniques of the period beforehand, they could make sure to wring every indulgence out of the collection they wanted. The illustrations also

37 Lucas Cranach the Elder, woodcut illustrations from *Dye Zaigung des hochhlobwirdigen Hailigthumbs der Stifft-Kirchen aller Hailigen zu Wittenburg* (1509).

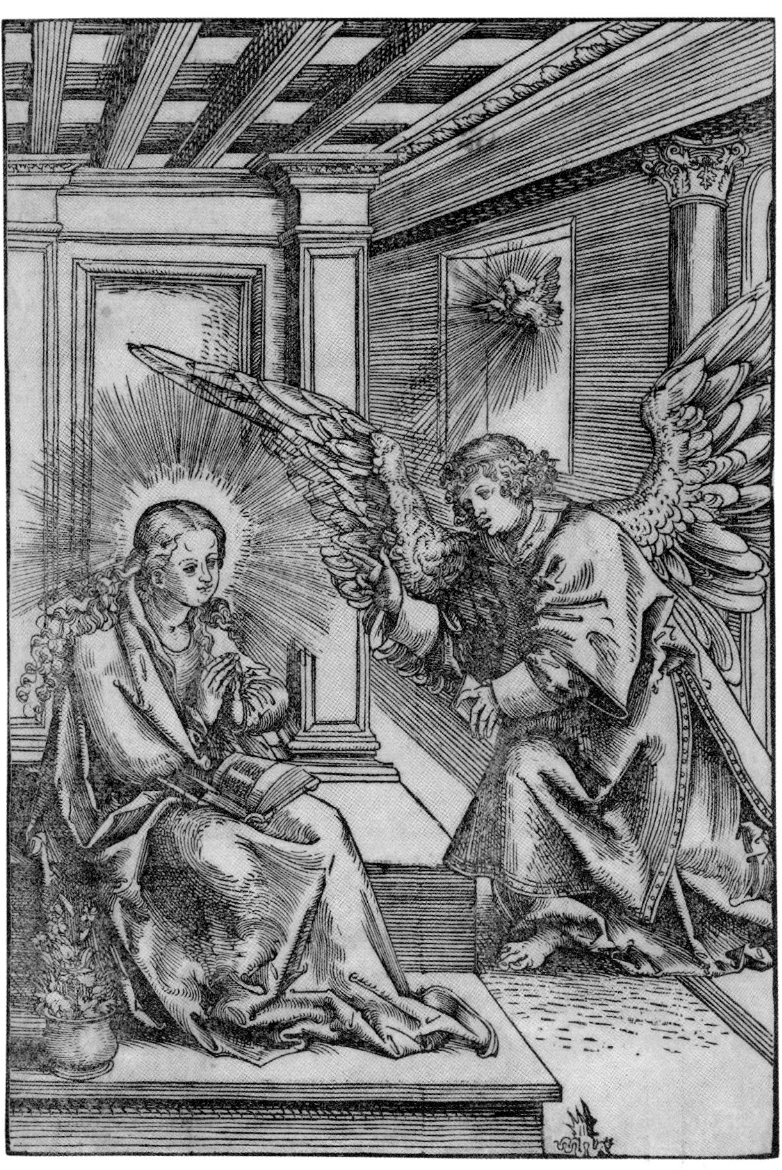

38 Lucas Cranach the Elder, *Annunciation, c.* 1512, woodcut.

helped assure a believer that they were giving the appropriate devotional attention (with appropriate names for saints) to the correct set of fragments. Though the book's claims of helping regular people attain salvation may have been in earnest, a Heiltumsbuch was nevertheless part of the monetization of faith.

In the process of promoting the Wittenberg relic collection as a worthy pilgrimage destination, the *Wittenberger Heiltumsbuch* also advertises many other things. Like a museum guide, the book is organized into eight sections or rounds (*Gänge*) of relics, perhaps only allusively, or perhaps literally corresponding to corridors or walkways through the collection. On the page illustrated here featuring two reliquaries, the number of relic fragments is carefully tallied at many levels: first according to saint-part or object of origin ('From St Leopold's legs 2 fragments', 'From a rib from St Leopold 1 fragment' and so on); then within the reliquary as a whole ('A total of 53 fragments'); and finally, at the end of each section, the total number of fragments within that section (in the case of the third section, 343 fragments).[13] At the very end, the book lists the total number of fragments in the entire collection – 5,005! – and reminds the viewer that each fragment bestows a hundred days of indulgence, and each of the eight sections a hundred days and a year. The rhetoric here indicates that believers should be impressed both by the sheer numbers in Friedrich's collection and by his generosity in allowing believers to obtain salvation by exposure to these objects.

For those who were more experienced on the pilgrimage circuit, Cranach's woodcuts provided information about another impressive aspect of the elector's collection: its range of artistic sensibilities. Relics were often not displayed in simple boxes but housed in elaborate reliquaries like the two shown here. That is, artists often honoured holy fragments by designing appropriate conditions for their display. The two examples on this page alone show many of the most common features of reliquary design from the late Middle Ages to the early sixteenth century.

At the bottom left appears an arm-style reliquary that houses the 'large bone' of the arm of the sainted Holy Roman Emperor Henry II (973–1024). Even though this type of arm reliquary is made of metal, the mimetic design uses form to indicate the relic within. Because the description clarifies that 'hand and apple' (remember that 'apple' and 'sphere' are interchangeable, as in the Judgement of Paris paintings) are gilded, it is possible that the rest of the object is made of a different material. In particular, the middle strip of the forearm, with its overlapping curved lines, might represent an area of transparency. From the twelfth century onwards, and especially in the fourteenth century, the use of rock crystal became common in reliquaries, to promote the kind of 'transparency and clarity' praised as beautiful in writings of the time.[14] Believers could see the preserved body parts, suspended within pleasing forms worked with precious metal and viewed through a material redolent with divine light.

In the upper part of the page shown here is a reliquary of a more theatrical style. It places a figurative statuette of St Leopold atop a drinking horn made from a rare object known as a 'griffin's claw'. Though it is unclear what animal Friedrich's horn came from, a similarly proportioned reliquary made later in the sixteenth century and now in the British Museum is made from polished buffalo or steer horn mounted in gilt silver.[15] However, given the amount of material supposedly contained in the Wittenberg relic (no longer extant) documented here – including an 'entire' limb from St Lazarus among 52 other fragments – one imagines it must have been larger than the average steer's horn. In any case, the point is that this was a common reliquary type: a container made from a supposedly rare but natural substance, ornamented with a silver or gilt silver mount and with other figuration. In this case the ornamental component included not only the figurine of St Leopold and fittings, but also a pair of lion's paws emerging from lions' mouths to stabilize the object. This type of reliquary uses artistry not to display the relics within, but to stage the object itself with a rich ornamental drama.

Finally, the diversity of relics in the *Heiltumsbuch* consolidated Wittenberg's range of access to the history of Christendom. For example, St Leopold, who would be made patron saint of Austria in the seventeenth century, had been recently canonized in 1485 and was known for his role in founding regional monasteries rather than seeking worldly power as an emperor. Thus, the upper reliquary participates in the rhetoric of local cultural history so appreciated by German elites of the time. Containing some relics from the Holy Roman Emperor Henry II, it naturally accompanies the emperor's arm reliquary below on this page. But on the next page readers would find a relic primarily devoted to St Eulogius of Córdoba, martyred in the ninth century in the caliphate of Al-Andalus. Each of these saints had a particular cluster of virtues and stories appropriate for particular spiritual needs. In other words, Friedrich's collection both reflected particular interests in regional history but also appealed to visitors of diverse backgrounds and spiritual states. Cranach's Heiltumsbuch for his patron showed off Wittenberg's spirituality as cosmopolitan and comprehensive.

## CRANACH AT THE BIRTH OF THE REFORMATION

Before giving an account of Cranach's trajectory of visually defining the Lutheran movement, it is important to mention that he continued producing art in contexts faithful to the Roman Church, especially but not only in the service of Cardinal Albrecht of Brandenburg. Illus. 40 represents a typical devotional image of the Virgin produced in Cranach's workshop, which would seem to fly in the face of recent Lutheran texts (some of which

Cranach himself had co-printed) curtailing the worship of the Virgin. Cranach's portrait of Albrecht as St Jerome (illus. 39) shows off the cardinal's sophisticated humanist artistic taste: it participates in the trend of portraying oneself as a historical figure; it acknowledges Dürer's and other recent Northern European painters' images of the saint as the Christian humanist par excellence, adapting this motif from Venetian precedents for this purpose; and it of course proudly represents the hallmarks of a Cranach, with the segmented foliage wall, civilization in the airy corner, and wood-play in the panel's foreground. Cranach was not playing both sides so much as working in service of clients in a period when artists did not feel obliged to represent their innermost convictions, especially when responding to patrons' commissions.

Alongside such more traditional Roman Christian works, though, the bulk of Cranach's religious-themed work from 1520 onwards intended Luther's followers and potential followers as its audience.[16] I say 'religious-themed' rather than 'religious', because Cranach's first major work in service of reform, like others before and after, was not meant for prayerful attention or sober reflection upon religious principles. A collaboration with Melanchthon, Luther and the canon lawyer Johann Schwerdtfeger, the 1521 *Passional Christi und Antichristi* (Passion-Guide of Christ and Antichrist) was a printed pamphlet with perhaps slightly more emphasis on scorn for the papacy than affirmation of true Christian values.[17]

This pamphlet presents an outspoken and relatively uncomplicated set of thirteen antitheses between Christ and the pope (that is, the Antichrist). Each opening (of two pages) contrasts two images within a loose theme. For example, the opening illustrated here, the sixth image-pair in the series, contrasts the varying means of locomotion undertaken by Christ and pope as they bear their respective crosses. Even illiterate or partially literate

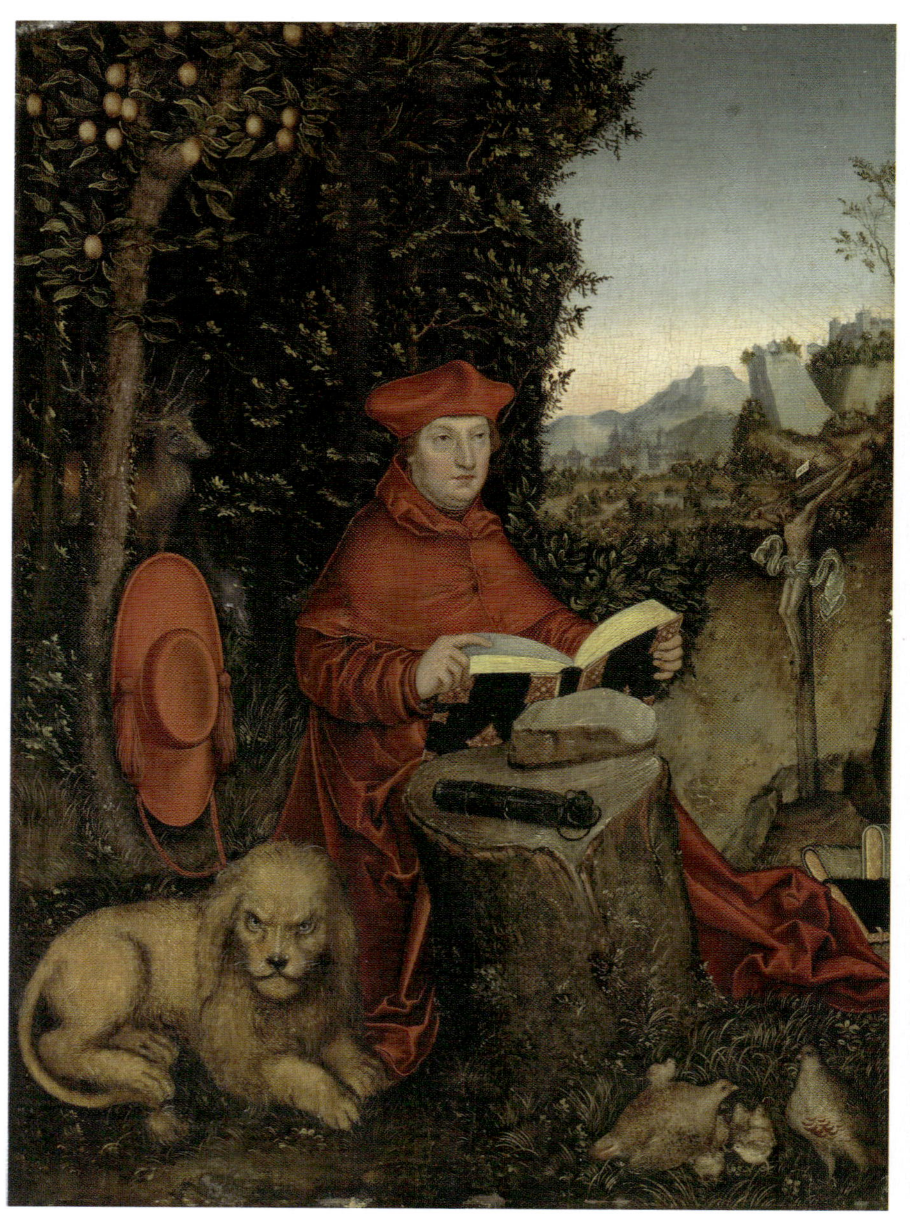

39 Lucas Cranach the Elder, *Cardinal Albrecht von Brandenburg as St Jerome in a Landscape*, *c.* 1527, oil on panel.

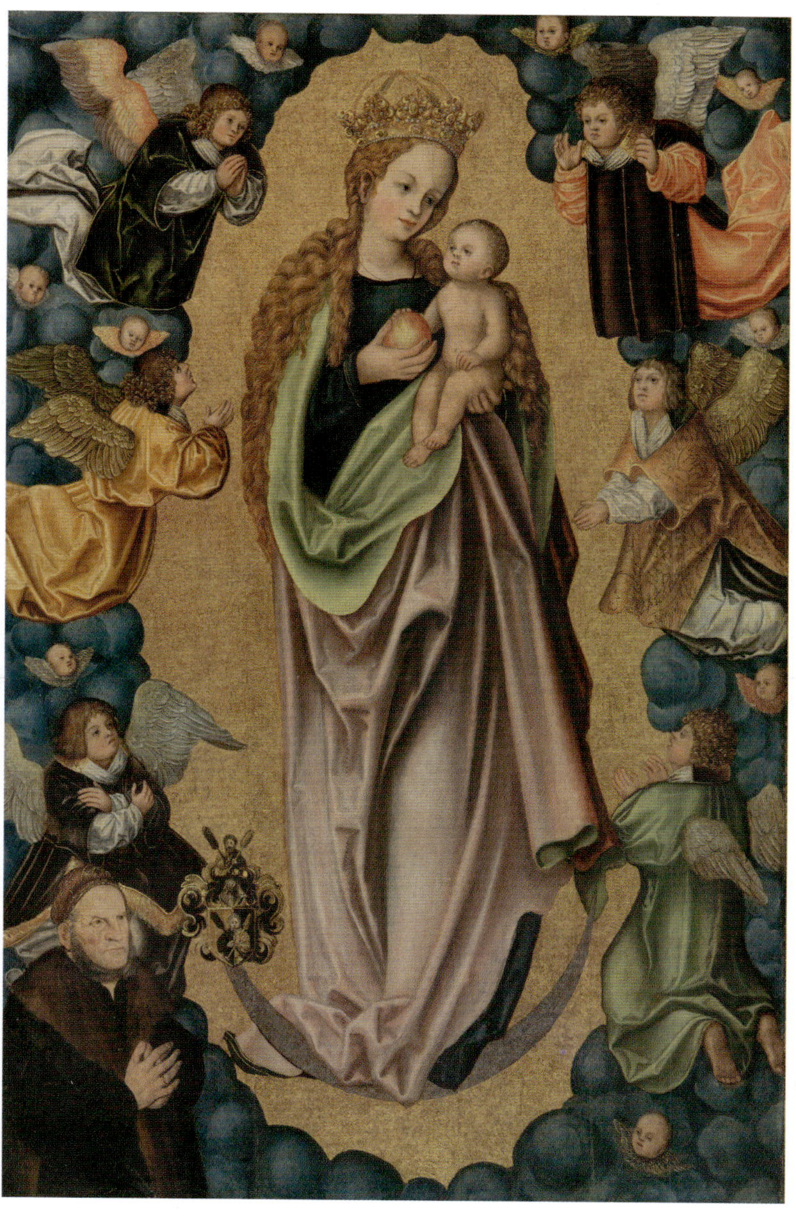

40 Lucas Cranach the Elder, *Virgin on the Crescent Moon Worshipped by the Donor Hieronymus Rudelauf*, before 1523, oil on panel.

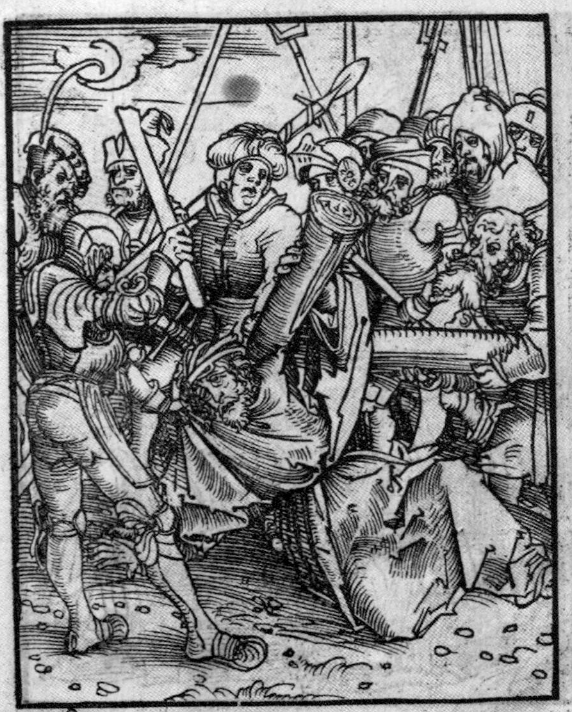

Ihesus fatigatus ex itinere sedebat sic supra fontem. Iohannis. iiij.
Si quis vult venire post me: abneget semetipsum, tollat crucem suã,
& sequatur me. Matthei. xvi.
Et baiulans sibi crucem, exiuit in eum qui dicitur Caluarie locus, Iohã.
xix.

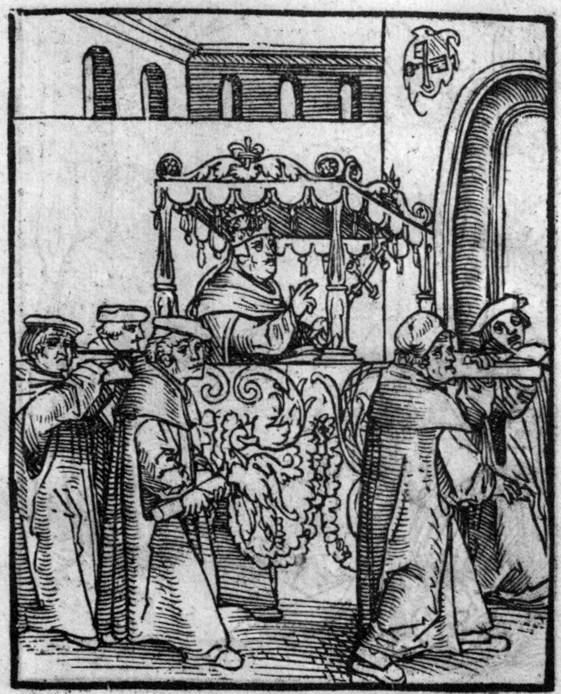

Capitulū. Si quis suadente diabolo & similia satis supercꝗ probant
quam libenter Papa crucem aduersitatis toleret, quū omnes quicunꝗ
manus in sacerdotes iniiciunt, maledicit, & diabolo tradit. Sic etiam fert
crucem Papa, vt baptisati Christiani cogātur eum humeris suis portare.

B iij

41, 42 Lucas Cranach the Elder, *Christ Carrying the Cross* and *Christians Carrying
the Pope Carrying a Cross*, woodcut illustrations from Luther, Melanchthon and
Schwerdtfeger, *Antithesis figurata vitae, Christi et Antichristi* (1521).

audiences could easily discern the pamphlet's distinctions; perhaps they would be intrigued enough to ask a more educated member of their family or a friend to explain the finer points of the writing. (Contrast, for example, the earlier woodcut Cranach made on behalf of reformer Andreas Karlstadt.)[18]

For this Latin version, Melanchthon and Schwerdtfeger selected and assembled various texts below the woodcuts: paraphrases of Bible verses, commentary on canon law and citations of both. In this example, the 'Si quis suadente diabolo' on the pope's side is from a major long-standing legal text, the *Decretum*. The passage introduced by these four words ('If anyone, by the Devil's persuasion') declares that whoever lays a malicious hand on clerics is subject to anathematization – that is, being made separate from God and thus united with the Devil – unless the one causing the harm is the pope himself. On the left-hand side

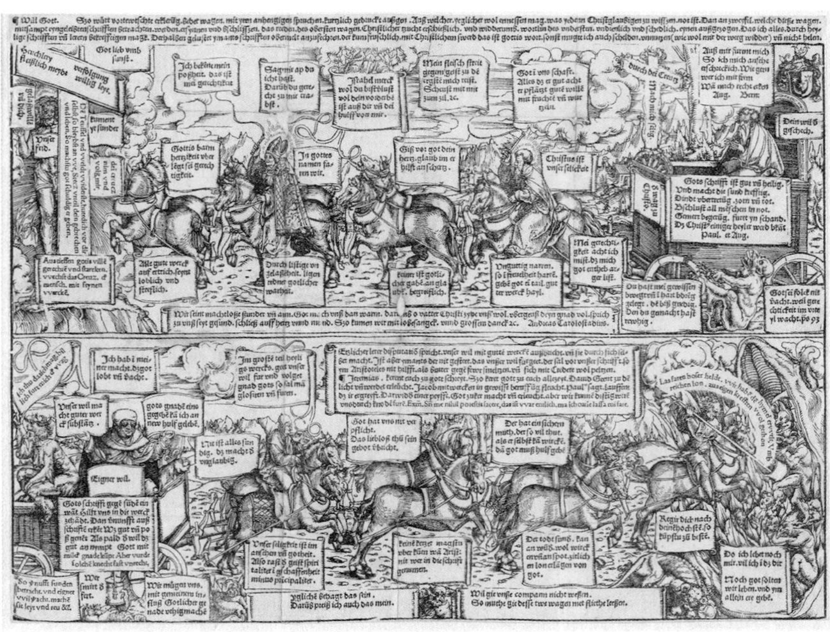

43 Lucas Cranach the Elder, *Himmelwagen und Höllenwagen des Andreas Bodenstein von Karlstadt*, 1519, woodcut. This woodcut of 'The Heaven-wagon and Hell-wagon of Andreas Bodenstein von Karlstadt', hailed as 'almost

are three versions of passages from scripture accompanied by citation. I say 'version' because the texts depart slightly, often in word order, from the standard Vulgate Bible available at the time.

Taken out of context as they are here, all three texts on the left can be interpreted to refer with varying levels of literality to the burden of Christ's cross: Christ's fatigue at the well with the Samaritans; his prophetic injunction to his disciples to take up his cross and follow him; and his actual carrying of the cross to Calvary.[19] The relationship of cited text to image on the right is less direct, and more bitter. The fact that the severe punishment of anathema is ordered upon any who attack the pope 'proves how [un]willingly the pope tolerates the cross of adversity', in contrast to Christ's substantial endurance of suffering. Furthermore, 'the Pope carries the cross in such a way that baptized Christians must carry him upon their own shoulders.' That is, while Christ suffers for the good of believers, the Antichrist pope *creates* suffering for believers.

The German edition was even more popular, with still looser biblical paraphrases (accompanied by citations). The Bible verses, decontextualized in service of polemic, nevertheless found anchor in the citations following each verse. The pamphlet was cheap, costing about 'six thaler'. It must have been successful: there are at least three different versions dated to 1521; some scholars estimate it reached about 20,000 people.[20]

These were fraught times for those who had begun to follow Luther's ideas. One of the chains of inspiration for the *Passional* began with Pope Leo X's papal bull of 15 June 1520, *Exsurge domine* (Arise, O Lord), which denounced Luther's ideas from the Theses and other publications as heretical and gave Luther sixty days to recant. Instead of recanting, in October 1520 Luther published a pamphlet, *Adversus execrabilem Antichristi bullam* (Against the Antichrist's Execrable Bull), followed by a second, more thorough

certainly the very first piece of visual propaganda for the Reformation', perhaps directs its many sharp texts at a highly educated audience; or perhaps, as some scholars suggest, it is a poor early effort at visual persuasion.

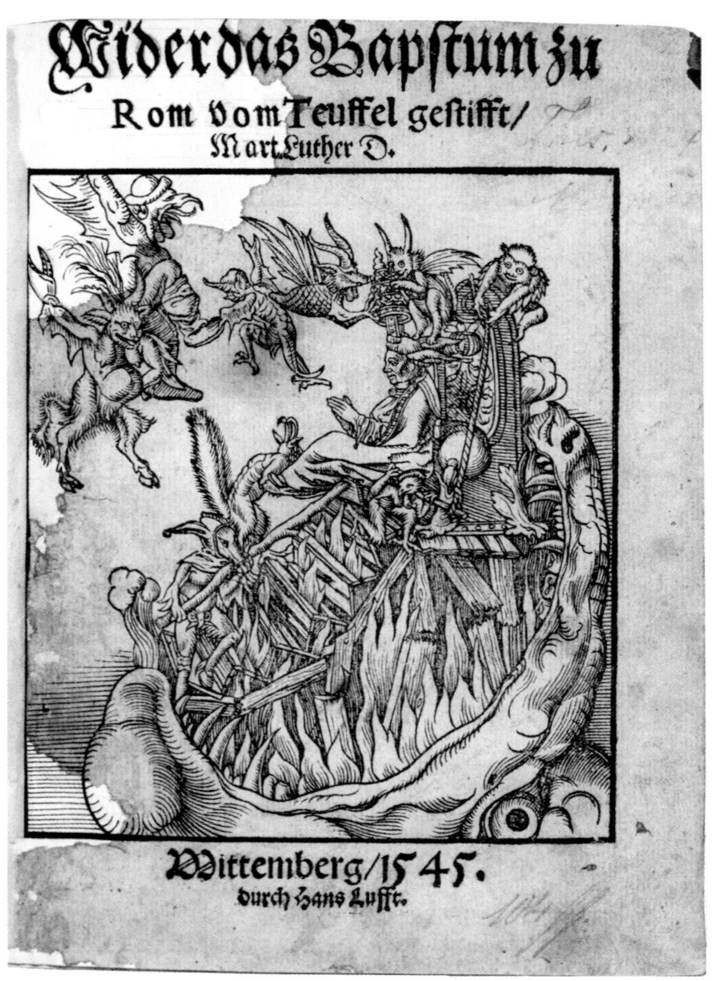


pamphlet in November, *Assertio omnium articulorum per Bullam Leonis X. novissimam damnatorum* (Affirmation of all the Articles Condemned by the Latest Bull of Leo X).

It was in response to Luther's extraordinarily bold refusal to back down that the pope initially excommunicated Luther in early January 1521. (The *Passional'*s commentary on anathematization

44 Martin Luther, *Wider das Bapstum zu Rom vom Teuffel gestifft*, 1545, woodcut. Though Cranach was not the most prolific of the many woodcut designers who provided illustrations for satirical Lutheran texts over the decades, he

assumed that everyone would know about this outrage.) Elector Friedrich intervened, and it was decided that Luther should appear and be permitted to argue his case publicly at a months-long convocation of regional leaders known as an Imperial Diet. This Diet, which began later that January, was held at Worms, an imperial free city of the Holy Roman Empire now in the Rhineland-Palatinate, about a fortnight's journey from Wittenberg by wagon. In April 1521, Luther appeared at the Diet and, after reconsidering the case against him, nevertheless recanted only some of the vitriol of his tone and none of his critiques of Church corruption.

Though Friedrich had negotiated Luther's safety in travelling to and from the Diet, the elector did not trust the pope or his allies not to attempt – perhaps with violence – to arrest Luther. Friedrich himself therefore arranged a fake 'abduction' of Luther by highwaymen; these hired men escorted Luther to Wartburg Castle in Eisenach in present-day Thuringia, between Worms and Wittenberg. There Luther remained for almost a year (*pace* a secret visit to Wittenberg in December) until early March 1522.

Despite the threats against Luther, his stay in Wartburg Castle was a kind of scholarly residency that freed him from pastoral obligations to his church and gave him time to focus on further publication projects. The most notable of these was his German translation of the New Testament, known as the *Septembertestament* because it appeared in September 1522 (almost certainly at Cranach's press). The *Passional* was published in Latin prior to Luther's residency at Wartburg Castle, but possibly came out in German during that time, as Luther first mentions it by its German name proudly in a letter to Melanchthon of 26 May 1521 (incidentally the same day that the pope released the Edict of Worms, which urged the capture of Luther and condemned any defence of him).[21]

turned back to book illustration in the year before Luther's death for his treatise 'Against the Roman Papacy Founded by the Devil'. This title page image places the papal throne across the maw of hell, attended by demons.

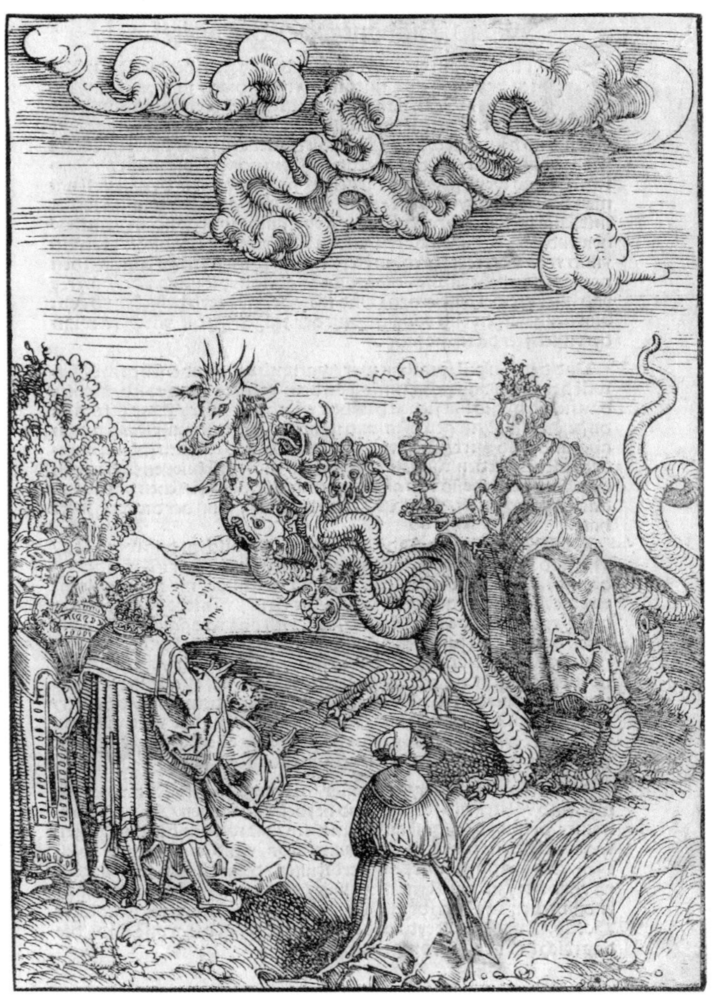

Though no correspondence between Luther and Cranach survives from this time, from the *Passional* onwards, Cranach was the primary print-designer for Luther's message. Following the production of the *Passional*, Cranach proceeded with illustrating the *Septembertestament*.[22] Along with 24 initial woodcuts by Cranach,

45 Lucas Cranach the Elder, *The Whore of Babylon*, woodcut illustration from Martin Luther, *Das Newe Testament Deutzsch* [*Septembertestament*] (1522).

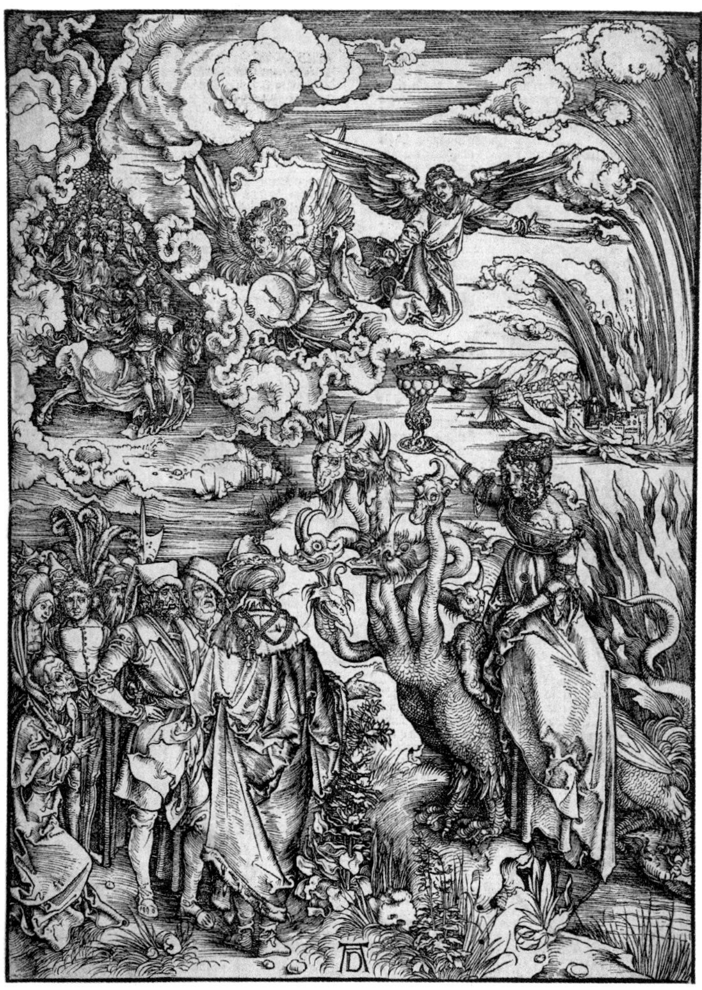

the book contains 21 full-page illustrations of the final book of the New Testament, the Book of Revelation or Apocalypse. Here Cranach is looking back to one of the most famous achievements in printmaking of his time, Dürer's 1498 pamphlet publication of an illustrated *Apocalypse*.

46 Albrecht Dürer, *The Whore of Babylon*, woodcut illustration from *Apocalipsis cu[m] figuris* (1498).

Comparing these two renderings of the so-called whore of Babylon shows Cranach's sensitivity to function and visual context. Twenty-six-year-old Dürer was taking the occasion of widespread awareness of the impending half-millennium (1500) to demonstrate the dynamism and power of the woodcut medium in its 'revelation' of the divine. Lines of varying thickness fill almost the entirety of the rectangular borders of the composition; the page ranges from deep black to white, distributing the sense of contrast almost equally between foreground and background, earth and sky; there are no broad undifferentiated passages. Like all Dürer's pictures in this series, it is, as one might say in the early twenty-first century, a lot. He had a lot to prove, for himself and for art, and for the emerging concept of Germany.

Though Cranach also suggests a stormy sky, he simplifies the scene, most obviously by including fewer figures. The sky's outburst of curly cloud is large, therefore legible, and isolated, ushering in no vignettes or angels; the landscape is not interrupted by bursts of flame or tufted shorelines but consists in regular grasses, rolling hills and cursory parallel strokes of sea. The biggest difference is in the evenness of tone. To some extent this is due to the way the blocks were inked and to quality of impression, but even in a crispier impression, Cranach's print does not range so violently from concentrated regions of darkness to bright white. This placid, simpler rendition of the whore of Babylon reflects Cranach's goal: rather than prove himself as a virtuoso artist, Cranach, nearly forty, strives here to provide fit company for Luther's new rendering of the most important text in all Christian lives, and to assist in establishing Luther's renegade authority within a new Christianity. If Cranach borrows from elements of Dürer's renowned series, it is not so much to compete with it as to claim the Dürer *Apocalypse*'s full-page appeal for Luther's movement, to situate Luther's work within a proud, continuous German cultural context. The illustration had to be good, but not distracting;

in being visually easy to parse it would keep readers focused on the text.

Compared with the *Passional* before it, and with the next set of Bible illustrations Cranach's workshop produced for Luther's full Bible translation of 1534, this image does not much directly target the pope. The whore of Babylon's headgear is a three-tiered crown, but unlike in the 1534 version of this image, the tiers of this crown diminish with each layer, rather than curving cleanly upward like the papal tiara. (That said, the papal reference is present in the crown's triplicity, which distinguishes this figure from that of Dürer's precedent woodcut.) The ruler in profile on the left, gesturing at the whore of Babylon – perhaps one of the many worldly rulers said to have 'fornicated' with her in Revelation 17:2 – resembles the recently deceased (1519) Holy Roman Emperor Maximilian I, but it is not really a portrait. The similarity feels as much a recognizable sign of imperialness as satire of the dead.

Another way to think about Cranach's streamlined approach to this image, indebted to Dürer but distinct from that precedent, is that it is confident in the words it accompanies. The text of Chapter Seventeen of Revelation, like much of that book, is chock full of specific references to figures and events that do not easily hang together in a causal narrative. The book, in which John of Patmos describes the visions 'revealed' to him of the end of the world, asserts itself as prophecy precisely by distancing itself from the plausibility of everyday life and by assembling myriad age-old symbols. Famously, many of the busy features of Dürer's rich woodcut, absorbingly difficult to parse, make Revelation's strange details manifest, pushing the limits of plausibility in a way that matches the ambition of prophecy proper.

But many of these details, in the case of Chapter Seventeen's account of the whore of Babylon, are presented in the text not as within John's vision, but as part of what the angel tells John will happen or has happened. In a way, foreshadowing a characteristic Lutheran confidence in scripture, Cranach mirrors the text more closely than Dürer. He shows us the whore of Babylon as described, anchoring the text in a clear scenario, but leaves most of the visualization of the guiding angel's (and Luther's) words to the reader. Scripture here does not stand alone, quite. But Cranach's image is not a parallel replacement for each facet of the text, either. Instead, he provides a visual prompt, putting the image in the role of a focusing lens or vessel that helps the reader experience the text for themselves.

## LAW AND GRACE: HOW REPETITION AUTHORIZED THE LUTHERAN STYLE

So far, much of the work discussed in this book has been about imagery Cranach inherited from ancient, Italian or earlier German precedents, and then transformed for his own purposes. However, as he continued to produce work in Luther's ambit, Cranach became responsible for depicting Lutheran theological doctrine in its own right, distinct from anti-papist satires or fresh renditions of traditional Christian themes.

Cranach's most important new subject was that of Law and Grace (also known as Law and Gospel), a theme that arguably formed the core of Lutheranism's visual repertoire. Emerging in the late 1520s, the same years in which Cranach's workshop began to massively produce variants on a theme – like Lucretia on a black background or the pastoral Venus with Cupid as Honey Thief in the last chapter – Law and Grace was the first Lutheran subject-matter to receive this standardized treatment. The subject-matter was possibly or even probably influenced by an earlier 1520s print from Paris or Antwerp based on Luther's preaching on this subject, but the subject did not become popular until Cranach adopted it as a workshop topos.[23] Two drawings for this composition, one lost during the Second World War, attest to Cranach's attempts to work out the deployment of its complicated iconography in space.[24] Once Cranach popularized it, the subject spread to other media made by other makers, from elite relief sculpture to stove tiles.[25]

The image presents its viewer with a choice between two options. Will the viewer, like the naked man on the left, allow the burdens of Christian law (associated with the strictures of the Old Testament) to usher him into hell, where a grey demon waits amid blood-red flames? Or will the viewer, like the bearded and thus perhaps notionally maturer and wiser nude man on the right, heed the New Testament's doctrine of salvation through Christ's sacrifice on the cross and subsequent Resurrection, attaining the Grace symbolized by Christ's red blood? The correct answer is obvious. The composition's largest organizing device is the tree at its centre, withered on the side of the law and flourishing on the side of grace.

Law and Grace provides the clearest example of an unusual quality mentioned earlier as a hallmark of the Cranach workshop and shared by many early Lutheran images, especially relief sculptures by fellow Lutheran artist Peter Dell the Elder: a disjunctive virtual space. When one looks at a Law and Grace painting – unlike, say, Cranach's renditions of the Nymph of the Fountain – one finds it difficult to imagine its space as a plausible continuous reality. The example illustrated here, which is located in Gotha, is more coherent than most, but it still looks more like a collage of different scenes pasted alongside each other than a unified virtual world. This is not just because Cranach has in fact composed the painting of different scenes from different parts of Scripture; Renaissance paintings often gracefully integrated multiple disparate events into a single landscape. One can only speculate on whether this disjunction would have registered on the general audience to whom woodcuts of the scene might have been sold at the market.

*Overleaf:* 47 Lucas Cranach the Elder and workshop, *Law and Grace*, 1529, oil on panel.

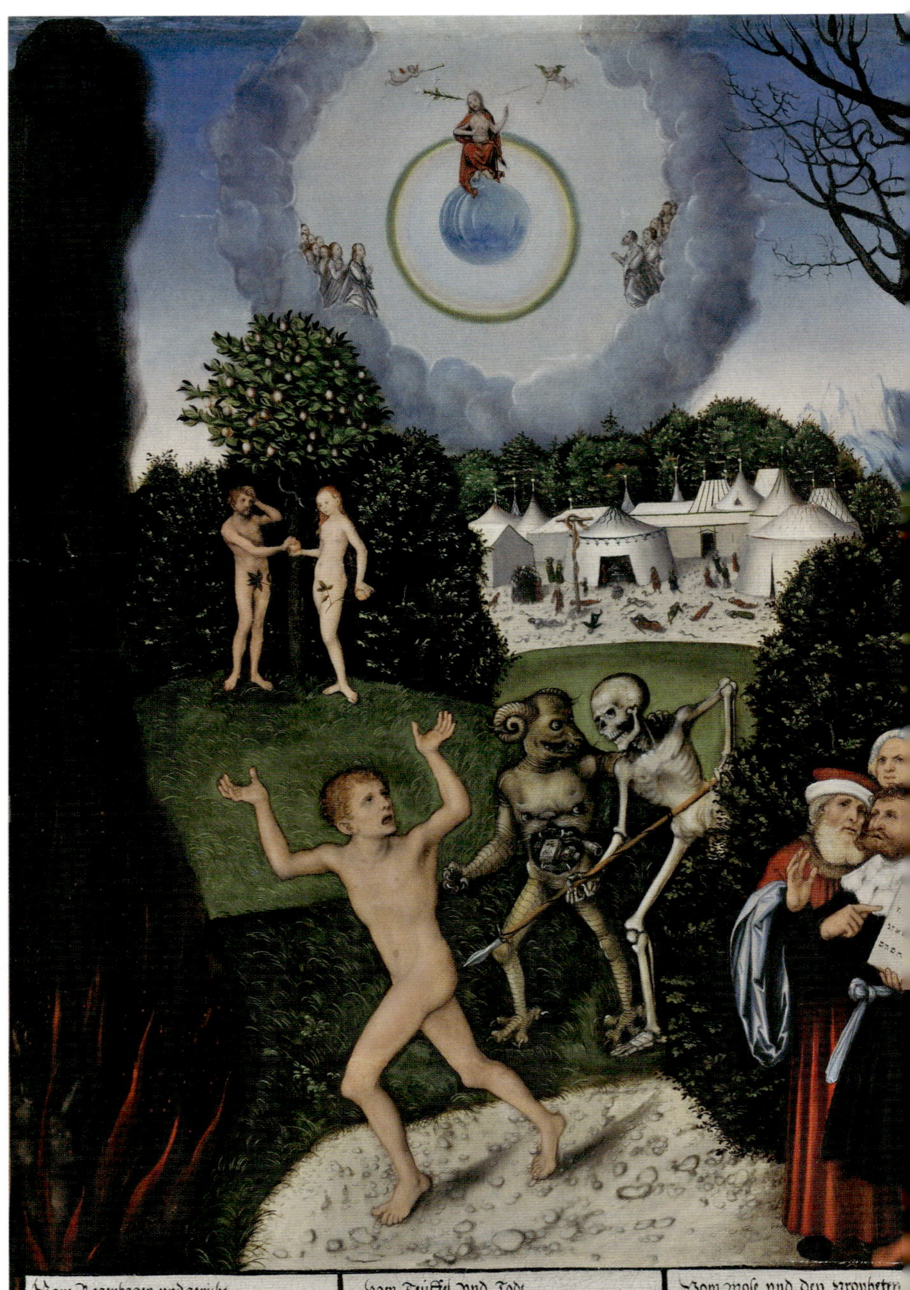


Vom Regenbogen vnd gericht.
Es wird Gottes zorn offenbart vom himmel vber aller
menschen Gottlos leben vnd vnnrecht. Roman.1.
wier seind allzumal sünder vmdt mangelm des preises
das sie sich Gottes nicht rühmen mügen Roman.1.

Vom Teuffel vnd Todt
Die Sunnde ist des Todes spiess aber das gesetz ist der sinden
krafft.1. Corinth.15.
Das gesetz Richtet zornn ahn. Roman.4.

Vom Mose vnd den propheten
Durch das gesetz kömet erkentnus der sü
Matthei.11.
Das gesetz vndt propheten gehen bis au

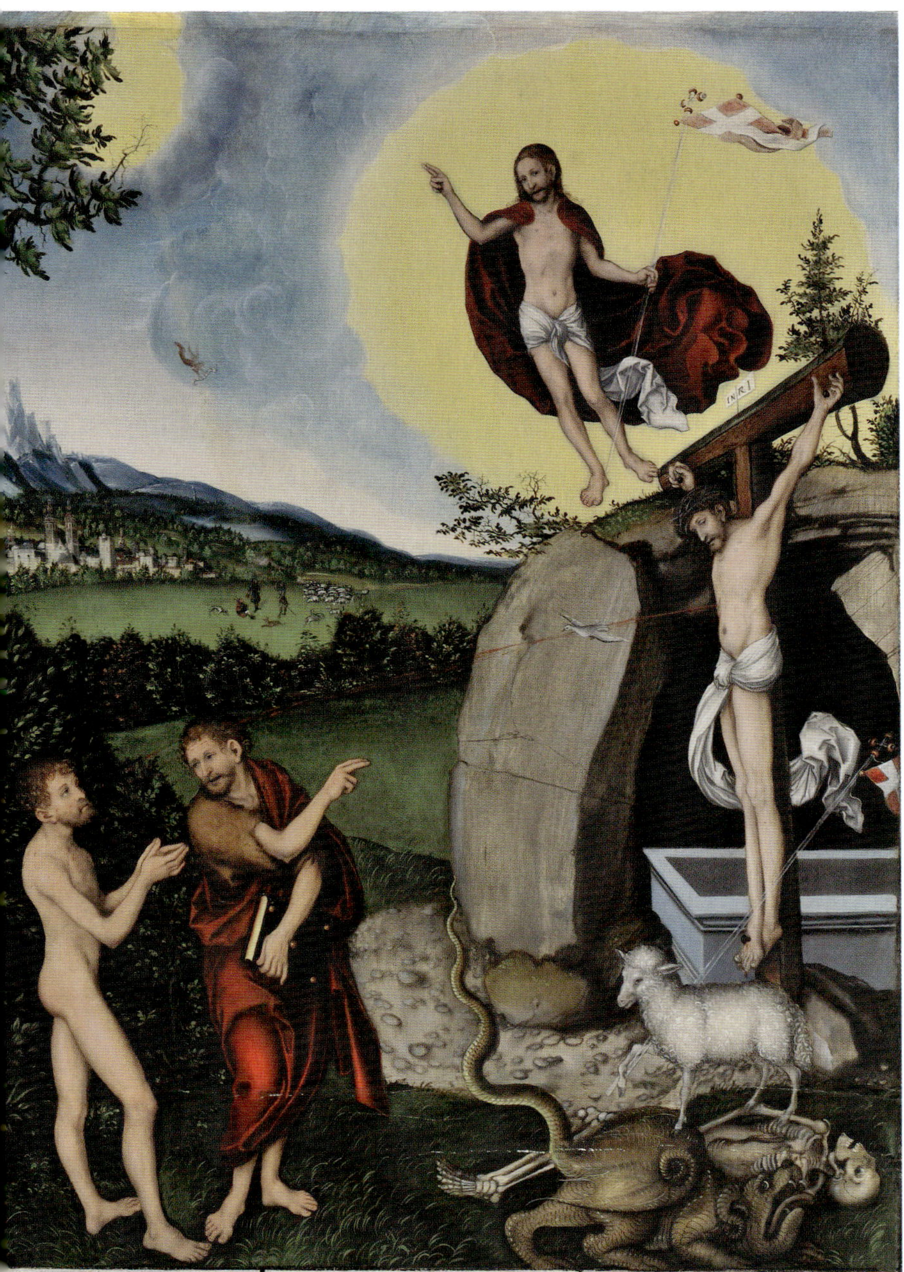
Vom Menschen
...chte lebet seines glaubens Roman·1·
...n das ein mensch gerecht werde den glauwen
...rch des gesetzs Roman·3·
Vom Teuffer
Sihe das ist gottes Lamb das der welt sünde tregt
Sant Johannes Baptist Johannis·Z·
In der heiligung des geistes zum gehorsam vnd besprēg
ung des blutes Jesu Christi amen·1·petri·1·
Von Tode Vnd Lamb
Der Tod ist verschlungen ynn sieg Tod wo ist dein spiß
Helle wo ist dein sieg: danck hab Gott der vns den siegt gegeben
hat durch Jesum christum vasern herten·1·Corinth·15

But as we have already seen, Cranach knew how to make a plausible illusion of continuous space. Here he chose not to.

The result is that the viewer is extraordinarily aware of the dependence of each scene not only on the scripture (with its careful citations) below, but also on the theology, based on Luther's preachings, that has assembled these particular scenes into a whole. It is the power of scripture and Luther's teachings, and through these the power of faith in Christ, that makes this picture come together. Power rooted in faith rather than illusion is in keeping with Luther's general ideas about the importance of images in Christian practice. Unlike other reformers like Zwingli and Calvin who would take stricter stances against the use of images, Luther believed that images could potentially have a positive function for a righteous Christian believer. If the essence of an image already came 'from a believer's heart', the material image could witness or provide a memory prompt for that content. Against gore and enthusiastic about image captions, contemptuous of pedants who needed images to represent a plausible reality (to the point of questioning, for example, why a wooden door to hell would not catch fire), Luther was indifferent to the simulation of the real world. For Luther, providing a visual anchor for core elements of faith was the main task of an image.[26]

With its clear captions and discrete vignettes, *Law and Grace* certainly fit this brief. Its intelligible layout would be a crucial part of rendering its novel composition and meaning accessible to a broad audience. For new Lutherans, this picture may have been the earliest visualization of a theme they had encountered in sermons – whether published or delivered from a pulpit – but many of the individual figures and vignettes in this painting would have been familiar, repurposed from traditional art in local churches and printed imagery available at book fairs. Some viewers might not have previously seen the background iconography of the brazen serpent, the snake curling around a pole

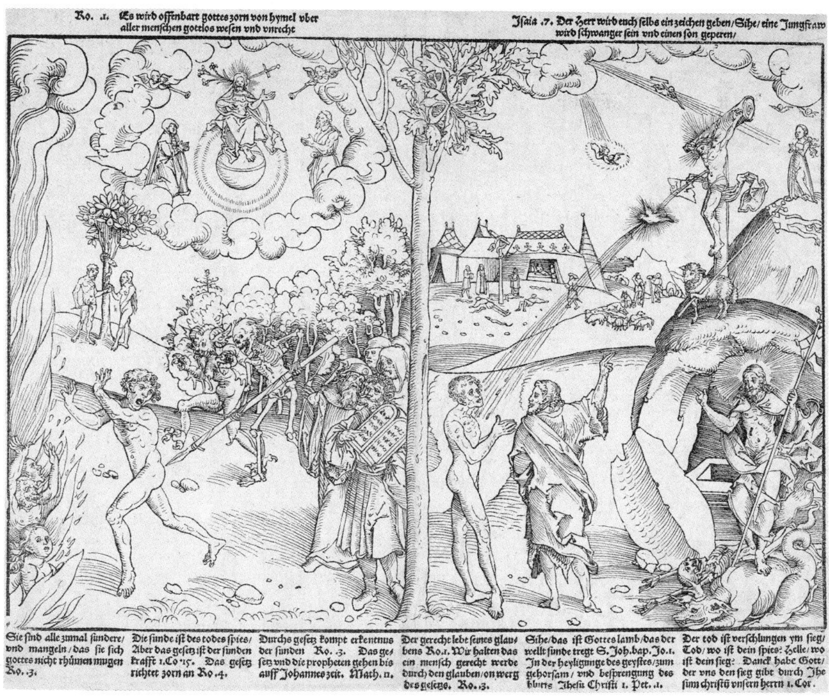



above prone bodies in front of several white tents. (In this scene, taken from the Book of Numbers 21:6, Moses cures a plague of lethal snakebites by following God's instructions to erect an artificial serpent in brass and mount it on a pole.) But most of the other vignettes were familiar, either as a whole or as recombinations of recognizable figures like the Paschal Lamb of the Resurrection and the Devil. Once Cranach had worked out the complex composition, he translated a simplified version of this scene onto a woodblock for wider dissemination.

But Cranach's design was not directed only to the churchgoing and market-going masses: he ensured that these works would have learned resonance as well. The binary composition is itself in some ways so primal as to make historical tracing of this visual

48 Lucas Cranach the Elder, *Law and Grace*, 1529, woodcut.

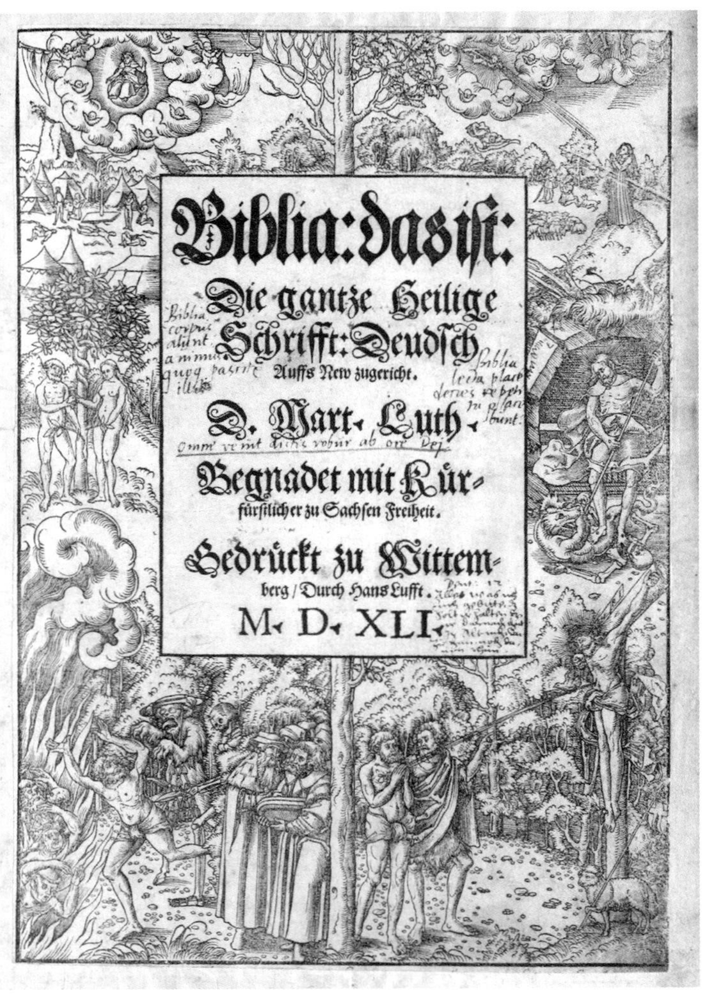


rhetoric feel foolish. One thinks most readily of the Last Judgement binaries of damned and saved souls that similarly relegated the damned to the left and the saved to the right on church and cathedral pediments (the spaces above doorways). But Cranach's image would have appealed also to humanist elites in its reference

49 Lucas Cranach the Elder, *Law and Grace*, title page of the Luther Bible (Wittenberg, 1541).

to the pagan theme of Hercules at the crossroads.[27] In this type of scene, popularized by widely circulating engravings associated with Andrea Mantegna and by a 1498 interpretation by Dürer, a young Hercules chooses between virtue and vice, between good and evil.

*Law and Grace* would also recall Cranach's *Judgement of Paris* imagery for humanist social circles. The important difference here is that ambiguity has been removed. Paris may not be able to make the right choice, but this viewer must. Though *Law and Grace* is packed with references to familiar Christian figures, the overall structure is streamlined and clear. Adhering to the law (and by extension, the trap of pay-for-salvation schemes offered to law-breakers by the Roman Church) will usher the viewer towards damnation; as Luther taught, the grace of Christ alone saves.

Cranach's construction of this theme for clear repetition in paint and print would become the central model for Lutheran imagery. By remixing old iconography into a new composition, Cranach both packed *Law and Grace* with familiar anchors for

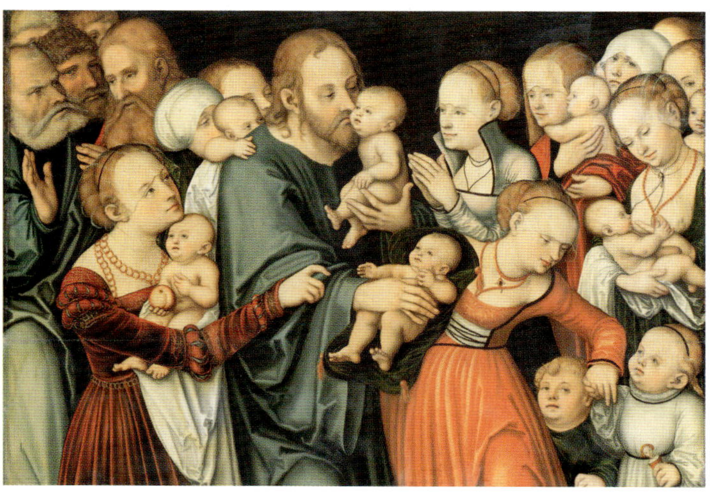

50 Lucas Cranach the Elder, *Christ Blessing the Children*, c. 1535–40, oil on panel. This also oft-repeated subject-matter, often smaller in scale, offered a more domestically relatable Lutheran message about the availability of grace to all.

viewer attention and organized those figures into a framework that itself became a symbol. This binary composition centring on a bifurcated tree would come to signify Lutheranism itself, Lutheranism as the hinge of salvation.

Of Law and Grace paintings made under Cranach's direct supervision, seven survived in oil on panel into the twentieth century. There are also three known illuminated manuscript versions, title pages for printed Bibles of 1541. This, again, is typical of Cranach's workshop production in these decades: multiple versions of the same subject, multiple similar treatments of the same subject, everything branded by a set of certain shared conventions.

The extensive production of Law and Grace pictures established the authority of Lutheran imagery by shifting the basis of that authority from tradition to repetition, as I will explain here. Sixteenth-century painting (like paintings of previous centuries in Christian Europe) counted on the recognizability of subject-matter. Today, many a non-expert museum goer, confronted with Renaissance galleries in a major museum, utters aloud a thought that may be suppressed by more expert museum goers: 'All these Madonna-and-child paintings look the same. One has the kid holding a pear and another has a thicker halo, but what's the difference?'

Now, differences between paintings of the same subject-matter have provided generations of Renaissance art historians with careers. But in the sixteenth century, for paintings to do their work in society, sameness was equally important: it guaranteed legibility and connection to a shared Christendom. When these paintings of the Madonna and Child were located in individual churches and chapels, they were representative of the scene for a given community, whether that community was a wealthy family, a congregation or a particular society or guild's space within a larger congregation. In this context, where a given painting of the Madonna and Child might have been the only one around, the play of recognizability (typically in Cranach's versions, the Madonna would be on the upper right and the child on the lower left in her lap) and variation (what object in the child's hand, what backdrop, what textiles and so on) was crucial. An individual painting's distinctiveness would speak to a community and/or patron's particularities, while its broadly recognizable iconography and composition anchored the community or patron in a larger tradition of Christendom, which transcended the communal context across space and time. It is no surprise that variation would emphasize the identity of an individual community or patron, and that increasing importance would thus be placed on variation in the sixteenth century, as an art industry emerged for wealthy consumers and as print culture spread access to images beyond local contexts. But one must also remember that repetition itself in this context stood in for the authority of shared, long-standing heritage.

When Cranach adopts this play of recognizability and variation and makes it the engine of his newly invented Lutheran subject-matter, he achieves an unprecedented result. The authority of tradition, associated with repetition, becomes associated in turn with his own repeated inventions. This is a transference of the basis of visual authority: even though artistic repetition's authority is supposed to derive from its connection to tradition, here an authoritative sense of tradition derives from repetition itself.

Nowhere is this transfer of authority from tradition onto repetition more visible than in Law and Grace. With this subject, Cranach has created a new series that explicitly rejects tradition. In other words, these paintings explicitly thematize Lutheranism's divergence from the older Roman tradition. In his various Law and Grace productions, Cranach has reshuffled the contents of that older tradition and extracted them from their previously standard compositional schemes. All that remains is the repetition itself, which establishes the new standard.

## MASS-PRODUCED PORTRAITS

Plentiful as Law and Grace pictures were, the most repetitive motif of Lutheran visual culture lay not in new iconographic inventions, but in portraits of Martin Luther himself. Again, portraiture of non-rulers was still somewhat novel at the beginning of the sixteenth century, especially in Germanophone lands. Cranach was one of the early well-respected practitioners of humanist portraiture, but he was hardly alone. Cranach's true innovation was in going from depicting wealthy scholars like Johannes Cuspinian on commission to producing regular portraits of his friend, the excommunicated priest, to be translated for painted copies and wide print distribution (illus. 5, illus. 51).[28]

Cranach's portraiture practice shifted over his career. Witty, sophisticated humanist portraiture dominates his early work. These paintings were intended for a group of like-minded intellectuals and perhaps for university students and colleagues. Later, Cranach harks back to the age-old tradition, familiar from ancient Greece and Rome, of distributing a relatively straightforward likeness of a ruler. Remarkably – perhaps in a kind of anti-papal parallel – Cranach starting in 1520 (with an earlier engraving of Luther in the traditional garb of an Augustinian monk) applies this tradition to the distribution of the likeness of a rebel leader, one in defiance of worldly power.[29]

Of course, Luther was backed by the power of the Saxon electors and other Germanophone princes at this point; they, too, appeared in woodcut and engraved portraits for broader distribution, some designed by Cranach and others by contemporaries. It is they whose stove-tile portraits spread as far as one of Henry VIII's castles in East Sussex.[30] But the distribution of print portraiture of Luther was extraordinary in its time. Luther was not the ruler of any territory. Comparable only to the executed Florentine friar Girolamo Savonarola – who, unlike Luther, did seize political power (within a republican framework)

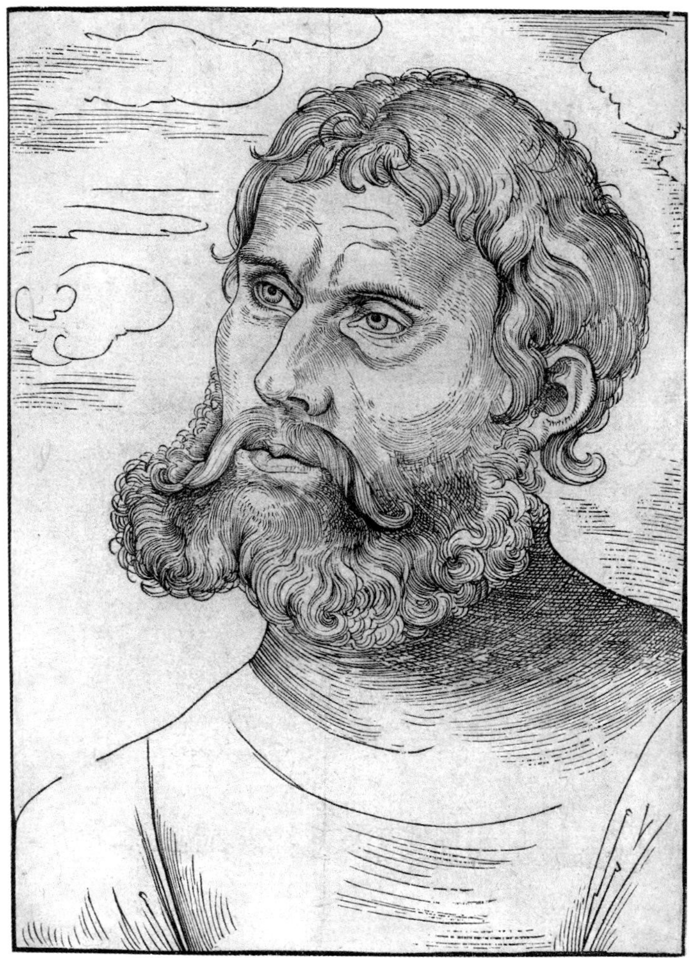

for a time – the outlaw Luther inspired many painted likenesses. Savonarola was painted by his follower Fra Bartolomeo only as Savonarola awaited execution in 1498; printed adaptations of this portrait followed later in the sixteenth century. Some think Cranach's image of Luther disguised as Junker Jörg was produced to reassure followers that Luther still lived in hiding, but

51 Lucas Cranach the Elder, *Martin Luther as Junker Jörg*, 1522, woodcut.

perhaps it was, similarly to Savonarola's portrait, a likeness made by a follower who feared for the life of a preacher and friend he profoundly admired.

From 1522 onwards, there were several moments around which the Cranach workshop produced multiple standardized portraits of Luther: a paired roundel or small rectangular panel for his pathbreaking 1525 marriage (as an ordained priest) to Katharina von Bora; the classic three-quarter view of Luther, who looks back at the viewer, from 1528–30 or so, also paired with Katharina; 1532's three-quarter Luther, who looks into the distance he faces, paired not with his wife but with his fellow leader Philipp Melanchthon; a more grey-haired version of the same in around 1540, also paired with Melanchthon; and the deathbed portrait, based on a 1546 drawing by Lukas Furtenagel, who had previously been part of Cranach's workshop. Each of these standardized portraits spoke to a particular phase in the larger narrative of Luther's reforms. His unprecedented marriage is only the most obvious fixed point.[31] It is also important to track the shift (around the time of negotiations at the 1530 Diet of Augsburg) from the open, accessible married preacher to the visionary scholar partnered with his brilliant, precocious sidekick Philipp Melanchthon, with whom, in the next iteration, he would go grey.

That pairing itself was unusual. It was not unheard of for scholarly friends to have matching portraits commissioned in the same way married couples did. The most well-known examples are the 1517 portraits by the Flemish painter Quinten Massys of Desiderius Erasmus and Pieter Gillis, which they sent to their friend Thomas More. But it was again unusual for anyone but rulers to have such matching portraits widely disseminated. That portraits of Luther and his wife, or Luther and Melanchthon, all people of ordinary birth, circulated in what must have been dozens of painted copies is unprecedented in the history of European art.

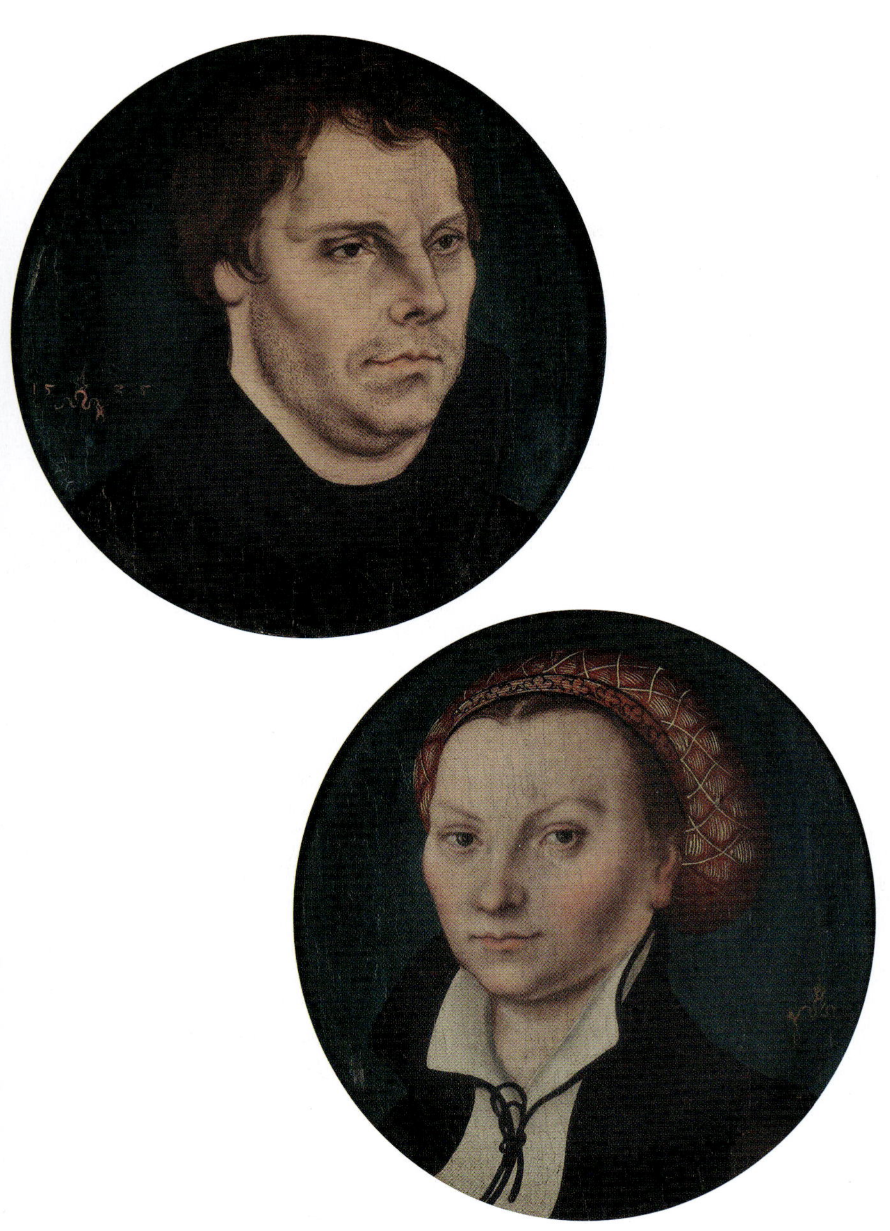

52, 53 Lucas Cranach the Elder, *Martin Luther* and *Katharina von Bora*, 1525, oil on panel.

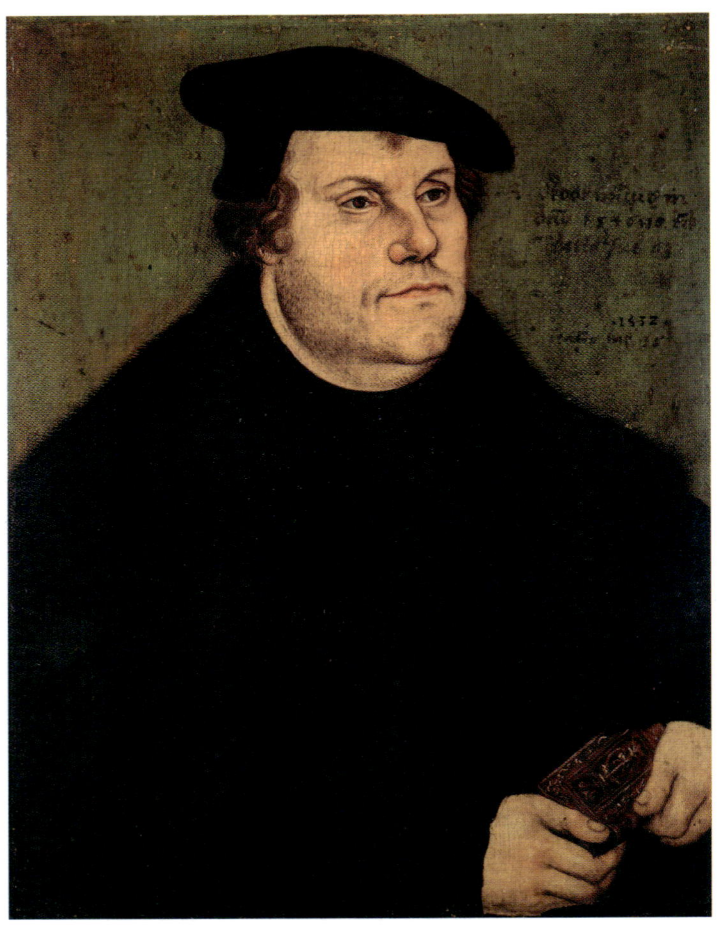

Though other artists like Dürer and Hans Holbein the Younger (operating within that Steelyard community of Hanseatic Reformation admirers in London in the 1530s) also circulated images of Reformation leaders, Cranach's paintings provided the official standard. One could even argue that they are among the early materials of celebrity culture. The historian Ulinka Rublack has summarized the preparation of a 'ground for an emotional

54 Lucas Cranach the Elder and workshop, *Martin Luther*, 1532, oil on panel.

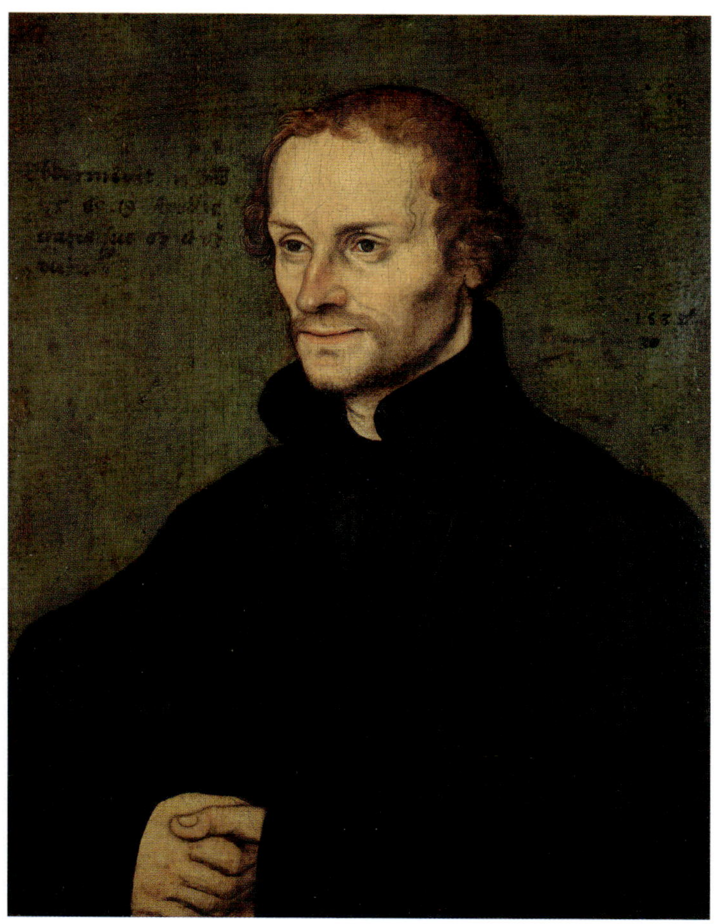

investment in famous people' starting in 1400, which intensified with the emergence of print imagery. Elsewhere she discusses the emergent importance of autograph inscriptions (among other paraphernalia like letter-seals) to the followers of Lutheran reform-ers.[32] The repetition and recognizability of Cranach's paintings and woodcuts would have lent them that same communal authority that transferred (via repetition) to pictures of Law and Grace.

55 Lucas Cranach the Elder and workshop, *Philipp Melanchthon*, 1532, oil on panel.

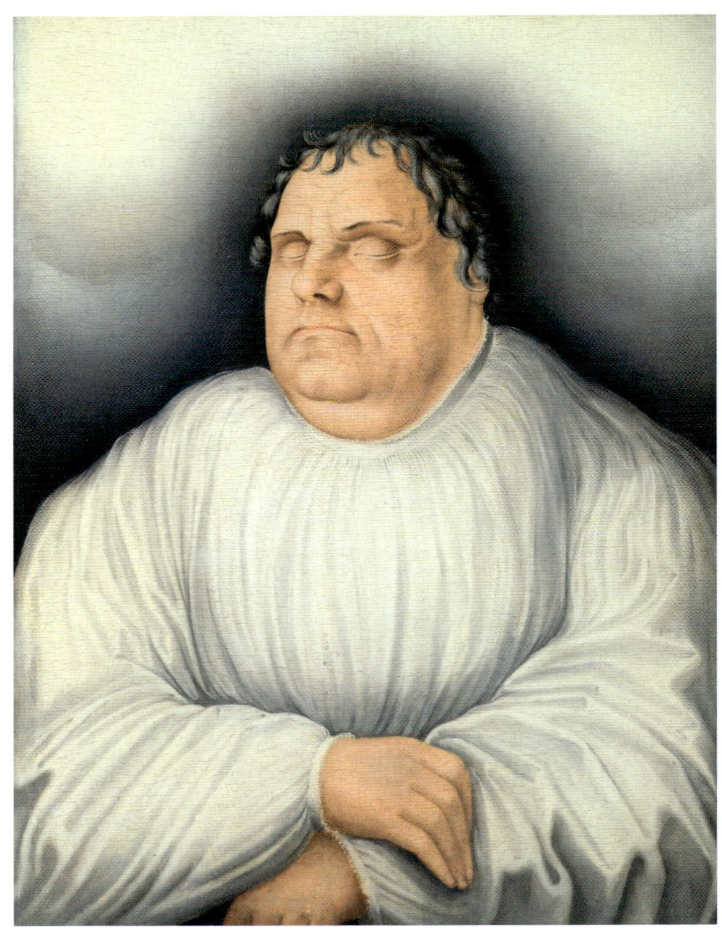

The celebrity Cranach promoted was a celebrity attached to theology. To own a printed image of Luther was to affirm one's theological affiliation, openly or not: one could paste the image on a highly visible wall, as prints are sometimes seen in contemporaneous images of interiors both public and private, or one could keep the image hidden, as one might have in cities where the Roman Church still held sway. Not as radical as, say, the

56 Workshop of Lucas Cranach the Elder, *Martin Luther on His Deathbed*, c. 1574, oil on panel.

Anabaptists (many of whom believed in a direct personal relation to God, immediate of the shared experience of the rite of Mass), nor as endowed with mainstream authority as a noble ruler like the elector of Saxony, Luther was by the late 1520s – in the wake of the Peasants' War – a moderate countercultural figure. His image must have been displayed in places where figureheads of local allegiance – local lords – might have once been, displacing governmental affiliation with a spiritual one.

In light of this new culture of affirmation by means of celebrity likeness, Cranach's embedded portraiture takes on a new valence. Recall the *Wittenberg Altarpiece* (illus. 2), begun the year after Luther's death, in which Luther appears as a wine-receiving apostle towards the right (illus. 6). Again, despite the altarpiece's late date, this is not 1546's already well-distributed deathbed-Luther, but instead the youthful Junker Jörg version (illus. 51). (He sits roughly above where a version of the standard grey 1540s portrait stands preaching in the predella.) The insertion of this youthful figure from 1521 would have brought the Wittenberg community back to the earliest iterations of Luther's celebrity at precisely the moment the continuity of the movement was threatened. The familiar visual hallmark of the foundation of Lutheran reform – Luther freshly excommunicated, in hiding – appears as if present at the Last Supper, that is, at the foundation of Christianity itself. This rhetoric, this aligning of foundations, would not have been effective unless the visuals were well known. With the help of mass portraiture and its codification of fixed points in Luther's narrative, faith transmuted grief into a confidence in Luther's ongoing place in sacred time.

## THE LUTHERAN STYLE OF VIEWERSHIP:
## THE WEIMAR ALTARPIECE

Lucas Cranach outlived not only Luther, but also the uncertain early days of the Reformation, when it was not clear whether the movement would be a blip or the birth of a new faith. Cranach trained two talented sons, Hans (1513–1537) and Lucas the Younger (1515–1586), to continue his workshop's brand. They probably began taking a significant role in the workshop in their teens. Scholars of the Cranach workshop have remarked for hundreds of years now how difficult it is to distinguish the work of the sons from the father.[33] After participating in some of the renovation projects at the Saxon elector's stronghold, Torgau Castle, young Hans travelled to Bologna later in 1537. Though the cause of death has gone unrecorded, he never came home; he was only 24 years old.

At this point, though Cranach (as I will continue to refer to the father) still ran the workshop, Lucas the Younger began to take a greater role. The *Wittenberg Altarpiece* of 1547 is a work

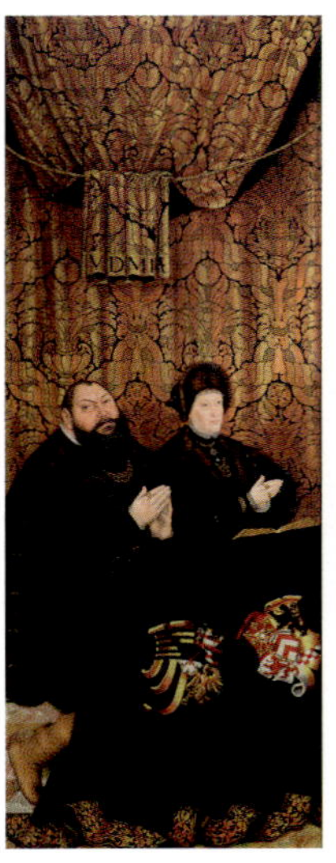
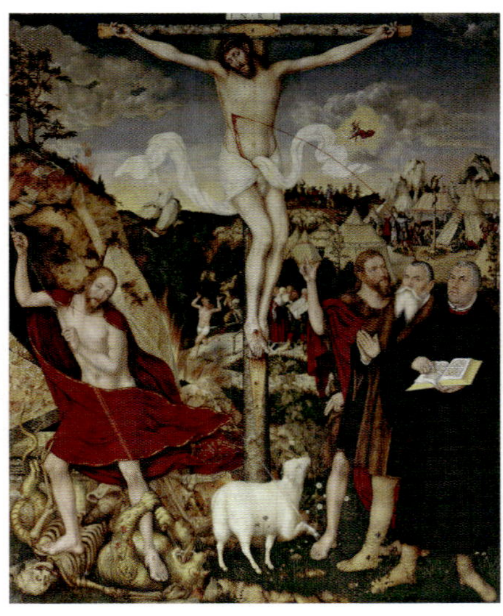
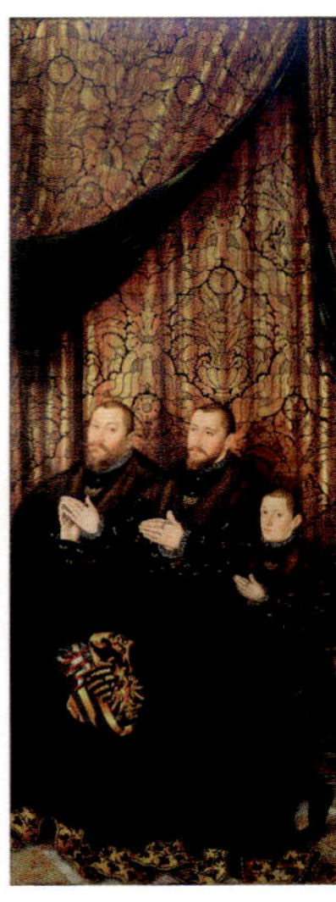

57 Lucas Cranach the Younger and workshop, *Weimar Altarpiece*, 1555, oil on panel.

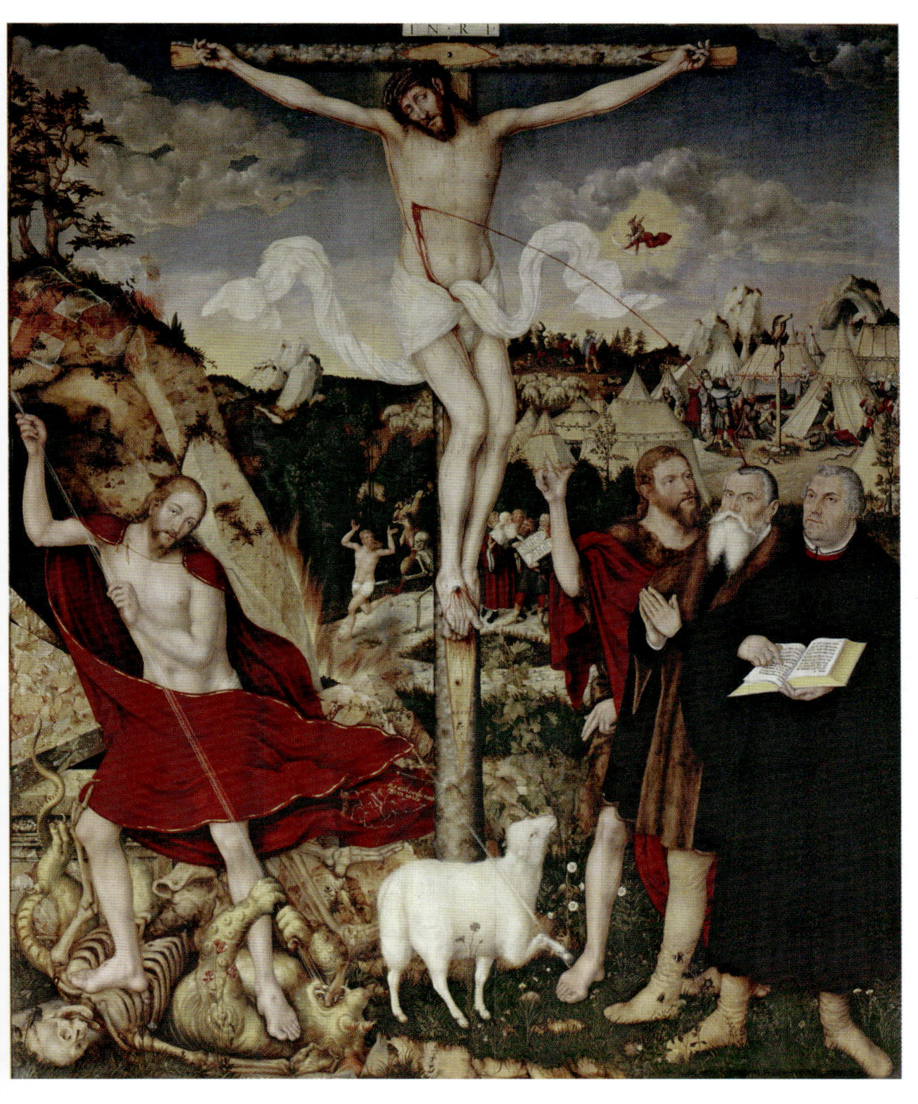

58 Crucifixion and Resurrection attended by Luther and Cranach, central panel of illus. 57.

primarily designed by the inventor of Lutheran art, but its execution was probably overseen by the first artist trained in Lutheran art from the moment he started making marks on surfaces. Like his father, Lucas the Younger would play on the variation and repetition so central to the community-building of a religion, but his understanding of the standard Christian image was in large part the Cranach workshop standard.

The central panel of the *Weimar Altarpiece*, completed in 1555, two years after Cranach's death, is Lucas the Younger's monumental variation on his father's trademark Law and Grace imagery.[34] Among the anthropomorphous figures of the foreground are not only John the Baptist, the crucified Christ and the resurrected Christ the Redeemer, but also Cranach and Luther (in his circa 1540 guise as a clear-faced, learned elder). Here one remembers the intimacy between these two men, who had both passed away within living memory. Collaborators and friends, Cranach and Luther had a relationship perhaps closer than any other in history between religious leader and artist – one can imagine them celebrating marriage, baptism and beers together. There is much to say about the prominent posthumous presence of these two men in this monument and the double vision it must have induced in its earliest viewers: these two friends from the community's everyday life also stood as artist and preacher, guarantors of Lutheran continuity and salvation.

But first, to fully appreciate the rhetoric of this altar shrine, one must look back both to the ordinary disposition of scenes in a *Law and Grace* (illus. 47) and to the innovation of an early Vienna-period Cranach *Crucifixion*. Cranach was about thirty years old when he painted this latter panel, around the same age as his son when Lucas the Younger finished the *Weimar Altarpiece*. In this *Crucifixion*, in a manner unprecedented at the time for a painting of this scale, Cranach altered the viewer's approach to Christ's crucified body. Fifteenth-century and earlier depictions of the

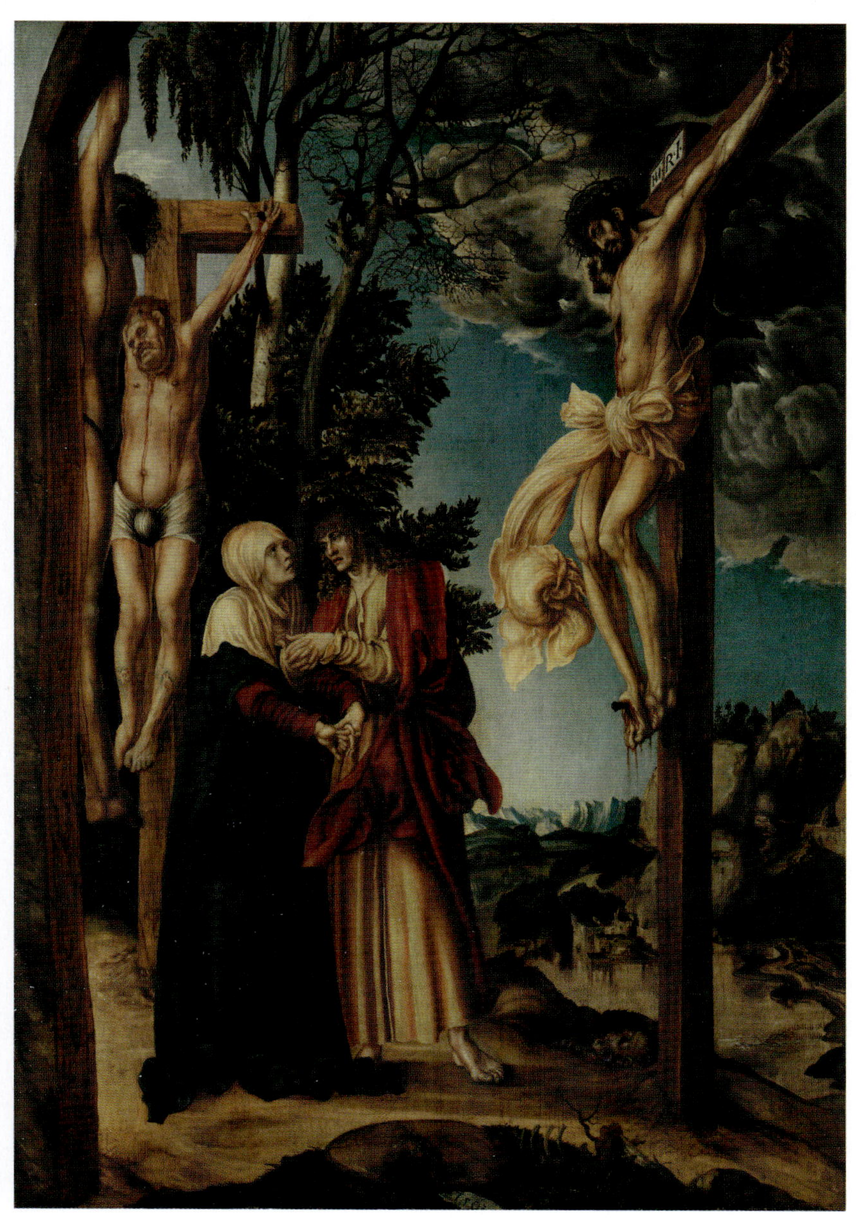

59 Lucas Cranach the Elder, *Crucifixion*, 1503, oil on panel.

Crucifixion were typically frontal, showing the crucified Christ flanked by a modular set of holy figures who could be chosen to suit a particular context of display. This cultic format for the Crucifixion emphasized the scene as a divine event with which the viewer could connect directly. It was common around 1500 for painters to instead decentre subject-matter in order to make a painting feel less staged, more connected to the serendipities of everyday life. Crucifixions start to appear in paintings set at an angle.[35]

Cranach in 1503 participates thoroughly in this shift: he turns the Crucifixion almost completely sideways. The viewer is placed as if struggling up the hill of Golgotha, just happening on a stormy day to come upon two people grieving a criminal.[36] This criminal's extraordinarily beautiful loin-wrapping, though, gusting elaborately with its own wind, anchors the crucified Christ firmly in his typical iconography. This is certainly Christ at his moment of ultimate sacrifice, even if witnessed in a biome north of the Alps.

The cost of this twist is that the viewer does not engage the crucified Christ directly; the usual flanking figures are now the ones presented frontally, closer to the centre of the composition. Viewers of this painting would model themselves on Mary and John, on the suffering of loved ones and the role of that grief in the worship of Christ: an appreciation for the extended costs of human salvation.

This part of the conceit lies at the heart of Cranach's Law and Grace compositions more than 25 years later. The viewer does not confront the salvific sacrifice offered by the crucified Christ directly, but rather through identification with the nude figure near the image's centre. Taking direction from John the Baptist, that nude man is the one who turns and receives Christ's Grace.

Of course, given the diagrammatic nature of Law and Grace images, they give no sense of the anecdotal, no sense that a viewer could have been wandering near the Danube and randomly come across Law and Grace's mayhem, with hellfire and the Devil in the corners and two different ascended Christs in the sky. Any convincing realism in Cranach's rendering of flesh or textiles finds its anti-realist counteraction in the captions below. There is nothing accidental about Law and Grace: it represents the very intentional choice to embrace grace-as-salvation, the choice at the heart of Lutheranism's rejection of the old ways.

In the *Weimar Altarpiece*, Lucas the Younger, asserting his faith's *replacement* of the old ways, keeps the iconography of Law and Grace but (re)turns the frontal cult image of yore towards a new Lutheran viewer. Cranach had helped depict a similarly frontal crucified Christ some years before, in the predella of the *Wittenberg Altarpiece*. But here in the *Weimar Altarpiece*, instead of the cult image's being offered to the viewer in the context of the interchange between preaching Luther and attentive crowd, the crucified Christ appears as the unifying motif of established sacred Lutheran imagery.

This reclaimed cult image also asserts the central role of artistry to the Lutheran faith — and not just by inserting Godfather Cranach into the main scene. The palette recalls both Cranach's early Danube-era pictures as well as the storm-darkened, golden light of Venetian-inspired painting, popular in Saxony. Beyond this confident treatment of earlier styles, Lucas the Younger shows off his merits as a painter throughout: there are many worthy passages here, for example in the lower left. Carnations bloom alongside the sucker- or infundibulum-like growths on the vanquished Devil's arm, their petals crinkling against the monster's wrinkles; nearby, the soft, clean nail-wound of the Resurrected Christ's left foot contrasts the stab of His crystal flagstaff into the Devil's mouth, its tongue flung at a matching angle.

To some extent Cranach, like many well-known sixteenth-century painters, thematized artistic processes and artistic presence regularly. It was standard in Cranach-workshop *Crucifixion* paintings from at least the 1520s onwards for the cross, as it does here, to demonstrate the preparation of raw tree material to bear a figure, paralleling the preparation of wood to bear painted figures. Nor was it unheard of for Cranach to appear in religious scenes over-seen by his son; he appears, for example, in the lower left of *Elijah and the Prophets of Baal* of 1545, bearing ritual wine jars for the sacrifice.[37]

Yet here it is Christ's blood, unconsubstantiated into wine, that interacts with the embedded portrait of Cranach. Christ's blood arcs so vigorously towards Cranach's head that it splatters, ricocheting more than a finger's width off his hair in some direc-tions. In Law and Grace pictures, the nude male figure – the one meant to stand in for all humans, headed towards salvation – is the one who receives the spurt of blood, generally more diffuse than in the *Weimar Altarpiece*. Cranach did not invent the recep-tion of Christ's arcing, spurted blood by onlookers.[38] But Law and Grace pictures codified this spurt as a transmission of grace itself.[39]

In the *Weimar Altarpiece*, the way the arcing blood splatter almost becomes the curve of one of the serpents in the background scene adds yet another layer of meaning: an inversion of salvific processes from older traditions to new. The artificially wrought brass serpent possesses the power to nullify the dangers of the living serpents it represents. Inversely, the Cranach workshop's rendering of blood through the artifice of paint affirmatively channels the salvific power of Christ's grace. As if to emphasize this inverse parallel, the winged-serpent workshop signature is painted onto the prepared wood of the cross in the direct path of the blood dripping from Christ's feet. In sum, the picture argues that painting should not be understood as the direct object of devotion (as the brazen serpent in the background was mis-understood in 2 Kings 18:4). Painting, like Christ's blood – and here, *as* it – was a vehicle for divine salvation.

Viewers familiar with this iconography again have no choice here. Whether as early Lutherans in Weimar's City Church or internet admirers in the twenty-first century, initiated viewers, having already chosen to be saved, are conditioned to identify with the nude figure. The wrong choice appears in the middle-ground: Lucas the Younger has preserved the binary structure of Law and Grace but turned the previously central scene of law, where Moses holds its tablets, into a small vignette behind Christ's feet. The hell awaiting that unhappy chooser, running in a loincloth with arms akimbo, is not even available to viewers; hell's flames – much more skilfully painted than in standard Law and Grace pictures – feather out beautifully but harmlessly from behind a rocky outcropping. Viewers of the altarpiece have already been redeemed from Adam and Eve's original sin, and so no longer need to look at their Fall; neither is there any Last Judgement awaiting in the sky. The viewers have already been judged, favourably.

The mood of this painting is unusual. Early Renaissance religious painting in Northern Europe often emphasized the suffering of figures, in keeping with devotional practices of empathetic suffering on the part of the viewer. Other images (like Cranach's nudes, along with, for example, well-known works by Hieronymus Bosch or Hans Baldung) tricked the viewer into revelling in their own iniquity, making the viewer complicit in sin by encouraging their fascination. The *Weimar Altarpiece* is different. There is a comparable sense of artistic triumph, of the role of the artist in salvation, perhaps, in Dürer's Christlike *Self-Portrait* of 1500. In this painting, the icon format of a frontal holy face becomes one with the face of the artist. But Dürer's famous self-staging swallows the viewer in a singularity of identification, a channelling of Christ-as-divine-artist isolated in a single moment. Though the *Weimar Altarpiece*'s claim for the artist's mediation of salvation is similar, the altarpiece instead opens its triumph up to plurality

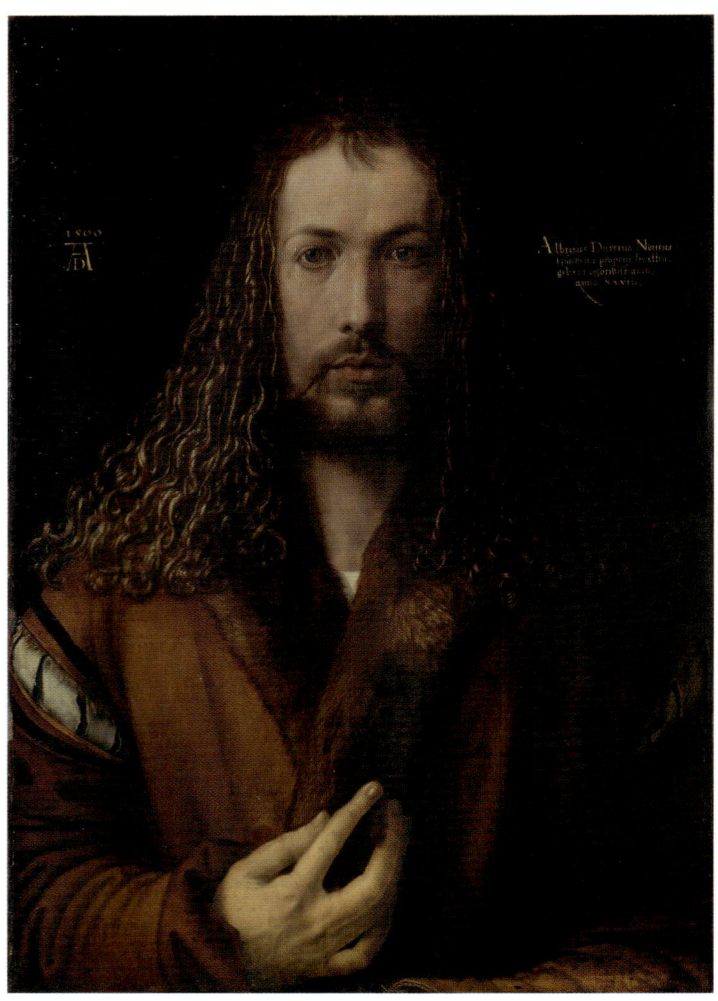

and community in a space where lived history coexists comfortably with sacred time.[40]

The subtlest parallel of the *Weimar Altarpiece* is the one between (on the one hand) the angel's Annunciation to the Shepherds in the farthest background, just below Christ's billowing

60 Albrecht Dürer, *Self-Portrait with Fur-Trimmed Robe*, 1500, oil on panel.

loincloth on the right, and (on the other) Cranach and Luther's communication of grace to future and potential Lutherans in the front. Cranach and Luther's announcement here exemplifies a new kind of religious painting: not painful, nor inimical, nor heroic. Lutheranism here styles salvation as both accessible and enjoyable. The best-painted parts appear at eye level. Whether through the artist's relish in the defeated and repugnant enemies of humankind in the left foreground, or through the delicate, careful rendering of a flowery meadow on the right, this painting invites everyone to the end of suffering, sin and death. Viewers accept by looking, and the pleasure of this looking affirms that painting itself can be grace.

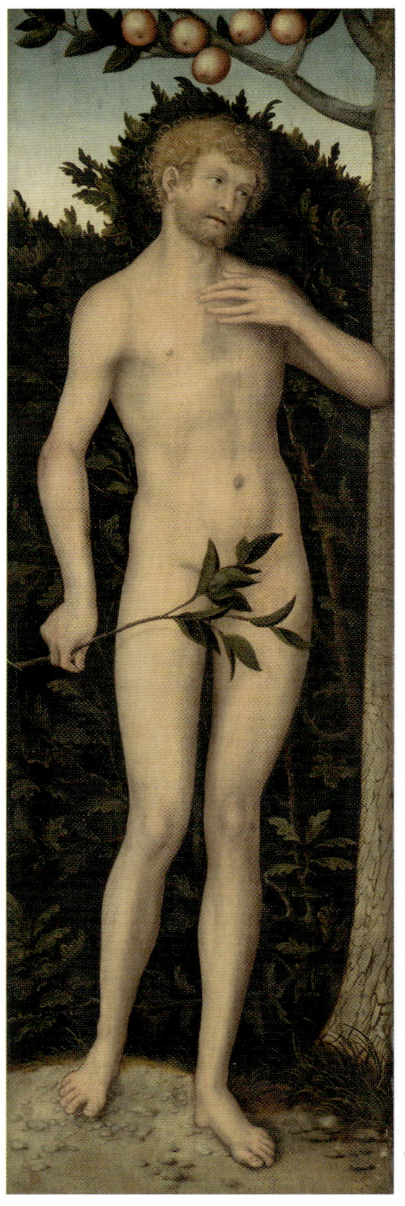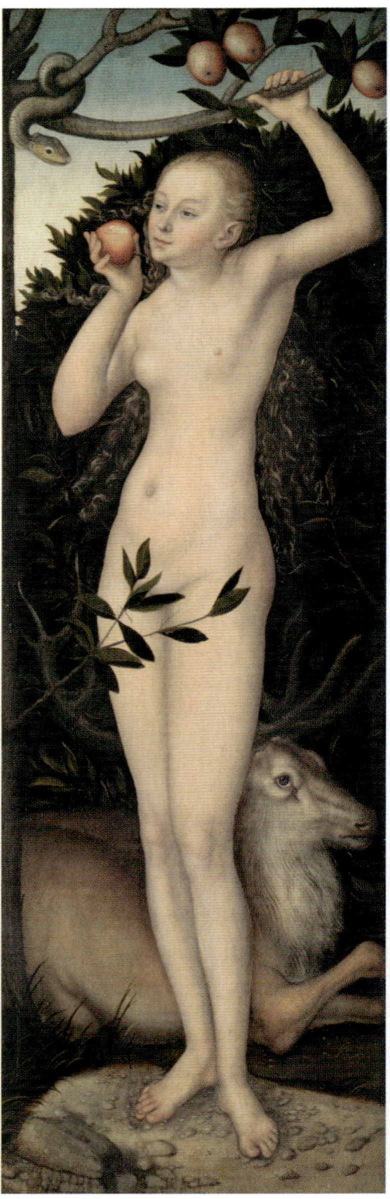

61, 62 Lucas Cranach the Elder and workshop, *Adam* and *Eve*, c. 1535, oil on panel.

# The Women Look Back

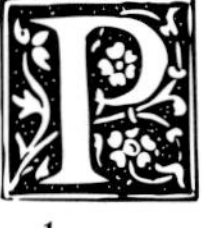leasure is of course not always about grace. The pleasure of representation often came alongside the dangers of knowledge. In Cranach's paintings, he gave his clientele – mostly university men and electors – the thing they most wanted to know. In Cranach's oeuvre, the tempting nude body of a woman often figured an ancestral German past, the powerful heritage with which so many of Cranach's clients sought to connect. But Cranach also depicted women's engagement with viewers' gazes in ways that reveal his notion of painting's role in communal salvation.

## THE FALL OF THE PERFECTED SELF

Germans' desire for their past was dangerous, for the past was pagan. But the quest for knowledge in general presented a danger in popular understandings of Christian traditions, too. The subject of at least 36(!) surviving paintings attributed to Cranach or his workshop is the foundational Christian image of the potential wickedness of the pursuit of knowledge: Adam and Eve, also known as the Fall of Man.[1]

The backstory for this event occurs in Genesis 2:16–17, in which God gives his one rule to Adam, the newly created first person. Everything in the Garden of Eden, Adam's perfect home, is available to him for consumption – with one exception. He is not supposed to eat from the 'tree of the knowledge of good and evil'. (Many biblical scholars agree that here 'good and evil' is a rhetorical expression intended to mean 'everything', the way one might say 'I want to know it all: the good, the bad and the ugly,' but interpreters in the sixteenth century, like Luther, tended to emphasize this tree as a source of particularly moral knowledge, knowledge of right and wrong.) By the beginning of Genesis 3, Eve has been created and, in her conversation with the serpent, shows she is also aware of the rule God gave Adam. The serpent tells her to ignore the rule, because eating from the tree of knowledge would make a human like God (Genesis 3:5). She takes the serpent's advice.

Luther, following other theologians, understood this moment as the birth of sin.[2] By learning the difference between good and evil, right and wrong, Adam and Eve came under the yoke of the law. In the Law and Grace images that promoted Luther's theology from the end of the 1520s onwards, the main Lutheran critique of law is that it powers sin: the images often include citations of Paul's first letter to the Corinthians on this topic, a favoured passage in Luther's sermons (1 Corinthians 15:56). In other words, without the law, without knowledge of right and wrong, there would be no sin. Because Cranach's Law and Grace paintings emphasized the triumph of divine grace over the force of the law, viewers could remember their core belief that Christ would save them from the consequences not only of particular sins, but also of sin as a concept. If they could receive Christ's grace, the breaking of worldly rules would not matter.

In many of Cranach's versions of Adam and Eve, as here, the apple already has bite marks from Eve. There are other versions in which she or Adam are about to bite into the fruit, but even then it is clear that the damage has been done. Because the serpent has convinced Eve that she ought to have knowledge, she has already opened up the path for sin to enter the world. Cranach's

many images of Adam and Eve, and even the larger paintings of
the Garden of Eden called *Paradise*, include this moment of the
Fall. They show not Eden per se but a landscape already un-Edened
by sin.

Eve is in Christian theology the very definition of a primordial
woman, so it is no surprise that Cranach renders her with his
formula for an ancestral German nymph or pagan goddess: with
long curling golden hair, elongated proportions and no adornment
or clothing. Her bite mark in the apple indicates bodily health
and vigour: this is a body with almost none of sin's ruin. Adam
and Eve here represent perfect fleshly forms. Following loose
Neoplatonic ideas that conceived of the world as increasingly
imperfect emanations radiating in space and time from a perfect
creator, Cranach's viewers would not have imagined Adam and
Eve as first drafts or test prototypes, but rather as the fullest
version of what humankind was intended to be.

Other artists had different ideas about what these full, flaw-
less humans should look like. The peer to whom we have often
returned, Dürer, published a famous engraving of the pair in 1504.
This vision of the perfect body is in thrall to the forms of Greco-
Roman antiquity surviving in Italy. Heavy as statues, rendered as
composites of discrete parts, these bodies (despite their dutiful
contrapposto) do not flow as Cranach's do, but rather accumulate
volume from antique fragments. The animals refer back to ancient
medical concepts of the four humours, here in the moment at
which they are about to come unbalanced for all time: the origins
of disease. (The rabbit is sanguine, the ox phlegmatic and the
elk melancholic, and the cat-and-mouse pair highlights the cat's
choleric nature.) The least antique aspect of the image is the goat
in the upper-right corner, its four feet crammed onto a precipice
too narrow for balancing or turning back. This goat is about to
literalize the Fall. The blank space around it, unusual for Dürer
– the only unworked part of the copper plate that produced this

print – is the only part of this image left undetermined by the accrual of antique forms and symbols. That small unknown corner is perhaps humankind's meagre future.

Cranach's panels, despite the impending disaster they represent, are more relaxed and simple, reliant on the familiar vocabulary of timeless German wilderness he established in earlier pictures. The setting consists of the usual moonscape ground

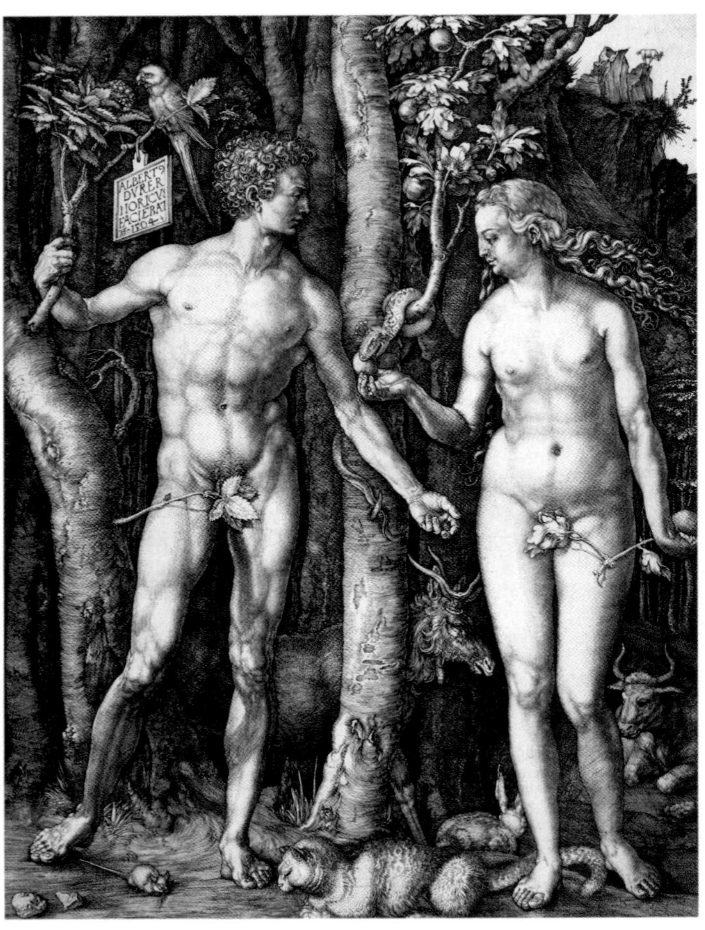

63 Albrecht Dürer, *Adam and Eve*, 1504, engraving.

and pastoral reserve-blocks of greenery, minus the typical backdrop of civilization, which would be by definition post-Edenic. Though some of Cranach's other versions of the scene are somewhat busier, here the elements are basic. Cranach in the 1530s has much less to prove than Dürer in 1504; Cranach by default adheres to his own invented German deep past rather than to Italianate imitations of dug-up ancient statues and recently edited Latin codes of symbolism.

The only optional extra feature of Cranach's scene is his most common addition in multiple versions of the subject-matter: a stag staring out at the viewer from the middleground, here behind Eve. This stag may be best understood as a symbol for Christ and for coming redemption.[3] Animals often look directly at the viewer in Renaissance paintings, but this is also a quality typical of self-portraits. This stag, whose beard resembles Cranach's later beard, may even foreshadow the *Weimar Altarpiece*'s assertion of the artist's Christlike role in facilitating salvation. How unlike the foreclosed, diagrammatic feel of Dürer's engraving this feels, even as Cranach also forces his viewer to witness the moment of doom that reverberates in the mortality, fallibility and temptation of the ongoing present.

Offering a dangerous pleasure familiar from Cranach's oeuvre, the figures emphasize sensuality. The leaves of the tree of knowledge across their hips and thighs are particularly alluringly splayed, drawing a viewer's eye into the push-and-pull of concealment. Though the unblemished, hairless skin behind those leaves adopts the anatomical properties of childhood to convey innocence, the artistry of the leaves – their sensitive play of lightly serrated textures, rich greens and light and shadow – is all about artifice and sophistication.

But the desire for Eve also differs from the desire induced by a *Nymph of the Fountain* or *Venus with Cupid as Honey Thief*. The desire for Eve – and for Adam – is a desire for the self, the self in its earliest state, prior to culture or any difference besides sexual difference.

Here is one of the tricks of Cranach's German-ness: through the sheer force of authorizing repetition (as with the Law and Grace images), the German wilderness and its inhabitants are assumed to be the originary default of creation. There is no need for special iconography for Eden – no fountain, no four rivers, nor incongruous animal species cohabiting in peace. The German forest *is* the first forest, continuous, shifting only in its staffage across the many world-eras.

This continuity would make it easy to understand Adam and Eve as oneself, especially if one were among Cranach's Germanophone audience. These figures offer themselves as perfected selves, the self as one might be if one had never suffered, especially not from the consequences of failing.

Counterbalancing the desire for self-perfection is the evidence of the first rot. Even if Eve is the only one who has bitten so far, the aftermath has affected them both. The red in both Adam and Eve's cheeks signals the beginning of lust. Adam's hand goes to his chest, which is also just beginning to flush as if with sexual

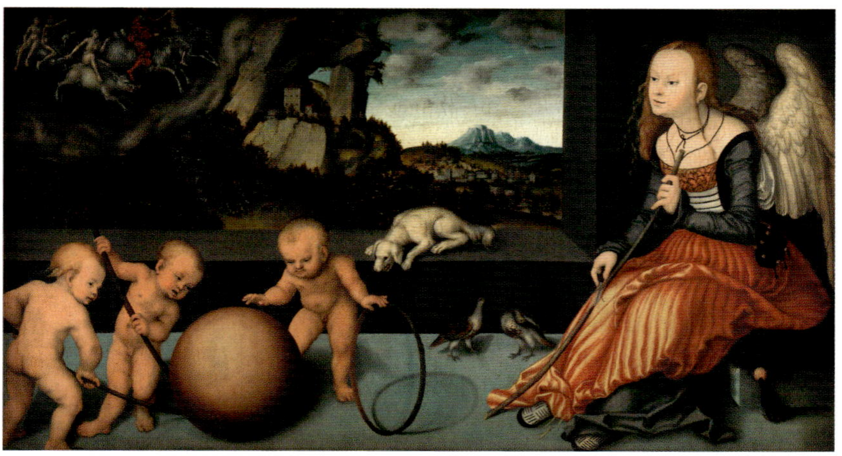

64 Lucas Cranach the Elder, *Melancholy*, 1532, oil on panel. Saxon governess Melancholy also gazes with judgement as she oversees putti/children who perhaps stand in for humankind. Her artistic labour, carving, directs itself

activity. His gaze slips from her face to her breasts. He is perhaps beginning to cover himself out of his first feelings of shame (though he has not yet advanced to the sewing of fig leaves reported in Genesis 3:7). His hold on the fig branch is loose, lacking conviction, an almost masturbatory grip suited to a broader object, one closer to the size of the forbidden branch Eve holds, itself an ersatz snake.

Would women viewers of these panels have seen their perfected selves in Eve, as I suggest? Perhaps. Certainly, this Eve shares the blame with her partner, rather than being only a temptress. A female viewer of this particular version might have been cheered by the thought that the first sin comes accompanied by the sign of its redemption in the stag at Eve's feet. Christ is on her side.

But it is Eve's facial expression that most complicates and perhaps boosts her potential as a target of self-identification and self-perfectibility for a woman viewer. As in many of Cranach's examples from the 1520s onwards, Eve's bite has put her in a certain mood. Her eyes are not lidded by desire or a recent drowse, nor is she staring plainly at the viewer with an invitation or moral challenge. Eyes narrowed, head tilted, she is looking at her partner with full knowledge of right and wrong. She is judging him.

## WOMEN ON TOP: THE HERITAGE OF CRANACH'S EROTIC KNOWLEDGE PICTURES

The same appraising look, rotated on a forward tilt, appears on the face of one of King Solomon's wives in Lucas Cranach the Younger's 1537 *The Idolatry of Solomon*. This scene of heretical devotion is part of a series of at least three images, all the same size, now in Dresden's Gemäldegalerie Alte Meister. Lucas the Younger presumably made all three paintings for the elector of Saxony; the other two depict *Samson and Delilah* and *David and Bathsheba*. The paintings have been attributed to Lucas the Younger on the basis

---

toward the master-switch with which she will punish overambitious mortals for attempting to use similar tools to steer the imperfect orb of the world toward the perfect abstraction of a circle. Its skew shadow foreshadows failure.

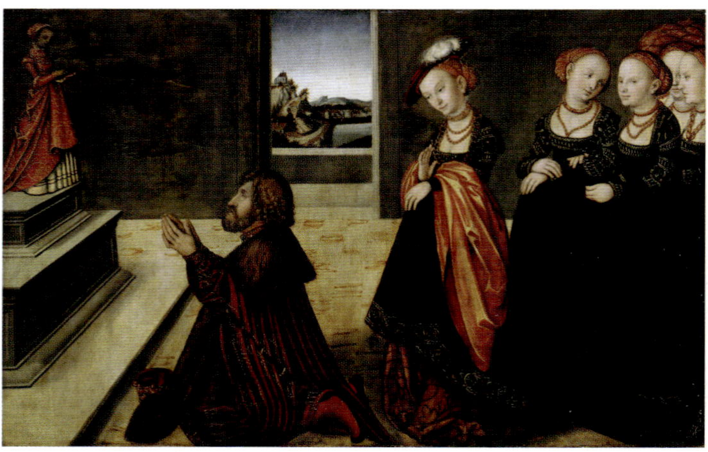

of both style and the underdrawing visible through infrared reflectography.

This series of paintings comes from a popular genre, Power of Women or *Weibermacht* pictures.[4] At its core misogynistic or even gynophobic, the *Weibermacht* genre warned men of the dangers of letting women have too much (sexual) power over them. Popularized by print series early in the century, including multiple versions by Lucas van Leyden (1494–1533) and, closer to home, by Hans Burgkmair (1473–1531) in 1519, this subject-matter often first found expression in paint north of the Alps in the Cranach workshop.[5] Lucas the Younger's horizontal *Bathsheba* and *Samson* panels in the series are reworkings of vertical panels by the father in the late 1520s; it is known that in 1513 Duke Johann the Constant of Saxony, brother of Elector Friedrich III and future elector and father of Elector Johann Friedrich, commissioned an *Idolatry of Solomon* for his second wedding – specifically, for his nuptial bed.[6] Though Lucas the Younger was not yet born at the time, and was unlikely to have spent time in his future elector's bedchamber, it is possible he was aware of the commission and referred back to it here as he does in his other adaptations of his father's work.

65 Lucas Cranach the Younger, *The Idolatry of Solomon*, 1537, oil on panel.

Lucas the Younger's three *Weibermacht* panels are joined by a painting of an identical size and a relatively similar painting style, *Three Pairs*. *Three Pairs* entered the records of the electoral collection at the same time as the *Weibermacht* images, amid a group of eighteen paintings originally from Johann Friedrich's electoral residence at Torgau.[7] Perhaps it was part of the same commission. This painting depicts three heterosexual couples gathered around a table with a glass of water and grapes and apples on a platter. Two couples cross a vast divide in age, featuring mouth-breathing, sparse-toothed elders cuddling with a younger woman and man, respectively. These two young–old couples are part of a popular trope in imagery and literature often referred to as the 'ill-matched pair'. Lucas the Younger's rendition of the trope features a third, better-matched pair. This couple on the right, closer in age, are discussing the other two pairs: he waves two fingers towards them in the opposite of a blessing, while she stares with a slight frown.

We now have many clues for the original context for *The Idolatry of Solomon*. The horizontal format is somewhat atypical

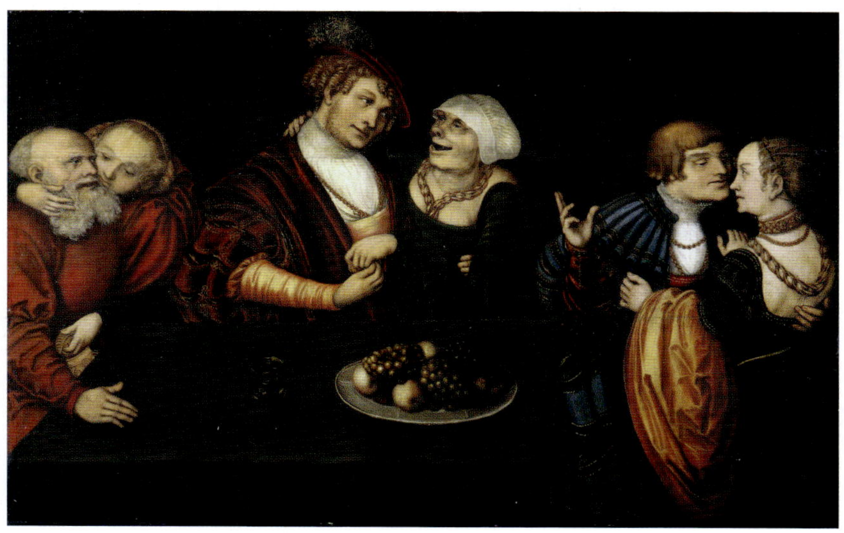

66 Lucas Cranach the Younger, *Three Pairs*, 1537, oil on panel.

and makes it plausible that these paintings were intended for a domestic context specifically designed for their display, whether a marital bed or a room that served as a backdrop for male social engagements. The unusual inclusion of a well-matched couple in the *Three Pairs* painting suggests that the set of four paintings – if it was a set – did not indicate any particular disharmony of the sexes at home. Though the *Weibermacht* genre functioned to mock and denigrate female power, it is important to note that Johann the Constant and Johann Friedrich both had happy marriages documented, especially in the latter case, by surviving lengthy correspondence. These men had these paintings not because they were extraordinary misogynists, but because visual reminders of the proper gendered hierarchy of a Christian household were the norm for interior decoration among the wealthy.

Lucas the Younger's *Idolatry of Solomon* is the most self-referential of the images that might have hung in Elector Johann Friedrich's gender-themed room. The image is based on the opening of 1 Kings 11, which tells the story of the downfall of Israel following from King Solomon's lapse of faith in his old age.

King Solomon loved many foreign women along with the daughter of Pharaoh: Moabite, Ammonite, Edomite, Sidonian, and Hittite women, from the nations concerning which the Lord had said to the Israelites: 'You shall not enter into marriage with them, neither shall they with you; for they will surely incline your heart to follow their gods'; Solomon clung to these in love. Among his wives were seven hundred princesses and three hundred concubines; and his wives turned away his heart. For when Solomon was old, his wives turned away his heart after other gods; and his heart was not true to the Lord his God, as was the heart of his father David. For Solomon

followed Astarte the goddess of the Sidonians, and
Milcom the abomination of the Ammonites . . . Then
Solomon built a high place for Chemosh the abomina-
tion of Moab, and for Molech the abomination of the
Ammonites, on the mountain east of Jerusalem.

What follows from this turn to idolatry, by God's divine punishment, is the division of the tribes of Israel and the loss of David's
kingdom under the reign of Solomon's son.

Lucas the Younger's painting, like many renditions of
Solomon's idolatry from the fifteenth and sixteenth centuries in
Europe, features the moment in which Solomon literally 'follows'
another god, that is, worships an idol. Also on the scene, unusu-
ally, are several ladies-in-waiting. Though one or two such ladies
in the wife's retinue appear in other Idolatry of Solomon precedents, here the pile-up of elaborate headdresses and decolletages
on partially visible figures in the upper right-hand corner suggests
also the plenitude of women mentioned in 1 Kings 11, a broader
community. In some precedent renditions of this scene, the idol
in question is one of the many male gods mentioned in the passage above (Milcom, Chemosh or Moloch/Molech). But in many
versions, as here, the lesson of the dangerous woman is doubled:
Solomon's Sidonian wife has led him to worship a female goddess,
Astarte.

The Israelite king kneels before Astarte in the pose of a traditional donor portrait in altarpieces, as for example in Cranach
altarpieces from the 1510s. Again, these donors often appeared
in the wings of an altarpiece, offering prayer to a divine scene or
figure in the centre panel. But Lucas the Younger's Solomon also
has the pose of one of the three kings or three magi from typical
Adoration of the Magi paintings. Like one of the eastern kings,
he has placed his gold-filigreed crown or cap on the floor before
him, as if to submit his political power as an offering to the divinity.

That divinity is the most unusual part of this image. Why is the goddess in this *Idolatry of Solomon* depicted as dark-skinned – as a Black African, with fuller lips and tighter curls in her hair than in the Cranach workshop's typical female figures – as a person who would have been described among Cranach's milieu as a 'Moor'? One possibility is that this is a so-called Black Madonna, a type of image of the Virgin with darker skin. There was a famous miraculous painted example in Częstochowa, Poland, within a fortnight's wagon journey from Wittenberg, past what was then known as Breslau (present-day Wrocław). But that painting bears little resemblance to the idol of Lucas the Younger's panel, which is clearly a sculpture. Astarte here is not merely dark-skinned, like medieval sculptural Black Madonnas, but also physiognomically more African. European Black Madonnas tended to have similar standardized features to other non-Black Madonnas in their ambit. In short, if there is resonance here between Astarte and Black Madonnas, it is secondary.

The primary resonance must have been with the line in the Song of Songs – an erotic poem spoken by Solomon and one of his wives, the Shulammite – in which the wife declares: 'I am black and beautiful' (Song of Solomon 1:5).[8] In other words, Lucas the Younger has applied the blackness of one of Solomon's wives in one part of the Old Testament to the goddess of another wife in another part (1 Kings). This is not to say that here the Song of Songs is itself literally understood as pagan, but rather that one of its verses has been repurposed from one wife of Solomon to another powerful female in his life. Compositional echoes between the Sidonian wife and her retinue facilitate this transference of quality. The Sidonian wife in particular, the foremost woman, the one who turned Solomon to the worship of her god, is almost identically mirroring Astarte in pose. Astarte's headdress is almost identical to the headdress of the Sidonian wife (beneath the brim of her hat) and her ladies-in-waiting. It is as if Solomon is worshipping a Black African version of his own wife.

The members of the Sidonian wife's retinue also resemble her. The wife shows a brilliant damask underskirt (with darker embroidery than Astarte's gown), a flashy satin-like sleeve or drape at her forearms and a feathered red velvet hat. But otherwise in face and ornament she looks like her servants. The two ladies immediately behind her wear dresses similar to hers, even as they lift its velvety train. In addition to the shared headdresses, they all also wear multiple golden chains, with one chain tight around the throat (like collared hinds) and one or more chains loosely spilling on to their chests. The faces are pale and identically reddened at the cheeks, with faint, fine eyebrows and high hairlines over moderately large ears. The women also share their mistress's sharp, knowing gaze, though they do not look at Solomon.

Most importantly, these women look like ladies of the Saxon court familiar from other Cranach workshop paintings (see, for example, another portrayal of one as a sacrohistorical figure, illus. 67). Though 1 Kings 11 tells of the dangers of interfaith marriage, Lucas the Younger's Solomon has – by appearances – not strayed far from the electoral domains. Through the doorway, beyond a balcony, a gothic cathedral sits atop a cliff. Is this the 'high place' Solomon built for the abominable false gods of non-Israelite peoples in 1 Kings 11? It looks instead like the most elaborate and iconic Christian architecture of worship. Perhaps the cathedral in the distance represents instead an abandoned house of the true faith. The balcony reveals that this scene takes place high above the land and water below. Lucas the Younger's *Idolatry of Solomon* may itself take place in one of Solomon's newly constructed temples. The construction is weak; pieces of the wall are already crumbling, presaging the fall of Israel to come.

The women are Saxon ladies, and the landscape and architecture correspond with Saxony. One could potentially read this

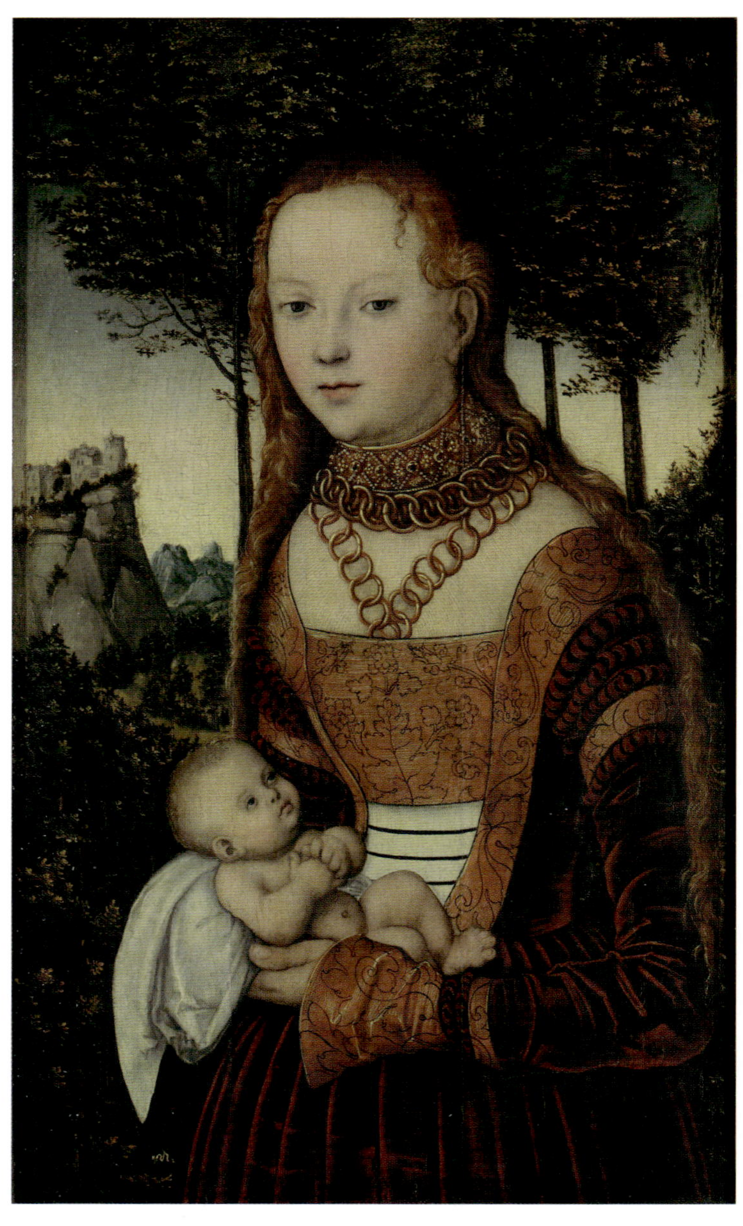

67 Lucas Cranach the Elder, *Young Mother with Child* (*Penance of St John Chrysostom*), *c.* 1525, oil on panel. It is noteworthy that this particular legend of the carnal sin of Eastern Roman patriarch and saint John Chrysostomos

painting as an allegory of being tempted away from the old faith of the Roman Church to the new faith of the Lutheran one. One function of Black Astarte is to eliminate this interpretation: she represents an otherness beyond interconfessional divides. (Though later in the sixteenth century, marrying between different Christian sects would become problematic, the issue seems not to have caused concern during Luther's lifetime.[9]) Black Astarte is not a Black Madonna, nor any other Christian image.

The Cranach workshop's pale Venuses, nymphs and other nude pagan women – as, for example, allegorized in the interchangeable rejuvenated nudes of the Cranach workshop's 1546 *Fountain of Youth* – offered not just a Germanized ideal of beauty, but the idealized German past. However, in the humanist project of uncovering antiquity, not every aspect could be assimilated into a clear path towards Christianity. As was written in Christian holy texts like 1 Kings and beyond, there were many other supposed gods besides the rightful one. Even as Cranach's role was to deliver to his often-learned clients art as a materialized form of the origin of German-ness, he and his son were also aware of the perils of such a delivery: devilry.[10]

In the context of the Cranach workshop's oeuvre of desirable women offering knowledge of the German past, this painting captures the spiritual danger of blending erotic desire with the intellectual desire for knowledge. Yet this *Idolatry of Solomon* holds little erotic appeal. It is the least beautiful of the three *Weibermacht* images in its series. Both *Samson and Delilah* and *David and Bathsheba* have alluring, sensual moments. The *Delilah* image is the most gracefully painted of the three, and of the various (less homogenous) ladies-in-waiting attending Bathsheba's bath, two look out, one over her shoulder in that promising pose, favoured in erotic imagery, that says 'even though my back is to you, I couldn't help but turn around because I wanted to see you.'

with the daughter of an emperor circulated largely if not exclusively in Western Christian contexts; it is not part of Eastern Roman or Orthodox lore about this historical figure.

By contrast, *The Idolatry of Solomon* is a picture of attractive women, rather than one that attracts its viewer to those women; they are not bared or available to the viewer. The painting looks like an allegorical frieze, the isocephalic row of women lovely but extraordinarily well covered. That covering has little sensuality to its texture – an oddity, since almost all prestige Renaissance painters, not just Cranach, used clothing as an occasion to show off their ability to make paint resemble textiles. These women wear a deep, featureless black, a colour rarely used for women's clothes in the Cranach workshop. This image is all about the iconography of beauty, without being particularly beautiful. Unlike the other *Weibermacht* pictures and much of the Cranach workshop oeuvre, *The Idolatry of Solomon* does not enact the threat of desire it describes.

The discomfort of otherness and particularly of Blackness may be one reason for this. Black Astarte might indeed be beautiful, but she is the most covered of all the female figures here, among the most fully clothed female figures ever produced by the Cranach workshop. Lucas the Younger did not intend for viewers to desire her. Made small, self-contained in a corner of crumbling walls, she is the opposite of the luscious, available Eve, who dominates her image, arms akimbo. This opposition should be understood as a contrast by parallel. Just as the tempting Eve holds out the apple, showing that she has bitten into the fruit of the knowledge tree, the demure Astarte holds a book. She holds it closed. In other words, Lucas the Younger's *Idolatry of Solomon* refuses to make Blackness tempting even when it comes in the form of a lore-bearing woman. In so doing, the painting reveals the Cranach workshop's commitment to the erotics of knowledge as a particularly white, German project.

## A SACRED GERMAN FUTURITY

Even as Lucas the Younger took a larger role in the workshop in the late 1530s, Cranach continued to lead it until around 1550, when he left Wittenberg. In 1547 – again, around the time of the completion of the *Wittenberg Altarpiece* – Moritz of Saxony's successful conquest of Wittenberg and Torgau had led to the imprisonment and deposition of his cousin Johann Friedrich. Around 1550, Johann Friedrich summoned Cranach, who was 72 years old, to accompany him in captivity in Augsburg, perhaps to counterbalance the invitation of Titian to the court of the Holy Roman Emperor Charles V there. Cranach had known Johann Friedrich, who was then in his late forties, since childhood, and Cranach seems to have truly loved his patron. He was said to have begged on his knees for merciful treatment of Johann Friedrich by Charles V.

Of all the things Cranach is known for, landscape is hardly foremost. Yet over his career the formula he established for consistent depiction of the natural world enables one of the most important themes of his work: that sacred history and the primal, timeless world of antiquity are both contiguous with the German wilderness and countryside. It is common in Renaissance painting to depict biblical or ancient people in a living Renaissance setting. What is less common – yet typical for Cranach – is to situate portraits of living people in a primordial setting suggesting biblical referents.

In a unique group portrait, Cranach worked with his son Lucas to depict *Martin Luther and the Wittenberg Reformers* surrounding their protector and patron, Elector Johann Friedrich. The panel has been cut off on the right-hand side and perhaps on all sides. (That said, seventeenth-century copies show the same composition, so the dismembering happened early in the panel's existence.) Though much smaller, a little more than

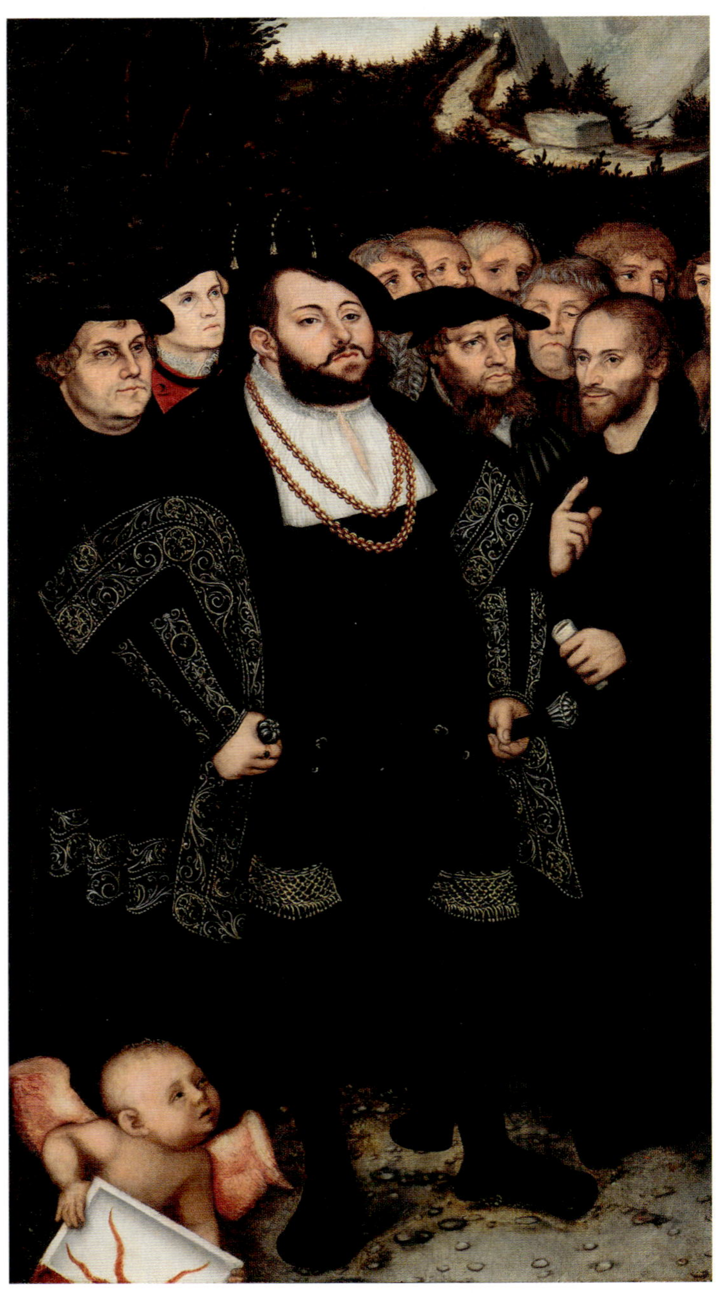

68 Lucas Cranach the Elder and Younger, *Martin Luther and the Wittenberg Reformers*, c. 1543, oil on panel.

70 centimetres (2 ft) tall, it must have been part of a triptych like the *Weimar Altarpiece*, which similarly includes portraits on the wings (illus. 57). But these portraits are unlikely to represent donors. First of all, most of these men are not of the wealthy donor class of noblemen and successful merchants: besides the front row of Luther, Johann Friedrich and Melanchthon, the figures include Georg Spalatin (immediately behind Luther) and Johann Friedrich's chancellor, Gregor Brück, who also advised Luther on legal matters.[11] Secondly, though some of the figures as a whole look solemnly, perhaps even fearfully, at whatever must have once appeared upward and to their left in the missing central panel – Melanchthon even looks out at the viewer and points towards it, in case the viewer needed more of a clue – they are not praying as a donor should. These are witnesses, not patrons.

They are in attendance at some event we cannot now re-construct. They are not witnessing the event from the gilded, curtained box seats of the *Weimar Altarpiece*, either. Above them, in the rearground, appears the bottom of a typical Cranach sheer cliff face. Before this cliff is a sarcophagus-sized and -shaped slab of stone. A path leads from that slab up the hill to a gateway, promising re-entry into the civilization so often depicted at the borders of Cranach's German wilderness. On the basis of this semi-biblical iconography, one might guess that the missing scene to which the reformers bore witness was a Resurrection. The slab thus doubles as a reference to the empty tomb and to Christ's authorizing statement in Matthew 16:18: 'On this rock I will build my church.' Regardless of what the missing image was, the naturalized imagery of the Resurrection in the background of this panel thematizes and authorizes the figures' resuscitation of Christianity itself by means of reform.

This inclusion of reformers in sacred time is subtler than in the *Wittenberg Altarpiece* (illus. 2). No one here is modelling the essence of a sacred ritual, or attending Christ's Last Supper. Cranach presents his friends and family in the same primeval forest that surrounds most of his biblical scenes and uses it to echo those scenes.

Though we may know less about Cranach's life narrative and personality than we would like, this painting did in fact include literal family members. Cranach was, again, the godfather of Luther's son; Lucas the Younger was married first to Barbara, the daughter of Gregor Brück (around the time this painting was made), and later to Magdalena Schurff, Melanchthon's niece. Cranach had collaborated with Spalatin – who has the same boyish face in *Martin Luther and the Wittenberg Reformers* that he had in a portrait Cranach made decades earlier, from 1509 – on an illustrated chronicle of Saxony before he ever really knew Luther.[12] In other words, Cranach was connected to each of the known figures in the painting in personal ways as well as professional.

Over his career, Cranach built upon his apparent genuine fondness for the learned world of university men and rulers to help create the greatest movement of his time. The Reformation precisely united scholarly interest in the past with political power and media distribution in the present to secure the institutionalization of a new form of Christianity (which the men in this painting would have argued was truer to the oldest, original form).

Cranach's interests followed his patrons, but surely conditioned them, too. By representing German antiquity in the same way as he represented the ideals of Reformed Christianity, he united the two defining notions of his time and place. The distance between Cranach's *Eve* and *Venus with Cupid as Honey Thief* was difficult to articulate on the basis of appearance. Using slightly different iconography, they both presented desirable female nudes in situations where the dangerous and tempting offerings of the natural world paralleled the dangers of erotic lust. The aesthetic problem (that a warning against forbidden desire inevitably elicits that desire) may have been universal, but Cranach resolutely set this problem in the context of the German desire for self-knowledge and self-affirmation.

While an extended discussion of the reception of Cranach's work in the context of later eras of German nationalism is not within the scope of this book, it is worth noting that Hermann Göring and Adolf Hitler had examples from Cranach of both an *Adam and Eve* and a *Venus with Cupid as Honey Thief* in the Third Reich's and Hitler's own collections, respectively. (Among other Cranachs seized by Göring was a portrait of Johann Friedrich in full finery.) Later, in East Germany, Cranach was understood by scholars as one of 'the forerunners of Socialist Realism', particularly marked by 'a deep attachment to common people and nature' and a 'genuine affirmation of life'.[13] Cranach's self-branding as the producer of a particularly German heritage has remained persuasive – for worse and for better – for centuries.

When Cranach earnestly portrays his own friends and family in a German landscape of the Resurrection, he does something no other Renaissance painter could: he depicts – indeed affirms – a whole community of the living as if they were truly part of the trajectory of humankind towards salvation. Other artists' portraits of popes and archbishops, no matter how grandiose, no matter how humanistically informed their references, no matter how disguised as biblical or early Christian figures, did not tend to simply imply that the people present were forging new moments in sacred history.

Using subtle cues in the scenery, and using the German wilderness landscape itself, Cranach asserts a claim more revolutionary (in the literal sense of overturning an order) than any other Renaissance artist: a sacred futurity shaped by his collaborators and by himself. If one pictures the Cranach workshop as a machine, the engine is the desire for access to a true German past, but the

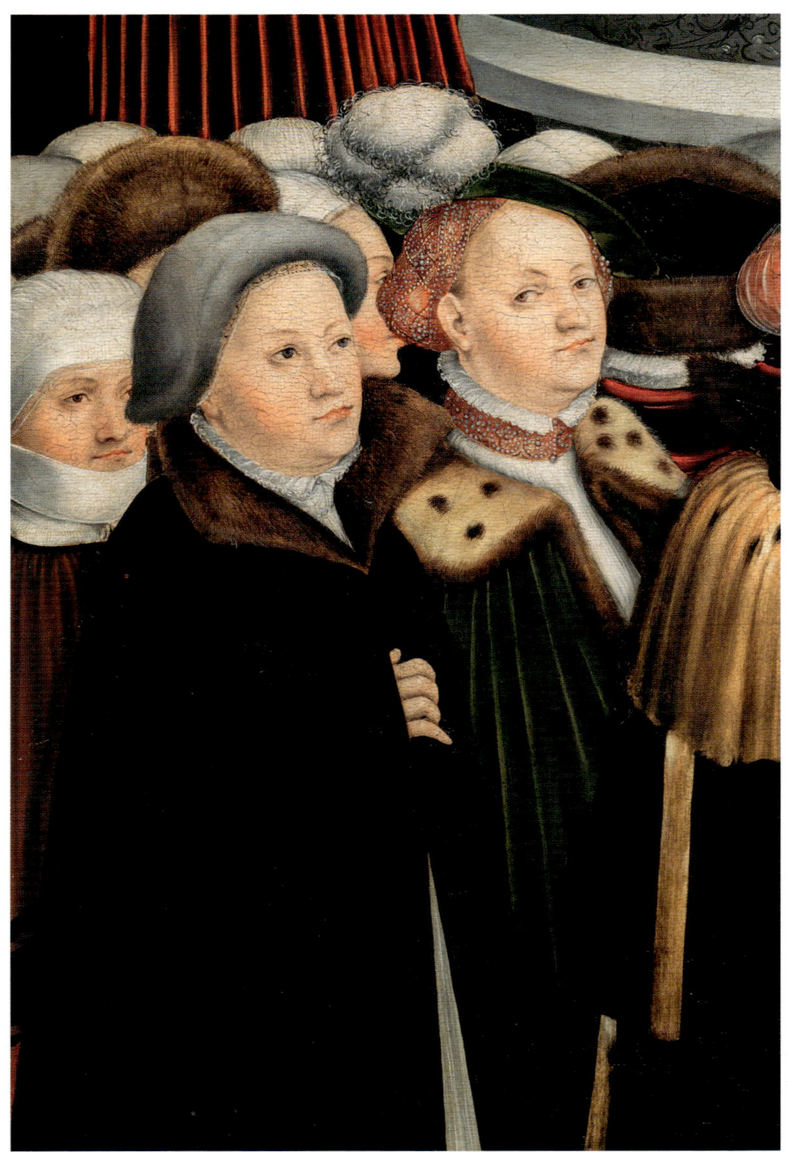

69 Woman from baptism scene looking out, detail of the left wing in illus. 2.

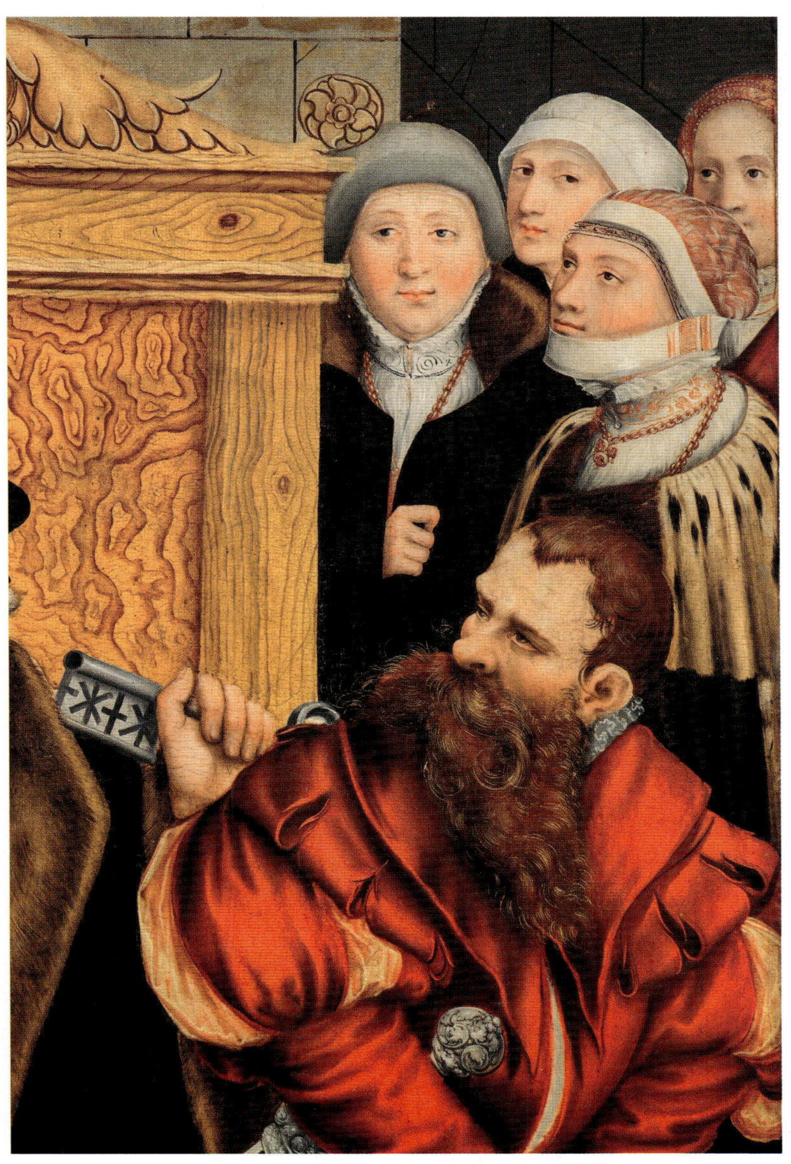

70 Woman from confession scene looking out, detail of the right wing in illus. 2.

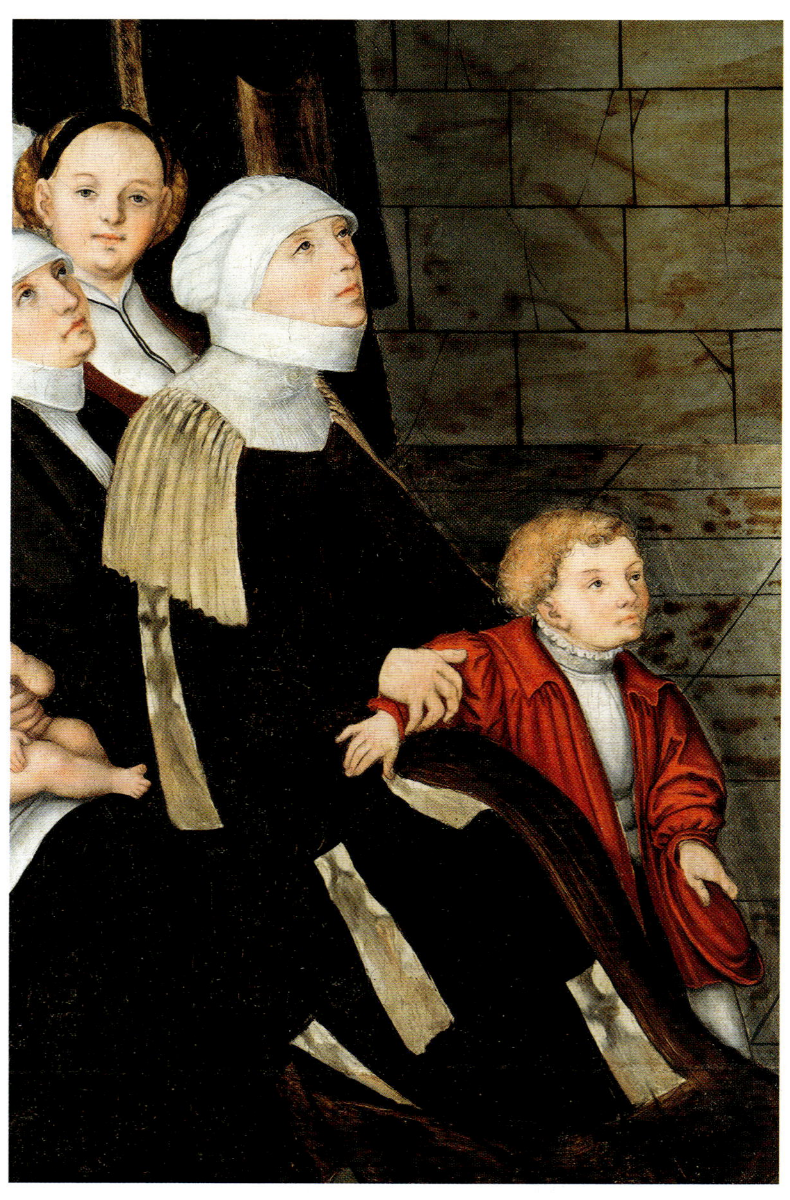

71 Woman from preaching scene looking out, detail of the predella in illus. 2.

output is grace – the fulfilment of the Christian promise to save humankind.

In most pictures like *Martin Luther and the Wittenberg Reformers*, in which communal figures from Cranach and Lucas the Younger's lives appear leading the way to the future of salvation, women do not appear. But in that boldest example, the *Wittenberg Altarpiece*, which shows community members present at a baptism and confession in the wings and at one of Luther's sermons in the predella at the bottom, women play a special role. In each of these panels, one woman in the group looks out at the viewer. These women – as conservatively dressed as Black Astarte or more so – direct the judgemental, alert gaze of Eve or the Sidonian wife at us.

These women take on a common role in Renaissance painting: the figure of the 'commentator' or 'admonisher', recommended by Leon Battista Alberti more than one hundred years earlier in his treatise on painting.[14] These figures essentially set the timbre of the painting: they represent the artist's recommendation for how the viewer should relate to the subject-matter. These wry, knowing women do not make such a relationship easy; they are not exactly welcoming. But their knowledge is different from the traumatic knowledge of Eve or the Sidonian wife, who know that they participate in the downfall of humankind or Israel. The knowing women of the *Wittenberg Altarpiece* possess a positive knowledge, confident of the rectitude of their faith.

As much as Cranach helped construct a visual culture that objectified and mocked women, he also endowed women with a special ability to cross temporalities. If *The Nymph of the Fountain* and Cranach's other pagan nudes stared from the deep past into Cranach's present, the community admonishers of the *Wittenberg Altarpiece*, perhaps in some cases real portraits of now-unknown women, stare out into the very future Cranach's Reformation promised. In their eyes, salvation may be guaranteed, but being ready for it is an eternal challenge.

SUMMARY

Cranach was a painter whose practices required collaboration. He worked together with learned scholars to devise their portraits and to illustrate their poetic aspirations of honouring and participating in the revival of German antiquity. He also worked with other artists and publishers on his more broadly distributed output of prints, as well as with his sons and other artists in his own workshop on an unprecedented mass production of paintings that further established his identity and what I have called his brand. He was reasonably well-to-do, but money does not seem to have been the motive. A well-liked tavern-keeper, shop-keeper and sometime mayor, he is a far cry from the lay concept (or typical film representation) of the Renaissance artist as an isolated genius. He did not just flatter patrons for a living; his life was earnestly interwoven with theirs. His grand Reformation altarpieces and those of his son after him – even at their most monumental, even when the electoral family is in attendance in the wings – tend to inspire not grandeur or awe but rather a sense of an integrated and enduring community.

The first recorded works by Cranach show him already with 'his people', with a community of scholars focused on recovering a German past in Vienna, a city that was the epicentre for such work. He began as a woodcut designer, but quickly focused on portrait painting. As he multiplied his success at the Saxon electors' court in Wittenberg, he built on past precedent in the relatively new genre of non-royal portraiture and innovated a new format that dominated Northern Europe portraiture for the rest of the century.

His other output for scholarly clients has been underappreciated for its focus on the female nude. Some 182 paintings of female nudes survive attributed to Cranach and his workshop alone, a number unmatched by any other sixteenth-century painter. The most popular subject-matter was Adam and Eve, the most Christian subject-matter, but most of the pictures applied ideals from Greco-Roman antiquity to women with tradition-ally German visual qualities, placed in the setting of a German forest. As was common in the first half of the sixteenth century, the theme of these nudes was often the dangers of female sex-uality, especially for male viewers. Cranach elevated this erotic desire for the female nude by bringing it together with his clients' scholarly desire for the culture of German antiquity.

Finally, and perhaps most importantly in terms of historical impact, Cranach provided nearly the entire visual apparatus of Luther's Reformation. There were other important artists who produced elite art for the movement's sponsors, like the sculptor Peter Dell the Elder and Dürer, who at the end of his life com-pleted a major commission aligned with Lutheranism; other artists supported reform but were too radical at times for the Lutheran community, like Sebald Beham. But it was Cranach who devised the core and most widely spread visual messages of the move-ment, whether in printed broadside, pamphlet and Bible illus-tration, or in large panels and altarpieces affirming the confidence, even pleasure, of the Lutheran path to salvation.

Cranach could not have had this impact without his previous successes as a portrait painter and humanist mythographer of German antiquity. Cranach godfathered the Reformation by inventing its iconography and then asserting it as tradition through sheer repetition. But he could not have made this assertion had he not already created a brand for himself in the mid-1520s, combining painterly skill and facility with antique iconography. It was this desirable humanist brand that grounded Cranach's establishment of a new Reformation tradition.

What model of Renaissance artist, then, does Cranach pro-vide? I began with his collaborative strengths. For all of Cranach's clear pride in his technical tricks – evident in his self-citation, especially in the 1546 *Fountain of Youth* – he was not in it for fame or to push the limits of what a maker of images might be able to do. It is a trope of Renaissance studies to talk about self-fashioning: the emergence of an individual's identity, legible through the social codes of his (usually not her or their) time. Artists and writers in particular are often understood as fulcrums of this practice, providing the images and texts that facilitated the expression of identity.[15]

Cranach certainly provided such images, but even in his portrait paintings his goal was never just the fashioning of a self. In his earliest portraiture, one gets the sense the parts he liked most were the esoteric attributes that would get people talking to one another about ancient symbolism in their university circles. His mythographic female nudes went beyond private erotics and evoked a shared quest for knowledge. Reformation believers put his portraits of their leaders (in paint, print or copies in other media) on their walls, in secret or open solidarity across German-speaking lands and beyond. Once he became the primary image-maker of the Reformation, Cranach, more than any other artist of his time, enabled an entire community to fashion itself.

# CHRONOLOGY

| | |
|---|---|
| 1459 | Conrad Celtis born in Wipfeld, Franconia |
| 1472 | Lucas Cranach born in Kronach, Franconia |
| 1483 | Martin Luther born in Eisleben, Saxony |
| 1486 | Friedrich III becomes elector of Saxony |
| 1492 | Celtis gives speech encouraging Germans to rival Italians in humanist study of Greco-Roman past, University of Heidelberg |
| 1497 | Emperor Maximilian I summons Celtis to University of Vienna |
| 1502 | First record of Cranach painting portraits of university clients in Vienna. University of Wittenberg founded by Friedrich III |
| 1505 | Cranach begins work in Wittenberg at the invitation of Friedrich III. Luther enters Augustinian monastery in Erfurt, Thuringia |
| 1506 | Cranach paints *Altar of St Catherine* |
| 1507 | Luther ordained as a priest in Erfurt Cathedral |
| 1508 | Friedrich III bestows upon Cranach the symbol of the winged serpent. Conrad Celtis dies in Vienna |
| 1509 | Cranach produces *Wittenberg Heiltumsbuch* and earliest surviving *Venus and Cupid* with a black background |
| 1512 | Luther earns doctorate in theology, accepts chair at University of Wittenberg |
| 1513 | Cranach's first son, Hans Cranach, born in Wittenberg |
| 1515 | Lucas Cranach the Younger born in Wittenberg |
| 1517 | Luther publishes 95 Theses against the sale of indulgences |
| 1518 | Philipp Melanchthon becomes professor of Greek at University of Wittenberg. Cranach paints earliest surviving *Nymph of the Fountain* |

| | |
|---|---|
| 1519 | Cranach first serves on Wittenberg city council and remains for 26 years |
| 1520 | Cranach receives exclusive apothecary privileges for Wittenberg area. Cranach's daughter Barbara born in Wittenberg; Luther is godfather. Luther publishes popular critiques of the Roman Church. Pope Leo X threatens Luther with excommunication |
| 1521 | Pope Leo X excommunicates Luther. Cranach completes collaboration with Melanchthon, Luther and Johann Schwerdtfeger on popular anti-pope pamphlet *Passional Christi und Antichristi*. Luther attends Diet of Worms. Friedrich III stages fake abduction of Luther and hides him. Diet of Worms confirms Luther as an outlaw |
| 1522 | Liturgical practice breaks down in Wittenberg; image-destroying riots begin. Luther returns to Wittenberg to restore peace, temporarily then permanently. Printer Melchior Lotter the Younger, sympathetic to Luther, leaves Leipzig and perhaps establishes printer's workshop in Cranach's house; Cranach and Christian Döring co-own press. Cranach illustrates, produces and sells Luther's rendition of the New Testament |
| 1525 | Friedrich III dies; his brother becomes Johann the Constant, Elector of Saxony. Peasants' War breaks out; Luther speaks against it; elector's mercenaries defeat farmers' armies. Luther, a priest, marries former nun Katharina von Bora, with Cranach as witness |
| 1526 | Luther's first child, Hans, is born in Wittenberg; his godfathers include Cranach. Diet of Speyer determines that, within the Holy Roman Empire, each prince should decide question of religious confession for his own state |
| 1528 | Melanchthon and friends publish adaptations of Theocritus's Idyll 19. Cranach produces first securely dated *Venus with Cupid as Honey Thief* with verses based on Idyll 19 |
| 1529 | Term 'Protestant' emerges as Luther-supporting states protest other states' failure to follow terms of Diet of Speyer. Cranach produces first dated Law and Grace images. Ottomans besiege Vienna, then retreat |
| 1530–31 | Formation of Lutheran Schmalkaldic League |
| 1532 | Elector Johann the Constant dies; his son, Johann Friedrich, becomes elector of Saxony. Cranach begins to produce |

|       |   |
|-------|---|
|       | pendant portraits of Luther and Melanchthon in great quantity; mass production believed to be facilitated by son Hans Cranach |
| 1537  | Hans Cranach dies, aged 24, in Bologna of unknown causes. Cranach winged serpent changes form (closed wings), perhaps marking new role for Lucas the Younger in workshop. Dating starts to become sporadic for workshop mass productions |
| 1541–2 | Cranach assists with visual aspects of Schmalkaldic League's military campaign against Duke Heinrich of Braunschweig-Wolfenbüttel |
| 1545–63 | Council of Trent; Lutherans send no representatives |
| 1546  | Luther dies in Eisleben. Holy Roman Emperor Charles V declares war on the Schmalkaldic League, with aid of papal armies. Cranach paints *The Fountain of Youth*. Cranach workshop begins *Wittenberg Altarpiece* |
| 1547  | Duke Moritz of Albertine Saxony openly sides with Charles V. *Wittenberg Altarpiece* completed. Wittenberg surrenders to Moritz's forces; Elector Johann Friedrich arrested along with other Schmalkaldic leaders; Moritz becomes elector of Saxony. Johann Friedrich imprisoned, mostly in Augsburg; Cranach initially refuses to accompany him in captivity; Cranach temporarily fired from court service |
| 1550  | Cranach transfers Wittenberg workshop to his son. Cranach travels to Augsburg and regains status as Johann Friedrich's court painter in captivity; paints Charles V and meets Titian |
| 1551  | Elector Moritz switches sides to ally against Charles V |
| 1552  | Johann Friedrich and other Schmalkaldic leaders freed. Cranach continues work as Johann Friedrich's court painter in Weimar, Saxony |
| 1553  | Cranach dies in Weimar |
| 1554  | Johann Friedrich dies in Weimar |
| 1555  | Diet of Augsburg affirms terms of 1526 Diet of Speyer; Peace of Augsburg begins. Lucas the Younger completes *Weimar Altarpiece*, including portrait of father |

# REFERENCES

Introduction: The Godfather of the Reformation

1  Bonnie Noble, *Lucas Cranach the Elder: Art and Devotion of the German Reformation* (Lanham, MD, 2009), p. 15.
2  Werner Schade, *Cranach: A Family of Master Painters*, trans. Helen Sebba (New York, 1981) provides the best overview of the family.
3  Michelle De Rusha, *Katharina and Martin: The Radical Marriage of a Runaway Nun and a Renegade Monk* (Grand Rapids, MI, 2017), p. 157.
4  Martin Luther, *D. Martin Luthers Werke: Kritische Gesamtausgabe* (Weimar, 1883), vol. XXX/1, p. 152. Hereafter this work will be cited as WA (Weimar Ausgabe) followed by volume and page number; translation into English is the author's unless otherwise noted. This passage is also cited by Keith Moxey, *Peasants, Warriors and Wives: Popular Imagery in the Reformation* (Chicago, IL, and London, 1989), p. 122, as part of a discussion about Luther's beliefs on gender in the context of marriage.
5  Martin Luther, *Das Tauffbuchlin verdeutscht* (Wittenberg, 1523).
6  For more information about Cranach's press venture with Christian Döring the goldsmith, see Alfred Götze, *Die hochdeutschen Drucker der Reformationszeit*, 2nd edn (Berlin, 1963), pp. 50–51, and Joachim Karl Friedrich Knaake, 'Ueber Cranach's Presse', *Centralblatt für Bibliothekswesen*, VII (1890), pp. 196–207.
7  For the best recent scholarly takes on this altarpiece, see Noble, *Lucas Cranach*; Joseph Leo Koerner, *The Reformation of the Image* (Chicago, IL, 2004), esp. pp. 329–30, 368–76; and, in German, Ingrid Schulze, *Lucas Cranach d. J. und die protestantische Bildkunst in Sachsen und Thüringen: Frömmigkeit, Theologie, Fürstenreformation* (Jena, 2004), pp. 32–51.
8  Augsburg Confession, Articles XI and XII, consulted at the Christian Classics Ethereal Library, www.ccel.org.
9  See Augsburg Confession, Article XXIV, for frequency of Mass and of the sacrament.

10   Martin Luther, 'Against the Heavenly Prophets', WA XVIII 37–214,
     pp. 99–100.

1  The Cranach Brand Emerges

1   I am grateful to Shira Brisman for this suggestion.
2   The date is given by a testimonial ('Zeugnis') by Matthias
    Gunderam in 1556 said to be located in the Wittenberg cupola or
    steeple. The Latin text is printed in Joseph Heller, *Lucas Cranach's
    Leben und Werke* (Nuremberg, 1854), pp. 279–82. For a German
    translation, see Christian Schuchardt, *Lucas Cranach des Aeltern: Leben
    und Werke* (Leipzig, 1851), vol. 1, pp. 18–20, 185–9 (Schuchardt
    interrupts the text with his biography).
3   Dieter Koepplin and Tilman Falk, eds, *Lukas Cranach: Gemälde,
    Zeichnungen, Druckgraphik* (Basel, 1974), vol. 1, p. 105.
4   Ibid., vol. 11, p. 748, nn. 2–3; Werner Schade, *Cranach: A Family of
    Master Painters*, trans. Helen Sebba (New York, 1981), p. 12.
5   The memorial is preserved in J. Heller, ed., *Lucas Cranachs Leben und
    Werke*, 2nd edn (Bamberg, 1844), pp. 279–80.
6   Armin Kunz, 'Cranach as Cartographer: The Rediscovered "Map of
    the Holy Land"', *Print Quarterly*, XII/2 (June 1995), pp. 125–7.
7   Koepplin and Falk, *Lukas Cranach*, vol. 1, p. 118.
8   By 1495, according to Schade, *Cranach*, p. 12.
9   Stadtarchiv Kronach, G 3, Gerichtsbuch 1492–1499: Acta Judicy,
    Indomo Civium, feria tertia post Letare anno etc. xcv, as transcribed
    by Dietrich Lücke, Monika Lücke and Anja Weigelt, https://
    lucascranach.org/en/DE_StA_Kronach_G-3_fol-112v-244r,
    accessed 28 March 2023.
10  Hambrecht, p. 361, Anh. 2., from the Stadtarchiv Coburg: B Nr. 135
    Stadtbuch der Stadt Coburg für 1482–1549, fol. 75.
11  Fedya Anzelewsky, 'Studien zur Frühzeit Lukas Cranachs d. Ä',
    *Städel-Jahrbuch*, XVII (1999), p. 125.
12  The Cranach Digital Archive show up 260 portraits when the
    search is limited to 'Bildnisse' and works by the master or the master
    and his Werkstatt. This number increases to 323 if you include
    portraits done by his workshop but before his death in 1553.
13  In considering these paintings, we are indebted to the doctoral work
    of Dieter Koepplin, 'Cranachs Ehebildnis des Johannes Cuspinian
    von 1502: Seine christlich-humanistische Bedeutung', PhD diss.,
    Universität Basel, 1973.

14  This project runs through Celtis's books *Norinberga* (1502), *Germania generalis* (1502) and *Germania illustrata*, with the latter unfinished at his death.

15  For an excellent recent account with bibliography, see the opening chapter of Christopher S. Wood, *Forgery Replica Fiction: Temporalities of German Renaissance Art* (Chicago, IL, 2008), pp. 1–24.

16  Koepplin, 'Cranachs Ehebildnis', p. 53, n. 152.

17  The most thorough account is still Koepplin, 'Cranachs Ehebildnis', pp. 86–261.

18  For this specific point, see Michael J. B. Allen, *Marsilio Ficino's Commentary on the Fatal Number in Book VIII of Plato's Republic* (Berkeley, CA, 1994). Two classic texts on occult Renaissance humanism are Frances Yates, *Giordano Bruno and the Hermetic Tradition* (London, 1964) and Frances Yates, *The Occult Philosophy in the Elizabethan Age* (London and New York, 1979), especially the earlier chapters of both books for fifteenth-century Florentine contexts.

19  Gunnar Heydenreich, *Lucas Cranach the Elder: Painting Materials, Techniques and Workshop Practice* (Amsterdam, 2007), p. 42.

20  Heydenreich, *Lucas Cranach*, p. 267.

21  Schuchardt, *Lucas Cranach des Aeltern*, vol. I, pp. 156–62.

22  See the transcriptions of various receipts and correspondence documenting Dürer's 'imperial liferent' in Jeffrey Ashcroft, ed. and trans., *Albrecht Dürer: Documentary Biography* (New Haven, CT, and London, 2017), vol. I, pp. 639–49.

23  Dieter Koepplin and Tilman Falk, eds, *Lukas Cranach: Gemälde, Zeichnungen, Druckgraphik* (Basel, 1974), vol. I, pp. 67–8, n. 19.

24  For the original text of the poem, see Reinhard Piper, *Das Liebespaar in der Kunst* (Munich, 1916), pp. 55–6.

25  'Frisch auff mein Herz, sey unverzagt:/ Die ich begert hab ich erjagt'. See previous note 24.

26  'willig gefallen in mein Netz'. See previous note 24.

27  This count is based on works within the Cranach Digital Archive attributed to Cranach the Elder, as of December 2020.

28  Heydenreich, *Lucas Cranach*, p. 270.

29  See the contract in the Staatsarchiv Weimar (StAW Reg. Bb. 4216, Bl. 60b): 'Cranach erhält eine Zahlung von 40 fl. 8 gr. durch den Hofkammerschreiber Stephan Strohl für einige zur Hochzeit Herzog Heinrichs von Sachsen ausgeführte Arbeiten'.

30  Marisa Bass, *Jan Gossart and the Invention of Netherlandish Antiquity* (Princeton, NJ, 2016), p. 65.

31  For more on Cranach's yellow and red pigments, see Heydenreich,
    *Lucas Cranach*, pp. 133–41.

32  The blue used for the portraits was based on azurite, probably
    mined in Wallerfangen and Goldberg; see Heydenreich, *Lucas
    Cranach*, p. 154.

33  Max J. Friedländer and Jakob Rosenberg, *Die Gemälde von Lucas
    Cranach*, 2nd edn (Basel, 1979), p. 136, no. 333.

34  David Gaimster, 'The Hanseatic Cultural Signature: Exploring
    Globalization on the Micro-Scale in Late Medieval Northern
    Europe', *European Journal of Archaeology*, XVII/1 (2014), pp. 71.


## 2  The Mythographer of Women: A German Renaissance

1  See Daniel Görres, catalogue entries no. 60 and 61, in Gunnar
   Heydenreich, Daniel Görres and Beat Wismer, eds, *Lucas Cranach
   der Ältere: Meister Marke Moderne*, exh. cat. Museum Kunstpalast,
   Düsseldorf (2017), pp. 148–9.

2  Inv. no. T9680, Hermitage Museum, St Petersburg.

3  Joseph Leo Koerner, *The Moment of Self-Portraiture in German Renaissance
   Art* (Chicago, IL, 1993), p. 320.

4  This count is based only on works within the Cranach Digital
   Archive attributed to Cranach the Elder or Cranach the Younger
   and their workshop during Cranach the Elder's lifetime, as of
   December 2020.

5  Inv. no. NG6680, National Gallery, London.

6  Τὸν κλέπταν ποτ᾿Έρωτα κακὰ κέντασε μέλισσα
   κηρίον ἐκ σίμβλων συλεύμενον, ἄκρα δὲ χειρῶν
   δάκτυλα πάνθ᾿ ὑπένυξεν. ὃ δ᾿ ἄλγεε καὶ χέρ᾿ ἐφύση
   καὶ τὰν γᾶν ἐπάταξε καὶ ἅλατο, τᾷ δ᾿ Ἀφροδίτᾳ
   δεῖξεν τὰν ὀδύναν, καὶ μέμφετο ὅττι γε τυτθόν
   θηρίον ἐντὶ μέλισσα καὶ ἁλίκα τραύματα ποιεῖ.
   χὰ μάτηρ γελάσασα· 'τὺ δ᾿ οὐκ ἴσος ἐσσὶ μελίσσαις,
   ὃς τυτθὸς μὲν ἔεις τὰ δὲ τραύματα ἁλίκα ποιεῖς;'
       This version of the Greek text is taken from Neil Hopkinson,
   ed. and trans., *Theocritus Moschus Bion* (Cambridge, MA, 2018), p. 270.
   The present author thanks Professor Athena Kirk for her assistance
   with the translation.

7  Pablo Pérez d'Ors, 'A Lutheran Idyll: Lucas Cranach the Elder's
   "Cupid Complaining to Venus"', *Renaissance Studies*, XXI/1 (2007),
   pp. 85–98.

8  Ibid., p. 89. The phrase Melanchthon used was 'sum . . .
   enarraturus'.
9  *Farrago aliquot epigrammatum, Philippi Melanchthonis, & aliorum quorundam
   eruditorum* (Hagenau, January 1528). This multi-author publication
   seems so far unmentioned in previous scholarship on Cranach.
10 *Epigrammata Graeca veterum elegantissima* (Cologne, 1528). The version
   Soter published in 1525 does not have these newer works.
11 Inv. no. G199, Staatliches Museum Schwerin. The '27' in the date of
   1527 appears quite different from the '15'; another '2' form seems to
   float oddly nearby; and the '27' is also partly painted over the wings
   of the winged serpent, which does not occur in any other Cranach
   workshop paintings that are also dated.
12 Four of the five moonscape versions of *Venus with Cupid as Honeythief*
   attributed to Cranach and/or his workshop read 'cuspite' instead of
   'cuspide', a spelling error or variant.
13 The line in the *Farrago* edition reads 'Furanti digitum sedula punxit
   apis': see *Farrago*, sig. E7v. 'Apis . . . sedula' would have been most
   famous from what was then the standard version of line 928 in Book
   XIII of Ovid's *Metamorphoses*, though the word 'sedula' there is now
   considered suspect by some scholars.
14 *Farrago*, sig. B2v.
15 This issue arises in Manfred P. Fleischer, 'Melanchthon as
   Praeceptor of Late-Humanist Poetry', *Sixteenth Century Journal*, XX/4
   (1989), pp. 570 and n. 43. Fleischer here misunderstands Max
   Töppen in *Die Gründung der Universität zu Königsberg und das Leben ihres
   ersten Rectors Georg Sabinus* (Königsberg, 1844). Fleischer claims that
   Töppen claims that Melanchthon wrote one of Sabinus's early
   orations, but Töppen actually ultimately discredits this seventeenth-
   century rumour (Töppen, *Die Gründung*, pp. 259–60).
16 The acute accent in the original (though amended here) is
   incorrectly placed on the ultimate syllable. See Georg Sabinus,
   *Georgii Sabini Brandeburgensis Poemata* (Strasbourg, 1538), sig. L6v.
   Interestingly, in the 1544 expanded edition of Sabinus's work, the
   second line has been emended again, to 'Concita furantem cuspide
   fixit apis', 'the agitated bee stabbed the thiever with his sting'
   (Sabinus, *Brandeburgensis Poëmata* (Strasbourg, 1544), sig. O8r).
17 The honeythief motif had pan-European appeal: it would
   be published in two textual variants beginning with the first,
   unauthorized version of the wildly popular *Emblematum liber* ('Book
   of Emblems') of Andrea Alciato in 1531. Later editions provided

a second illustration for the second variant that in some ways resembles Cranach's composition.

18  The National Gallery now refers to this painting by the title *Primitive People*.

19  Hesiod, *Theogony; Works and Days; Testimonia*, ed. and trans. Glenn W. Most (Loeb Classical Library) (Cambridge, 2018), pp. 127–39.

20  'μέγα νήπιος', in ibid., p. 131.

21  Pushkin Museum, Moscow, inv. no. F-603.

22  For accounts of these statue-types' relevance in this period, see Leonard Barkan, *Unearthing the Past: Archaeology and Aesthetics in the Making of Renaissance Culture* (New Haven, CT, 1999).

23  See Christopher S. Wood, *Albrecht Altdorfer and the Origins of Landscape*, 2nd edn (London, 2014), especially the chapter 'The German Forest', pp. 151–238. See also Larry Silver, 'Forest Primeval: Albrecht Altdorfer and the German Wilderness Landscape', *Simiolus*, XIII/1 (1983), pp. 4–43.

24  Wood, *Albrecht Altdorfer*, pp. 152–3. The most recent extended treatment of this subject-matter is Timothy Husband with the assistance of Gloria Gilmore-House, *The Wild Man: Medieval Myth and Symbolism*, exh. cat., Metropolitan Museum of Art (New York, 1980).

25  On the body types of these people and their relation to the 'underclass of rural Europe', see helpful comments by Christopher S. Wood, *Forgery Replica Fiction: Temporalities of German Renaissance Art* (Chicago, IL, 2008), pp. 300–301.

26  To some extent, these were also the terms of an Italian ideal female beauty. See Elizabeth Cropper, 'On Beautiful Women, Parmigianino, Petrarchismo, and the Vernacular Style', *Art Bulletin*, LVIII/3 (1976), pp. 374–94, but note the distinctions elaborated in the following discussion.

27  This drawing is in the Ambras album in the Kunsthistorisches Museum, Vienna (Winkler 663). See Wood, *Forgery*, p. 302; and Otto Kurz, 'Huius Nympha Loci: A Pseudo-Classical Inscription and a Drawing by Dürer', *Journal of the Warburg and Courtauld Institutes*, XVI/3/4 (1953), pp. 171–7. The drawing deviates from the standard inscription in a couple of alterations thought to have been made by Conrad Celtis himself. See Dieter Wuttke, '*Zu Huius nympha loci*', *Arcadia*, III/3 (1968), pp. 306–7.

28  Elisabeth B. MacDougall, 'The Sleeping Nymph: Origins of a Humanist Fountain Type', *Art Bulletin*, LVII/3 (1975), pp. 358–9. For more extended discussion of the sources, see Barbara Baert, 'The

Sleeping Nymph Revisited: Ekphrasis, *Genius Loci* and Silence', in
*The Figure of the Nymph in Early Modern Culture*, ed. Karl A. E. Enenkel
and Anita Traninger (Leiden and Boston, MA, 2018), pp. 149–76,
esp. pp. 153–5. For the genre of poetry, see Patricia Emison, 'Asleep
in the Grass of Arcady: Giulio Campagnola's Dreamer', *Renaissance
Quarterly*, XLV/2 (1992), pp. 271–92.

29  Dieter Koepplin and Tilman Falk, eds, *Lukas Cranach: Gemälde,
Zeichnungen, Druckgraphik* (Basel, 1974), vol. II, p. 631.

30  Wood, *Forgery*, p. 301.

31  Francesco Colonna, *Hypnerotomachia Poliphili* (Venice, 1499), sig. EIr.

32  Inv. no. AM-185-PS01, Gemäldegalerie Alte Meister, Dresden.

33  Wood, *Forgery*, p. 303.

34  One, now in a private collection, has a blank inscription field, but
it is likely that this field once possessed lettering (Friedländer and
Rosenberg no. 404).

35  Inv. no. 28.221, Metropolitan Museum of Art, New York.

36  Maryan W. Ainsworth, 'The Judgment of Paris', in *German Paintings in
the Metropolitan Museum of Art, 1350–1600*, ed. Maryan W. Ainsworth and
Joshua P. Waterman (New Haven, CT, and London, 2013),
cat. no. II, p. 54.

37  Helmut Nickel, '"The Judgment of Paris" by Lucas Cranach the
Elder: Nature, Allegory, and Alchemy', *Metropolitan Museum Journal*,
XVI (1981), pp. 122–3.

38  For reflections on this interchangeability as irony towards the
subject-matter, and a different take on Cranach's practice with
'variant' forms, see Berthold Hinz, '"Sinnwidrig zusammengestellte
Fabrikate"? Zur Varianten-Praxis der Cranach-Werkstatt', in *Lucas
Cranach: ein Maler-Unternehmer aus Franken*, ed. Claus Grimm, Johannes
Erichsen and Evamaria Brockhoff (Augsburg, 1994), pp. 176–8.

39  Inv. no. AP 2004.03, Kimbell Art Museum, Fort Worth.

40  Inv. no. 28:1932, St Louis Art Museum.

41  Nickel, 'The Judgment of Paris', p. 127. The following discussion of
alchemy is a modification of Nickel's argument, which convincingly
documents various sources of this alchemical lore that Cranach
and his associates might have accessed. Nickel does not, however,
mention Trismegistus. Closer examination of Trismegistus's
supposed texts in the period might help test Nickel's claims, which
have not seen much subsequent engagement from scholars.

42  Cranach received privileges to the pharmacy in 1520, according to
Werner Schade, *Cranach: A Family of Master Painters*, trans. Helen Sebba

(New York, 1981), p. 41. But Helmut Nickel repeats the account of Edeltraud Wiessner of Wittenberg's Stadtgeschichtliches Museum that Cranach bought the pharmacy from Martin Polich von Mellerstadt, which must have been earlier, since Polich died in 1513 (Nickel, 'The Judgment of Paris', p. 127, n. 21).

43 For a similar allegory of Mercury's powers within art, see Ashley West, 'Albrecht Dürer, Hans Burgkmair and the Practice of Early Etching', *Print Quarterly*, xxx/4 (2013), p. 395.

44 Christiane Klapisch-Zuber, 'The Fountain of Youth: Bathing and Youthfulness (Fourteenth–Sixteenth Century)', *Clio: Women, Gender, History*, XLII (2015), p. 179.

45 For an overview of contemporary representations, see Alison Stewart, 'Sebald Beham's "Fountain of Youth-Bathhouse" Woodcut: Popular Entertainment and Large Prints by the Little Masters', *Register of the Spencer Art Museum*, VI/6 (1989/1990), pp. 64–88.

46 On bathhouses of the time, see Klapisch-Zuber, 'The Fountain of Youth', p. 186.

47 François Rabelais, *The Complete Works of François Rabelais*, trans. Donald M. Frame (Berkeley, 1991), pp. 654–55 (Book 5, part 20).

48 The most recent English-language overviews of witch imagery in this period are Linda C. Hults, *The Witch as Muse: Art, Gender, and Power in Early Modern Europe* (Philadelphia, PA, 2011) and Charles Zika, *The Appearance of Witchcraft: Print and Visual Culture in Sixteenth-Century Europe* (New York, 2007). See also Koerner, *The Moment*, especially 'The Crisis of Interpretation', pp. 317–62.

49 For an excellent bibliographic overview of witchcraft in this period, see Allison Rowlands, 'Witchcraft and Gender in Early Modern Europe', in *The Oxford Handbook of Witchcraft in Early Modern Europe and Colonial America*, ed. Brian P. Levack (Oxford, 2013), pp. 449–67.

50 The drawings are in a separate pamphlet known as *Abbildung des Bapstum* (Wittenberg, 1545) intended to accompany Martin Luther, *Wider das Bapstum zu Rom vom Teuffel gestifft* (Wittenberg, 1545). The woodcuts also appear in a manuscript in the Staatsbibliothek zu Berlin, Ms. germ. fol. 1371.

51 I am grateful to Prof. Tamara Golan for access to her discussion of this work in her book chapter, based on her dissertation research, on Niklaus Manuel.

52 Thomas Murner, *Ein andechtig geistliche Badenfart* (Strasbourg, 1514), sig. LIII verso–LV recto.

53  Jeffrey Hamburger has noted that this figure resembles figures of
    Horace, who confronts a monstrous hag caricature as an example of
    the kind of chimeric monster he warns against in his *Ars poetica* in at
    least one surviving manuscript miniature of the twelfth century. For
    one example, see Jeffrey Hamburger, *The Birth of the Author: Pictorial
    Prefaces in Glossed Books of the Twelfth Century* (Toronto, 2021), p. 62,
    fig. 40.

## 3  The Look of Luther's Reformation

1  For a recent historical overview of Cranach and Luther's roles in the
   Reformation, see Steven Ozment, *The Serpent and the Lamb: Cranach,
   Luther, and the Making of the Reformation* (New Haven, CT, 2012).
2  The best biography of Martin Luther with a thorough focus on his
   religious intervention is Lyndal Roper, *Martin Luther: Renegade and
   Prophet* (New York and London, 2017). For a survey of the
   Reformation and its place in religious history, see John Bossy,
   *Christianity in the West, 1400–1700* (Oxford, 1985). For a survey
   more focused on theology, see Steven Ozment, *The Age of Reform (1250–
   1550): An Intellectual and Religious History of Late Medieval and Reformation
   Europe* (New Haven, CT, 1980). For a more recent overview of the
   Reformation with a more global orientation, see Lee Palmer Wandel,
   *The Reformation: Towards a New History* (Cambridge, 2011).
3  On the Cranach publication, see Joachim Karl Friedrich Knaake,
   'Ueber Cranach's Presse', *Centralblatt für Bibliothekswesen*, VII (1890),
   pp. 196–207, especially p. 202.
4  For a recent overview of this aspect of the Reformation, see Andrew
   Pettegree, *Brand Luther: How an Unheralded Monk Turned His Small Town into
   a Center of Publishing, Made Himself the Most Famous Man in Europe – and Started
   the Protestant Reformation* (New York, 2016). The classic art-historical
   text on illustrated Reformation prints is Robert Scribner, *For the Sake of
   Simple Folk: Popular Propaganda for the German Reformation* (Cambridge, 1981).
5  Luther wrote to Georg Spalatin in April 1525, 'optaram eam Lucae
   typis dari, qui vacant' (I would have liked to send it [the text] to
   Lucas's press, which is not busy); see Knaake, 'Cranach's Presse',
   p. 201. For a list of Wittenberg printers at this time, see Josef
   Benzing, *Die Buchdrucker des 16. und 17. Jahrhunderts im deutschen Sprachgebiet*,
   2nd edn (Wiesbaden, 1982), pp. 497–501.
6  For an overview of Cranach's graphic output, see Armin Kunz,
   'Der Graphiker als Hofkünstler: Anmerkungen zu Funktion und

Rolle der Druckgraphik am Beispiel Lucas Cranachs und seiner
Werkstatt', in *Cranach in Coburg: Graphik von Lucas Cranach d. Ä., Lucas
Cranach d. J. und der Werkstatt im Kupferstichkabinett der Kunstsammlungen der
Veste Coburg*, ed. Stefanie Knöll, Meike Leyde and Michael Overdick
(Regensburg, 2020), pp. 10–31.

7   See Grażyna Jurkowlaniec and Magdalena Herman, 'Introduction',
    in *The Reception of the Printed Image in the Fifteenth and Sixteenth Centuries*,
    ed. Jurkowlaniec and Herman (New York, 2020), pp. 3–4.

8   Kunz, 'Der Graphiker', p. 13.

9   The original title was *Dye Zaigung des hochhlobwirdigen Hailigthumbs der
    Stifft-Kirchen aller Hailigen zu Wittenburg* (Wittenberg, 1509). See sig.
    C4r. (Page references are made to the gatherings [signatures] of
    the book, reference to which can be found in the lower right-hand
    corner of right-hand pages, especially early in a gathering.) For a
    fuller account of this object, see Livia Cárdenas, *Friedrich der Weise und
    das Wittenberger Heiltumsbuch: Mediale Repräsentation zwishen Mittelalter und
    Neuzeit* (Berlin, 2002).

10  For background on this genre and its development, see Suzanne
    Karr Schmidt, *Interactive and Sculptural Printmaking in the Renaissance*
    (Leiden and Boston, MA, 2018), pp. 60–64.

11  Kunz, 'Der Graphiker', p. 19.

12  *Dye Zaigung*, sigs A2r–A3v and L4r, especially sigs A3r–A3v for the
    authorization of '*aplas*' ('*Ablass*', or indulgence).

13  *Dye Zaigung*, sig. D4r.

14  For an excellent overview with bibliography on this subject
    through 2017, see Claire Kilgore, 'Viewing Heaven: Rock Crystal,
    Reliquaries, and Transparency in Fourteenth-Century Aachen',
    MA Thesis, University of Nebraska–Lincoln, 2017.

15  Inv. no. WB.102, British Museum, London.

16  For discussion of a major commission from Albrecht of
    Brandenburg and some overview of Cranach's other work
    for Roman Church contexts, see Andreas Tacke, 'Cranach im
    Dienste der Papstkirche: Zum Magdalenen-Altar Kardinal
    Albrechts von Brandenburg', in *Cranach im Exil: Aschaffenburg um
    1540: Zuflucht, Schatzkammer, Residenz*, ed. Gerhard Ermischer and
    Andreas Tacke (Regensburg, 2007), pp. 107–22; and Tacke's
    dissertation 'Der katholische Cranach: zu zwei Großaufträggen
    von Lucas Cranach d. Ä., Simon Franck und der Cranach-Werkstatt
    (1520–1540)', PhD diss., Freie Universität, Berlin-West 1989
    (Mainz, 1992).

17  Philipp Melanchthon and Johann Schwerdtfeger, *Antithesis figvrata vitae Christi et Anti-Christi* (Wittenberg, 1521), sigs B2v–B3r. Luther had more of a hand in selecting passages for the German edition of the text, the *Passional*, which is the more common and popular title of the document.

18  Lyndal Roper and Jennifer Spinks, 'Karlstadt's *Wagen*: The First Visual Propaganda for the Reformation', *Art History*, XL/2 (2017), pp. 256–85.

19  John 4:6; Matthew 16:24; John 19:17.

20  Bodo Brinkmann and Gabriel Dette, 'Philipp Melanchthon and Johann Schwerdtfeger, Passional Christi und Antichristi', in *Cranach*, ed. Bodo Brinkmann, exh. cat., Städel Museum, Frankfurt, Royal Academy of Arts, London (London, 2008), cat. no. 43, p. 198.

21  Karen Groll, *Das 'Passional Christi und Antichristi' von Cranach d. Ä* (Frankfurt am Main, 1990), pp. 10–11.

22  For an excellent, more in-depth overview of Cranach's contribution to the history of Bible illustration, see the two chapters on Cranach in David H. Price, *In the Beginning Was the Image: Art and the Reformation Bible* (Oxford, 2020), pp. 85–160, 209–60.

23  The print dates from 1523 at the earliest. Once attributed to Geofroy Tory, it is commonly thought to be the first expression of these Lutheran ideas in print. See Heimo Reinitzer, *Gesetz und Evangelium: Über ein reformatorisches Bildthema, seine Tradition, Funktion, und Wirkungsgeschichte* (Hamburg, 2006), vol. I, pp. 17–36; the print is illustrated in vol. II, cat. no. 559, fig. 31; see also Mathias Weniger, '"Durch und Durch Lutherisch"? Neues zum Ursprung der Bilder von Gesetz und Gnade', *Münchner Jahrbuch der bildenden Kunst*, lv (2004), pp. 115–34.

24  Inv. no. C 2167 vermisst, Kupferstichkabinett, Dresden; and inv. no. 15202, Städelmuseum, Frankfurt.

25  See bibliography in Joseph Leo Koerner, *The Moment of Self-Portraiture in German Renaissance Art* (Chicago, IL, 1993), p. 366, n. 14.

26  For a summary of Luther's positions on issues of likeness versus witness, see Jennifer Nelson, 'Visualizing Sacred History: Peter Dell's *Resurrection* and Lutheran Image Theology', *Journal of Medieval and Early Modern Studies*, XLVI/2 (2016), pp. 351–4.

27  See Erwin Panofsky, *Hercules am Scheideweg und andere antike Bildstoffe in der neueren Kunst* (Leipzig and Berlin, 1930).

28  Another outlier portrait in this period is the profile chiaroscuro woodcut of the Augsburg merchant Jakob Fugger the Rich,

produced in 1511 by Hans Burgkmair the Elder. However, the chiaroscuro format increased the costs of mass production and would have gone against the general principle of the broadest possible distribution.

29  It is worth mentioning in passing here Hans Baldung Grien's adaptation of Cranach's 1520 engraving, in which Baldung depicts Luther as a saint with a halo – a treatment to which Luther would surely have objected. In Robert Scribner's great overview of the operation of Luther's image in early modern Germany, he notes that Baldung's portrait would have resonated with the popular cult of St Martin in Baldung's native Strasbourg. See R. W. Scribner, 'Incombustible Luther: The Image of the Reformer in Early Modern Germany', *Past and Present*, 110 (1986), p. 49.

30  David Gaimster, 'Pots, Prints and Propaganda', in *The Archaeology of Reformation, 1480–1580*, ed. David Gaimster and Roberta Gilchrist (Leeds, 2003), p. 133.

31  Merry Wiesner-Hanks says double portraits of the married couple 'ultimately hung in more than sixty churches and wealthy homes across northern Europe': Wiesner-Hanks, 'Martin Luther', 7 July 2016, in the *Oxford Research Encyclopedia of Religion*, n.p. (see the section 'Luther on the Marital Household'): https://oxfordre.com/religion/display/10.1093/acrefore/9780199340378.001.0001/acrefore-9780199340378-e-365, accessed 21 August 2021.

32  Ulinka Rublack, 'Celebrity as Concept: An Early Modern Perspective', *Cultural and Social History: The Journal of the Social History Society*, VIII/3 (2011), p. 402; and Ulinka Rublack, 'Grapho-Relics: Lutheranism and the Materialization of the Word', *Past and Present*, Supplement 5 (2010), pp. 144–166.

33  For the most recent debates, see three essays: Jørgen Wadum, 'Cranach, His Sons, and Their Workshop: The Never-Ending Problem of Hands (Part I)'; Hanne Kolind Poulsen, 'Cranach, His Sons, and Their Workshop: The Never-Ending Problem of Hands (Part II)'; and Karin Kolb, 'Zuschreibung im Cranach-Œuvre. Neue Überlegungen zu einem alten Problem', all in *Lucas Cranach der Jüngere und die Reformation der Bilder*, ed. Elke A. Werner, Anne Eusterschulte and Gunnar Heydenreich (Munich, 2015), pp. 192–9, 200–205 and 206–17, respectively.

34  Traditionally thought to have been begun by Cranach, the altarpiece's underdrawing reveals significant differences between

its production and that of works overseen by Cranach himself.
Thus the painting is now attributed to Lucas the Younger. See
Gunnar Heydenreich, 'Cranach? Fragen der Zuschreibung im Lichte
kunsttechnologischer Untersuchungen', in *Lucas Cranach der Ältere:
Meister Marke Moderne*, ed. Gunnar Heydenreich, Daniel Görres and
Beat Wismer (Munich, 2017), pp. 75–6.

35  On this shift, see Daniela Bohde, 'Schräge Ansichten bei
Kreuzigungen und anderen Passionsszenen', in *Fantastische Welten.
Albrecht Altdorfer und das Expressive in der Kunst um 1500*, ed. Stefan Roller
and Jochen Sander (Munich, 2014), pp. 85–7 and catalogue entries
on pp. 102, 104f., 106f., 108f., 110; and Mitchell B. Merback, *The
Thief, the Cross, and the Wheel: Pain and the Spectacle of Punishment in Medieval
and Renaissance Europe* (Chicago, IL, 1999), pp. 258–9.

36  A similar reading of this panel appears in Christopher S. Wood,
*Albrecht Altdorfer* (London, 1993), p. 184.

37  Inv. no. 1941, Gemäldegalerie Alte Meister, Dresden.

38  Koerner, *The Moment*, p. 407.

39  Friedrich Ohly, *Gesetz und Evangelium: zur Typologie bei Luther und Lucas
Cranach: Zum Blutstrahl der Gnade in der Kunst* (Münster, 1985).

40  Koerner also parallels Dürer's 1500 self-portrait with this altarpiece,
but in different ways; he draws different conclusions (Koerner,
*The Moment*, pp. 406–10). Though my analysis here differs from
his, my characterizations of Baldung and Bosch are indebted
to his discussions of those artists: see especially 'The Crisis of
Interpretation', in *The Moment*, pp. 317–62, and 'Enmity', in Joseph
Leo Koerner, *Bosch and Bruegel: From Enemy Painting to Everyday Life*
(Princeton, NJ, and Oxford, 2016), pp. 96–150.

## Coda: The Women Look Back

1  The count of 36 includes paired individual panels of Adam and Eve
as just one painting.

2  See Jaroslav Pelikan, 'Cosmos and Creation: Science and Theology
in Reformation Thought', *Proceedings of the American Philosophical Society*,
CV/5 (1961), pp. 464–9, esp. p. 467 and n. 23, which lists relevant
passages from Luther's commentaries about specific after-effects
of sin.

3  For numerous examples of the stag's association with Christ,
see Don Cameron Allen, *Image and Meaning: Metaphoric Traditions in
Renaissance Poetry* (Baltimore, MD, 1960), pp. 99ff.

4 For the best overview of this topos in the context of the German Reformation, see the chapter 'The Battle of the Sexes and the World Upside Down', in Keith Moxey, *Peasants, Warriors and Wives: Popular Imagery in the Reformation* (Chicago, IL, and London, 1989), pp. 101–26.

5 Dieter Koepplin and Tilman Falk, eds, *Lukas Cranach: Gemälde, Zeichnungen, Druckgraphik* (Basel, 1974), vol. II, p. 570.

6 Karin Kolb, 'Salomos Götzendienst', in *Cranach*, ed. Harald Marx and Ingrid Mössinger, exh. cat., Gemäldegalerie Alte Meister, Dresden (Cologne, 2005), cat. no. 6, p. 235; and Joshua P. Waterman, 'Samson and Delilah', in *German Paintings in the Metropolitan Museum of Art, 1350–1600*, ed. Maryan W. Ainsworth and Joshua P. Waterman (New York, 2013), cat. no. 12, pp. 59–62.

7 This was in 1657. Kolb, 'Salomos Götzendienst', p. 232.

8 In translations that would have been available in German or Latin to Cranach workshop members in the 1530s, the line would have read 'I am black, yet beautiful.'

9 For Luther's easy-going treatment of marriage, which he considered a worldly concern despite its spiritual importance, see Martin Luther, 'Vom ehelichen Leben', in *D. Martin Luthers Werke: kritische Gesamtausgabe*, 95 vols (Weimar: Böhlau, 1883–2009), vol. 10 part II, pp. 275–304, especially p. 283.

10 Note that Lucas the Younger puts the workshop's signature on the altar of the priests of Baal, not the Israelites, in the 1545 *Elijah and the Priests of Baal*, also in Dresden.

11 Scholars have not securely identified any of the other figures.

12 Various sections and versions of this are preserved in the Coburg Landesbibliothek (Ms. Cas. 9–11) and the Weimar Thüringisches Hauptstaatsarchiv, EGA, Reg. O 20/21.

13 See Tamara Golan, 'Mit dem Kreidestift und Farben: Revolutionizing Grünewald in the German Democratic Republic', *Art History*, XLI/2 (2023), pp. 2–34, especially pp. 17–20, quoting from a 1953 essay by Joachim Uhlitzsch.

14 I follow Victor Stoichita's interpretation of this figure in his *Darker Shades: The Racial Other in Early Modern Art*, trans. Samuel Trainor (London, 2019), p. 34.

15 Stephen Greenblatt, *Renaissance Self-Fashioning: From More to Shakespeare* (Chicago, IL, 1980).

# SELECT BIBLIOGRAPHY

This list represents some major (and/or often overlooked) studies and exhibition catalogues that will be of use for further investigation of Cranach.

Baert, Barbara, 'The Sleeping Nymph Revisited: Ekphrasis, *Genius Loci* and Silence', in *The Figure of the Nymph in Early Modern Culture*, ed. Karl A. E. Enenkel and Anita Traninger (Leiden and Boston, MA, 2018), pp. 149–76

Brinkmann, Bodo, ed., *Cranach*, exh. cat., Royal Academy of Art, London (2008)

Campbell, Caroline, ed., *Temptation in Eden: Lucas Cranach's 'Adam and Eve'*, exh. cat., Courtauld Institute of Art Gallery, London (2007)

Ermischer, Gerhard, and Andreas Tacke, eds, *Cranach im Exil: Aschaffenburg um 1540: Zuflucht, Schatzkammer, Residenz*, exh. cat., Stadt Aschaffenburg and the Katholische Kirchenstiftung St. Peter und Alexander et al., Aschaffenburg (Regensburg, 2007)

Grimm, Claus, Johannes Erichsen and Evamaria Brockhoff, eds, *Lucas Cranach: ein Maler-Unternehmer aus Franken*, exh. cat., Festung Rosenberg, Kronach (Augsburg, 1994)

Heydenreich, Gunnar, *Lucas Cranach the Elder: Painting Materials, Techniques and Workshop Practice* (Amsterdam, 2007)

—, Daniel Görres and Beat Wismer, eds, *Lucas Cranach der Ältere: Meister Marke Moderne*, exh. cat., Museum Kunstpalast, Düsseldorf (2017)

Knöll, Stefanie, Meike Leyde and Michael Overdick, eds, *Cranach in Coburg: Graphik von Lucas Cranach d. Ä., Lucas Cranach d. J. und der Werkstatt im Kupferstichkabinett der Kunstsammlungen der Veste Coburg*, exh. cat., Kupferstichkabinett der Kunstsammlungen der Veste Coburg (Regensburg, 2020)

Koepplin, Dieter, and Tilman Falk, eds, *Lukas Cranach: Gemälde, Zeichnungen, Druckgraphik*, exh. cat., Kunstmuseum Basel (1974)

Koerner, Joseph Leo, *The Moment of Self-Portraiture in German Renaissance Art* (Chicago, IL, 1993)

—, *The Reformation of the Image* (Chicago, IL, 2004)

Kunz, Armin, 'Cranach as Cartographer: The Rediscovered "Map of the Holy Land"', *Print Quarterly*, XXII/2 (June 1995), pp. 123–44

Marx, Harald, and Ingrid Mössinger, eds, *Cranach*, exh. cat., Gemäldegalerie Alte Meister, Dresden (Cologne, 2005)

Nickel, Helmut, '"The Judgment of Paris" by Lucas Cranach the Elder: Nature, Allegory, and Alchemy', *Metropolitan Museum Journal*, XVI (1981), pp. 117–29

Noble, Bonnie, *Lucas Cranach the Elder: Art and Devotion of the German Reformation* (Lanham, MD, 2009)

Ozment, Steven, *The Serpent and the Lamb: Cranach, Luther, and the Making of the Reformation* (New Haven, CT, 2012)

Price, David H., *In the Beginning Was the Image: Art and the Reformation Bible* (Oxford, 2020)

Reinitzer, Heimo, *Gesetz und Evangelium: Über ein reformatorisches Bildthema, seine Tradition, Funktion, und Wirkungsgeschichte* (Hamburg, 2006)

*Renaissance and Reformation: German Art in the Age of Dürer and Cranach*, exh. cat., Los Angeles County Museum of Art (Munich, 2016)

Schade, Werner, *Cranach: A Family of Master Painters*, trans. Helen Sebba (New York, 1981)

# ACKNOWLEDGEMENTS

This book was mostly written under the auspices of the Nellie McKay Fellowship at UW-Madison, as well as during a Clark Institute fellowship; many people are owed thanks for their direct assistance during this time. Suzanne Karr-Schmidt read early chapter drafts and was always available for consultation; Armin Kunz was extraordinarily generous with his authoritative command of all things Cranach. Tamara Golan made very helpful suggestions about 'witches'. Shawon Kinew and Felipe Pereda kindly allowed me to crash a conference on Titian at Harvard University that helped reshape the second chapter. Athena Kirk made time to assist with translating the ancient Greek we learned together long ago. Eileen Lagman, Nadia Chana, Kristina Huang and Juliet Huynh helped improve the third chapter and provided moral support. LiLi Johnson went out of her way to do fieldwork for me during times of limited pandemic travel. Steven Nadler both modelled good writing and gave good advice about it.

I am grateful to editors Michael Leaman and François Quiviger for their thorough attention to the manuscript, and to Shira Brisman for her extraordinary efforts towards improving it; any flaws which remain are my own responsibility. Finally, it is my pleasure to thank Christopher S. Wood, not just for his advice, but also for training me in the German Renaissance and for writing books without which this life of Cranach would not be possible.

# PHOTO ACKNOWLEDGEMENTS

The author and publishers wish to express their thanks to the sources listed below for illustrative material and/or permission to reproduce it. Some locations of artworks are also given below, in the interest of brevity:

Alte Pinakothek, Munich (CC BY-SA 4.0): 59, 60; Art Institute of Chicago: 61, 62; Bayerische Staatsbibliothek, Munich (CC BY-NC-SA 4.0): 37, 41, 42; The Cleveland Museum of Art, OH: 23; Forschungsbibliothek Gotha (Theol 2° 23/7): 49; Gallerie degli Uffizi, Florence: 24; Gemäldegalerie, Staatliche Museen zu Berlin: 35; Gemäldegalerie Alte Meister, Dresden: 11 (inner wings, central panel), 13, 16, 17, 54, 55, 56, 65, 66; Gemäldegalerie Alte Meister, Kassel: 30; Georg-August-Universität Göttingen, Kunstgeschichtliches Seminar und Kunstsammlung (photo Katharina Anna Haase, CC BY-SA 4.0): 10; Hamburger Kunsthalle: 43; Klassik Stiftung Weimar: 5, 20; Koninklijk Museum voor Schone Kunsten (KMSKA), Antwerp: 4; Kunsthistorisches Museum, Vienna: 33; Kupferstichkabinett, Staatliche Museen zu Berlin: 29, 40; The Metropolitan Museum of Art, New York: 12, 19, 34, 38, 46, 63; The Morgan Library and Museum, New York: 52, 53; Musée du Louvre, Paris: 18; Museo Nacional Thyssen-Bornemisza, Madrid: 32; Museum der bildenden Künste, Leipzig: 31; The National Gallery, London: 11 (outer wings), 14, 15, 26, 27; National Gallery of Art, Washington, DC: 51; Newberry Library, Chicago: 44; private collection: 39; The Pushkin State Museum of Fine Arts, Moscow: 28; Sammlung Oskar Reinhart 'Am Römerholz', Winterthur: 8, 9; Schloss Friedenstein, Gotha: 47; Schloss Stolzenfels, Koblenz: 1; Städel Museum, Frankfurt: 40, 50; Stadtkirche Sankt Peter und Paul (Herderkirche), Weimar: 57, 58; Stadtkirche Wittenberg, photos Jürgen M. Pietsch/JMP-Bildagentur: 2, 3, 6, 7, 69, 70, 71; The State Hermitage Museum, St Petersburg: 25; Statens Museum for Kunst, Copenhagen: 21, 22, 64; Toledo Museum of Art, OH: 68; © The Trustees of

# INDEX



Illustration numbers are indicated by *italics*